Cognitive Behaviour Therapy: A Practical Guide to Helping People Take Control

D0141289

Cognitive Behaviour Therapy: A Practical Guide to Helping People Take Control explores the premise that negative beliefs play an important role in the development and continuation of mental health problems. The book offers a new integrative model of causality for instigating change, based on giving clients control and choice over these beliefs, and therefore over their mood and behaviour.

This practical guide also focuses on the stigmas often attached to people with 'mental illness'. Danny C. K. Lam suggests that by providing both the client and the general public with a more accurate understanding of the nature and causes of mental health problems it is possible to de-stigmatise the 'mental illness' label. This will help the client improve self-esteem and the ability to manage personal and interpersonal difficulties and to take control of their problems and responsibility for recovery.

Divided into six parts, this book covers:

- stigma, prejudice and discrimination from societal perspectives
- the nature and cause of emotional upsets
- a therapeutic framework for change
- self-prejudice, personal and interpersonal issues
- good and bad methods of communication
- practical approaches to assessing problems
- methods of taking control.

This cognitive behavioural approach to mental health problems is an innovative contribution to the field. Illustrated throughout with clinical examples and practical advice, the book is essential reading for all of those involved in mental health, from nurses to counsellors, and from medical practitioners and social workers to ministers of religion.

Danny C. K. Lam is a Principal Lecturer at Kingston University, St George's, University of London, a CBT trainer and supervisor and a frequent contributor to the literature and CBT conferences. He is passionate about developing an effective practical approach in the treatment of mental health problems, including psychological assessment, cognitive case formulation, CBT techniques and relapse prevention.

Cognitive Behaviour Therapy: A Practical Guide to Helping People Take Control

Danny C. K. Lam

Routledge
Taylor & Francis Group

LONDON AND NEW YORK

First published 2008 by Routledge
27 Church Road, Hove, East Sussex BN3 2FA

Simultaneously published in the USA and Canada
by Routledge
270 Madison Avenue, New York, NY 10016

Routledge is an imprint of the Taylor & Francis Group, an Informa business

© 2008 Danny C. K. Lam

Typeset in Times by Garfield Morgan, Swansea, West Glamorgan
Printed and bound in Great Britain by TJ International Ltd, Padstow, Cornwall
Paperback cover design by Lisa Dynan

This publication has been produced with paper manufactured to strict
environmental standards and with pulp derived from sustainable forests.

British Library Cataloguing in Publication Data
A catalogue record for this book is available from the British Library

Library of Congress Cataloging-in-Publication Data
Lam, Danny C. K. (Danny Chung Kit), 1949–
    Cognitive behaviour therapy : a practical guide to helping people take
control / Danny C. K. Lam.
        p. ; cm.
    Includes bibliographical references and index.
    ISBN 978-0-415-39811-4 (hbk) – ISBN 978-0-415-39812-1 (pbk)
1. Cognitive therapy. I. Title.
    [DNLM: 1. Cognitive Therapy—methods. 2. Mental Disorders—therapy.
WM 425.5.C6 L213c 2008]
    RC489.C63L28 2008
    616.89'142–dc22

                                                              2007044379

ISBN: 978–0–415–39811–4 (hbk)
ISBN: 978–0–415–39812–1 (pbk)

For my father

Contents

About the author

Danny C. K. Lam is a Principal Lecturer at the Faculty of Health and Social Care Sciences, Kingston University, St George's, University of London. He qualified in mental health nursing, then graduated and worked as a chemist for a couple of years. He obtained his postgraduate certificate in education (PGCE) from the University of Wales, BSc in psychology from the Open University, MSc in health psychology from Middlesex University, MA in education (major in psychology) from the Open University and MSc in cognitive behaviour therapy (CBT) from the University of London. He completed his PhD at St George's Medical School, University of London.

His research interests are in the effects of biological, genetic and psycho-social explanations of 'mental illness' on therapists' clinical judgement, therapeutic process and alliance, and on the public's and clients' perceptions of individuals with mental health problems. He is also interested in the effects of mental illness stigma, prejudice and discrimination on health beliefs, self-esteem and self-image. He is passionate about developing an effective practical approach to the treatment of mental health problems such as psychological assessment and intervention, cognitive case formulation, CBT techniques and communication skills. He is a CBT trainer and supervisor and a journal reviewer. His publications and conference presentations reflect his research and clinical interests.

Foreword

Cognitive behaviour therapy: counteracting the poison of stigma and prejudice

Paul M. Salkovskis, Professor of Clinical Psychology and Applied Science, Department of Psychology, Institute of Psychiatry, King's College London

Cognitive therapy has its origins in the way in which Aaron T. Beck sought to apply basic cognitive models of the experience of emotion to 'Emotional Disorders' (Beck 1976). Within this cognitive framework, psychiatric 'disorders' are conceptualised as understandable problems arising from normal changes in normal emotional functioning. Normal processes result in apparently abnormal results. By the same token, the learning theory origins of behaviour therapy lie in the idea that normal learning and conditioning processes could lead to abnormal reactions in terms of emotions and behaviour. Contemporary cognitive behavioural theory and therapy is therefore firmly and deeply rooted in a normalising, non-pathological approach to emotional problems. However, the societal, social and clinical reality that people who seek help find themselves in is often quite different, with concepts related to abnormality and pathology constituting the norm. This is often the background which therapist and patient work against.

The fact that for the past century mental health problems have commonly been labelled as 'mental illnesses' in 'patients' requiring 'diagnosis' in 'clinics' can have the effect of distorting our view of the fundamentally normal processes which are involved in patterns of unduly negative thinking, emotional distress and counterproductive behavioural changes. It is, of course, an empirical question as to whether this is a good or a bad thing. It has become a burning question in the context of a mental health system which seeks to empower service users and carers, and which has begun at last to turn its attention to the vital issue of prevention.

So, do labelling processes really matter, and if they do, what can we do about it? In particular, what of the use of labels surrounding the concept of 'mental illness'? Cognitive theory tells us none of the words used to label people or actions are necessarily problematic in themselves; rather, it is the burden of meaning they carry which can have a problematic impact on the person who is labelled by others and by themselves. This issue lies at the heart of this thoughtful and highly practical book, which uniquely tackles cognitive therapy from the perspective of the impact of labelling and stigma. It considers the issue from the perspective of the person who seeks help, from that of those who seek to help them professionally, and from others including carers and the general public.

It has, of course, long been known that the use of 'labels' can both directly and indirectly affect the people to whom the label is applied. Such labels can be descriptive ('She is mentally ill') or causal ('He has a genetic defect which has made him mentally ill'). Although the focus here is on the negative impact of labelling, it should also be noted that labels, including causal labels, can have positive connotations (e.g. 'She is a hero'; 'He has a strong character which resulted in him becoming a hero').

Typically, the widespread use of labels carries the implication that a simple description (when correctly applied) can predict a range of other characteristics of the person and how they might react and behave. The idea that 'He is a hero' would lead the person to make guesses about him; for example, that he is unlikely to steal money. 'He is a criminal' might lead to opposite conclusions, which may or may not be justified. 'Joe the hero didn't declare his income for tax purposes' puts the two labels together; this more complex labelling process begins to convey the complexity of the individual in ways which make prediction less easy, but more appropriately convey the reality of the person. The use of a number of labels can converge with the level of complexity required for people we are closely acquainted with, and begins to approximate to a description of the person, which tends to leave much less room for misunderstanding and false prediction (hence making stigmatisation and prejudice less likely).

Thus labels and the descriptions that they can be shorthand for can be heuristic in the sense that they guide the way we think about the labelled person, with one characteristic tending to predict others. However, the simpler the label the more likely it is to mislead, as the use of simple labels leaves gaps which might otherwise modify one's judgements. This is not to say that labels cannot sometimes be helpful in allowing us to predict the behaviours of other people we may encounter. This is probably the reason why labelling is so widely used; we find the use of labels helpful as a way of simplifying a complicated world.

Heuristics of this type can be accurate, may be overly negative or overly positive in terms of the person labelled. The problem lies not in their use, but in circumstances where they introduce *systematic biases* in either direction, and where such systematic biases are likely to be unhelpful, such as when a person in distress seeks help from a professional who is required to provide it. There is now a great deal of evidence that both professionals and non-professionals tend to show overly negative biases in respect of particular causal and descriptive labels in the context of psychiatric problems. Such biases tend in turn to lead to overly negative expectations, and negative expectations further tend to lead to poorer outcomes in therapy and other helping activities. In other words, labelling can result in systematically distorted patterns of thinking about the person who is labelled both in others and in themselves. Cognitive therapy, as described in this book, is about putting distorted patterns of thinking into a helpful context in ways which enable the person to try new more helpful ways of thinking. This book is the first to consider the practicalities of helping people to change, using CBT from the perspective of stigma, self-stigma and labelling.

Diagnostic and causal labelling

Within psychiatry and psychology, the value of two types of label has been considered: 'disease' labelling (typically in the form of diagnosis) and causal labelling. Over the second half of the twentieth century debate has raged as to whether the use of such psychiatric and causal labels is helpful or harmful. Unfortunately, this debate has been characterised by strong beliefs and weak evidence.

The weight of *discussion* has tended to support the idea that labelling was a good thing, to the extent that mental health education campaigns drew comparisons between mental illness and physical illnesses such as diabetes in ways which conflated and widely propagated the two types of labels. It has been argued that the 'disease like any other' view is de-stigmatising, as it relieves the patient from any notion of 'blame' or even 'malingering'. Although such campaigns are usually keen to specify that evidence is central to the ideas they promote (e.g. that treatment is effective), they are not evidence-based in terms of how they seek to achieve their educational and de-stigmatising aims.

It may not be a coincidence that such health education campaigns have usually been financially supported in full or in part by the pharmaceutical industry, and that the analogy with biological diseases such as diabetes carry the implication that disease management requires the lifelong use of prescribed medication.

As will be clear from the chapters that follow, the *evidence* favours the idea that stigma tends to be lessened when mental health difficulties are perceived as arising from psychological rather than biological causes. By the same token, an emphasis on stress and distress as the defining components of mental health problems is more acceptable (and more likely to lead to appropriate help seeking) than diagnostic labels and the idea of mental illness as 'a disease like any other'.

The commonest justification for the use of biological explanations, with no foundation in research, is that in some way it is 'good for the patient'. Those advocating this position specifically argue that biological disease models are de-stigmatising and empowering relative to psychological models. Promoting the view that mental health problems have biological causes has become an established part of many programmes with the declared intention of reducing stigma.

There are other reasons why the promotion of biological factors is not necessarily in the best interest of those with mental health problems and their families. For example, genetic factors may be promoted (or over-promoted) as causal with little regard for the potential impact that such ideas may have (Rimes and Salkovskis 1998). Clinicians, sufferers and carers who uncritically consider genetic factors are likely to considerably overestimate these as a result of factors such as selective attention. Once a person is identified as having a problem such as obsessive compulsive disorder (OCD), relatives will for example recall Great Uncle George, who was very fastidious. Cousin Emily was diagnosed as having OCD. The patient's grandmother, when asked, recalls an aunt who checked a lot. Three cases in a family; that sounds like a lot. However, the context is that the collective recollection of family members of several generations can draw upon a potential pool of information about almost two hundred relatives; OCD is likely to occur at normal lifetime rates in at least eight of those. If milder obsessional-type behaviours (rather than handicapping levels) are included, the figure would rise to somewhere in the region of thirty. None of the examples given above are first-degree relatives, and when lay people consider genetic explanations such considerations seldom feature. Note also that genetic and biological explanations may have the effect of alleviating feelings of blame and guilt not in the patient but in parents.

Biological accounts stigma: if your brain is diseased, what does that say about you?

As described in this book, biological accounts can be problematic because they have been shown to have the unwanted effect of inducing pessimism regarding likely treatment outcome in patients, their carers and the general public. Attributing mental health problems to 'brain disease' and biological causes has additionally been shown to affect the extent to which sufferers are regarded as unusually unpredictable, potentially antisocial or even frankly dangerous by and to themselves and others. As described in the later chapters of this book, the brain is commonly understood to be the organ of the mind and the 'seat of the self'; a diseased brain for many comes to mean a diseased mind and diseased 'self'.

A key influence on this book is the research carried out by Danny Lam on issues relating to stigma and labelling. In an adult community sample the mere suggestion of 'psychological' but not 'biological' labels resulted in more positive views of mental health problems relative to controls (Lam et al. 2005). Anxious and depressed patients have also been shown to be similarly susceptible to biological labelling effects in experimental studies (e.g. Lam and Salkovskis 2007), showing that such effects may well be causal rather than merely correlational. The importance of clinicians' attitudes to causal factors in mental health problems lies both in their own expectations of patients' response to treatment (Lam and Salkovskis in press) and in the extent to which their causal beliefs are transmitted to patients. The way in which patients understand and accept such causal explanations may in turn affect not only their expectation of change but also their engagement and response in treatment. Understanding how causal labelling might affect younger patients with mental health problems is thus an important next step in research terms.

Not throwing out the baby with the bathwater

An implication of this work is, at first sight, unexpected. This book requires a thoughtful approach to the issue of labelling in the context of cognitive therapy treaments, which represent the strongest evidence-based treatments for problems such as anxiety and depression. It is clear that the brain is the organ of the mind, and that psychological problems occur in the context of a biological substrate, albeit one which is not necessarily diseased. We can reasonably criticise biological psychiatry for ignoring the mind, but we in turn ignore the fact that brain is the organ of the mind at our own peril.

What is lacking at present is sensible neuroscience-based approaches to establishing the role of biological and genetic factors and their interaction, in the type of way that this been done in complex trait research (Kovas and Plomin 2006). We know that disease/neuropsychiatric models (e.g. comparing OCD to neurological disease such as epilepsy or genetic problems such as Huntington's disease) have failed to help our understanding, and may well have been damaging in terms of stigma. Currently biological theories struggle to account for the specific phenomenology of OCD and the effectiveness of psychological treatment. This is not to say that biological factors are not relevant: the brain, after all, is the organ of the mind, and all psychological processes have a physiological substrate. The mistake, in my opinion, is to presume that the pathophysiological basis of OCD has already been established.

To progress our understanding of mental health difficulties, biological accounts need to be conceived of in a more subtle way. The fact that psychological theories and research are so well developed should provide a useful starting point, allowing consideration of the psychological/neuro-physiological interface. Such theories may be able to generate specific predictions based on the phenomenology of the problems being investigated, and therefore provide evidence to evaluate them. It thus seems extremely unlikely at this stage that any of the common mental health problems will be identified as a primarily 'caused' biological abnormality, making the interface between normal biological and psychological factors and how these normal processes can produce disordered reactions a particularly important area of interest. Such research may suggest ways in which psychological and pharmacological treatments might be combined synergistically in particular types of problem. Note that at present the CBT is the first-line treatment with the combination of psychological and pharmacological treatment being appropriate only in severe depression; in anxiety such a combination is, at best, of uncertain value, and at worst actually counterproductive (Barlow et al. 2001).

Stigma, prejudice and helping people to change

The development of a sensible integration of psychological and biological factors lies some way in the future, and so we are left with the task of dealing with the psychological issues by further linking understanding and treatment. In this book, Danny Lam has been able to bring together our understanding of the harmful effects of labelling (both descriptive and causal) and cognitive-behavioural treatments. The 'final common pathway' of this work lies in the issue of self-prejudice, which cognitive therapy is particularly well placed to help people to change. The issues of control and choice are rightly emphasised here. This book will help practitioners understand the basis of cognitive behavioural interventions in ways which will allow them to help people to choose to change. I am delighted to have been invited to write the foreword to this ground-breaking book, which will live up to its title: it is a practical guide to helping people take control.

Paul M. Salkovskis, London, October 2007

References

Barlow, D. H., Gorman, J. M., Shear, M. K. and Woods, S. W. (2001). 'Cognitive behavioral therapy, imipramine or their combination for panic disorder: A randomised controlled trial.' *Journal of the American Medical Association* **283**: 2573–2574.

Beck, A. T. (1976). *Cognitive therapy and the emotional disorders*. New York: International Universities Press.

Kovas, Y. and Plomin, R. (2006). 'Generalist genes: Implications for the cognitive sciences.' *Trends in Cognitive Sciences* **10**(5): 198–203.

Lam, D. C. K. and Salkovskis, P. M. (in press). '"Judging a book by its cover": An experimental study on the impact of personality disorder diagnosis on clinicians' judgements.' *Behaviour Research and Therapy*.

Lam, D. C. K., Salkovskis, P. M. and Warwick, H. (2005). 'An experimental investigation of the impact of biological versus psychological explanations of the cause of "mental illness".' *Journal of Mental Health* **14**(5): 453–464.

Rimes, K. A. and Salkovskis, P. M. (1998). 'Psychological effects of genetic testing for psychological disorders.' *Behavioural and Cognitive Psychotherapy* **26**(1): 29–42.

Preface

It has been suggested that problems of stigma, prejudice and discrimination are in part due to society or the majority of society being ignorant about the nature and causes of 'mental illness'. Biological and genetic explanations not only have been ineffective in the de-stigmatisation campaign to date, but also may have had the unwanted effect of maintaining the public's stigmatising attitudes and of clients stigmatising themselves in a self-fulfilling prophecy. Social stigma diminishes self-esteem, affects self-confidence and robs people with mental health problems of social opportunities, thus affecting treatment participation and outcome.

Part I of the book examines the issues of stigma, prejudice and discrimination from the societal perspective and suggests or illustrates practical ways to alleviate the negative impact of these issues.

Through the use of a CBT therapeutic framework, Part II not only illustrates the nature and causes of emotional upset, but also shows ways in which negative thoughts and unhelpful behaviour of people with mental health problems can be dealt with in a practical way.

Part III addresses the issues of approval and approval-seeking, perfectionism, healthy and unhealthy negative emotions, procrastination, self-criticism, setback and relapse, which therapists often have to deal with in therapy. These common issues underlie depression, anxiety disorders, eating disorders, substance misuse and other mental health problems, and can lead to clients stigmatising and judging themselves in a negative way, if these issues are not successfully dealt with.

Part IV examines communication issues and techniques or skills in relation to clients' responses to treatment, self-confidence and self-esteem. Although negative thinking is seen as the primary cause of mental health problems, an ability to communicate is a key factor for self-confidence and self-esteem, which, in turn, affect the way clients think and react. Being able to communicate thoughts and feelings effectively in social, work and family situations is one of the main contributing factors to their recovery. Otherwise, the problem of clients stigmatising and judging themselves in a negative way is likely to emerge.

Part V illustrates a practical CBT approach to the assessment of clients' mental health problems and to disputing negative and irrational thoughts. It also suggests ways to develop effective disputing techniques.

Part VI advocates new models of change to help people with mental health problems. These new models emphasise the importance of helping people with mental health problems to do better rather than curing disease. Control and choice are at the heart of these new models. A detailed case example of a client with panic disorder is used to illustrate ways in which the client learnt to take control and make choices in the way she thought and reacted to her anxiety problem.

Acknowledgements

I am very grateful to Paul Salkovskis for supervising my PhD studies, encouraging me to write this book and for his generosity in writing the Foreword. He has become not only a friend, but also a teacher for life. Having Paul as my teacher has been one of the most important aspects of my professional life and he has been the person most influential in shaping my understanding of CBT research and in the development of my thinking about good and effective CBT practice.

I would particularly like to thank Sue Spicer for her time and support in her careful reading of the text throughout the writing of the book. Her constructive suggestions and comments were invaluable in improving the readability and clarity of the book. Linda Cheng, Edward Maliki, Matthew Tong, Sandra Jago, Gillian Lim, Grace Lam, Andrew Lam, Kate Honeybill and William Au were helpful and supportive throughout, not just in reading the text, but also in offering their helpful views and suggestions in the shaping and development of the book.

Many clients offered invaluable and thoughtful feedback during the course of the writing of this book. In addition, every client with whom I have worked contributed to my understanding of how people change and to the development of techniques for their unique problems. Although I am unable to acknowledge them by name, this book is a product of their openness, their suggestions and all the hard work in our CBT sessions. They have taught me to be a better therapist and I hope that our experiences in working together have been reflected in this book.

Finally, the support, understanding and encouragement from my family – Sue, Andrew and Vincent – are always remembered with appreciation, gratitude and affection.

A personal experience by Danny C. K. Lam

I was shocked to find out that I had passed only one subject out of seven O levels taken. My body shook uncontrollably with fear and I was over-whelmed with anxiety, guilt, shame, anger and worry. I did not know what I could say to my family about my failure. I had brought shame on them, especially my father, who was a professor and the author of eight books. My grandfather was one of the few Western-trained doctors in Hong Kong a century ago. 'You're such a failure,' I told myself and felt sick and disgusted with myself. When I came out of the school and saw my father waiting for me, I almost had a panic attack and wanted to escape, but I seemed to have 'frozen' and was unable to move. He came up to me and then put his arm around me and said, 'I know the results. There is no need to say anything.' There wasn't any anger in his tone of voice, only dis-appointment and sadness, but he wasn't critical. He was calm, supportive and encouraging as he had always been. He asked, 'What do you want to do now, Chung Kit [my Chinese name]?'

Danny: Dad, I am sorry. I am such a failure.
Dad: Yes, you have failed badly in the examinations, but it doesn't make you a failure as a person. You have many positive qualities as a son, but you need to work very hard on your shortcomings. It is never too late.
Danny: What will people think about me?
Dad: Forget it. You have no control over their impressions about you. Don't waste your time and emotional energy worrying about what they think. Ask yourself what you want to do now.

Education and educational achievements are regarded as paramount in Chinese culture. Racked with shame and guilt, I went to one of the tallest buildings in Hong Kong to commit suicide, but I did not have the courage to carry it out. I was angry with myself for being a coward, not just a failure. I am glad now that I was a coward then. With the support and understanding of my beloved father, I went to England to study mental health nursing. On the way to the airport, we were in the back of a taxi and I will never forget what he said.

Dad: Chung Kit, you don't know anything about nursing. This is what you want to do and I support your decision. Whatever you do, take an interest in it and I have faith in you.

Danny: Dad, I will.

Dad: Even if you were 'trapped' in a room with four walls and no doors and windows, create a door for yourself to a better life and future.

His wisdom gave me my *first* exposure to the essence of 'cognitive behaviour therapy': to accept and be myself, not to worry about what other people think and get on with life. His wisdom also provided me with the drive to embrace my life with 'the use of cognitive behaviour therapy' in a personal and professional way. He was not just my father and my best friend, but he was also my 'CBT teacher and mentor'.

With great sadness, I left Hong Kong at the age of 19 (with five pounds in my pocket, a lot of anxiety and very little command of English) to start a new life in the United Kingdom, remembering the Chinese saying, 'A journey of a thousand miles begins with a single step.' Leaving Hong Kong was indeed a difficult and painful step in the journey. After the graduation ceremony where, at the age of 54, I received my PhD, I came down from the platform and Vincent, my younger son, came up to me and gave me a hug and said, 'Dad, well done. It has been a hard and long journey for you.' 'Yes, it has been,' I responded with emotion and tears in my eyes. My father's voice seemed to be buzzing in my ears: 'Chung Kit, you have done it. Well done.'

Part I

Societal perspective

Stigma, prejudice and discrimination

Chapter 1

Mental illness stigma

Stigma has its roots in *differences*. For example, society or the majority of society perceives individuals with a physical disability, HIV and AIDS as different. These individuals may also feel different. People are in reality different from each other, whether that difference is one of personality, physical appearance, illness and disability, age, gender or sexuality. Thus, it can be argued that it is not the difference itself (or a particular type of difference) that causes the stigmatisation, prejudice and discrimination; it is about how *acceptable* the difference is to society or the majority of society. People with 'mental illness' are, unfortunately, seen as one of the most unacceptable groups in society because of their perceived character.

The Oxford Dictionary defines stigma as a 'mark of shame, a stain on a person's good reputation'. When the difference is a mark of shame in the person's attributes or character, it discredits the person in the eyes of others (Franzoi 1996). People with 'mental illness' are discredited because they are wrongly perceived as having attributes of *unpredictability and danger* as part of their character. These attributes portray them as having little or no control over their mind and behaviour and as such they are not responsible for their aggressive and violent behaviour. The public may therefore be fearful of coming into contact with them; prefer to have as little to do with them as possible and view them as inferior, flawed, unworthy, and so on. These attributes are forms of labelling, signifying them as being different from the majority of society and the difference is emphasised through the process of discrimination and prejudice. There are forms of discrimination and prejudice which can be identified in the interaction between the 'normal' and the 'discredited' or the public and the mentally ill (Goffman 1990). Discrimination and prejudice in any form serve to separate and socially exclude individuals from society and from many of the benefits of society, such as equitable access to services like housing, education, health and social support. Prejudice and discrimination in this way thus serve as a form of social exclusion.

The public perception of people with 'mental illness'

Research shows that 'mental illness' is one of the most stigmatised conditions, and is more stigmatising than conditions such as homelessness, epilepsy, homosexuality, HIV and AIDS. There is little or no sign of stigmatisation being reduced, despite a range of health initiatives being used to de-stigmatise the condition since the late 1950s and the advancement of effective treatments such as drugs and psychotherapy.

Numerous surveys of the public's attitude towards 'mental illness' have revealed strikingly negative views of psychiatric and psychological disorders and the people who suffer from them. In one early attitude study involving four hundred individuals representative of the general population, Nunnally (1950) asked the participants to rate a number of different groups with respect to a list of bipolar objectives (e.g. good–bad, safe–dangerous, predictable–unpredictable). The objectives most commonly used to rate people with 'mental illness' were dangerous, dirty, unpredictable and worthless. Tringo (1970) conducted a survey to assess the relative acceptability of people with 'mental illnesses'. In the survey, the public was asked to rate twenty-one different disability groups with respect to their social acceptability. People with 'mental illness' were rated at the very bottom, just below alcoholism, mental retardation and a former convict. Gussow and Tracy (1968) showed that the two most horrible diagnoses that can happen to someone are leprosy and insanity; insanity (or mental illness) is viewed as the worse of the two. In other words, someone with leprosy is viewed more favourably than a person with mental illness.

Even now, people who are mentally ill are consistently portrayed as dangerous, unpredictable, dependent, unsociable, unemployable, unproductive, transient, flawed, unworthy, incompetent, irresponsible and socially undesirable (Day and Page 1986). There has been little change in public perception of people with 'mental illness' and recent research suggests that the stigmatising attitude is actually worsening (Sayce 2000). This inaccurate portrayal of clients' characteristics thus maintains the stigmatising attitudes of the public and influences their prejudiced and discriminatory reactions towards people with 'mental illness'. The impact of stigma and social exclusion can be devastating, leading to low self-esteem, poor social relationships, isolation, depression and self-harm.

Enacted and perceived stigma

Stigma can be categorised into enacted and perceived. Enacted stigma is the result of a person being stigmatised for certain attributes (e.g. dangerous, dishonest or flawed) or certain conditions (e.g. unmarried mother, HIV/ AIDS or homeless), whereas perceived stigma is a fear of being stigmatised because of these attributes or conditions. Scambler (1989) believes that people with epilepsy were much more likely to experience perceived (or self-perceived) than enacted stigma. There is evidence that, due to a better understanding of and more effective management or treatment of epilepsy, stigmatising attitudes towards the sufferers are diminishing (enacted stigma). However, people with epilepsy are still anxious about and fearful of being stigmatised, probably because of feeling ashamed of having this condition (perceived stigma).

There is mounting evidence that people with 'mental illness' stigmatise themselves because of enacted stigma. Social scientists are interested in the likely impact of stigma on their thinking and behaviour. One common observation is that stigma may become internalised, whereby stigmatised individuals may come to share the same beliefs as the majority of society and have a low opinion of themselves. They may believe that they are inferior, flawed, unworthy, incompetent, and so on. Some clients may accept that there is nothing they can do to change and get better because their condition is 'genetic, a disease of the brain, or the result of chemical imbalances'. What follows becomes a kind of self-fulfilling prophecy. They may act in unmotivated and pathological ways that confirm the expectations that they and society have of them. It is believed that societal expectations place subtle pressure on mentally ill clients to live up to those role expectations.

Through the stigmatising process, the 'mental illness/psychiatric label' has the unwanted effect of taking away clients' self-belief, undermining self-confidence, lowering self-esteem and increasing pessimism about recovery and the future. This is particularly so with clients not responding or not responding satisfactorily to drug treatment. It is believed that the stigmatising process may include clients either receiving professional diagnoses (e.g. you suffer from bipolar disorder), seeking psychiatric treatment, receiving drug treatment, or displaying behaviour consistent with the stereotyped image of people with mental health problems. For example, Christian, described below, could not quite shake off the stigma of 'mental illness' and often felt inferior to others because of the psychiatric diagnosis.

The case of Christian

Christian, aged 32, was a computer programmer. He did not go to university, but was quite good at computer programming and web design, largely through reading books and magazines and a lot of learning by trial and error. His friends thought he was good at what he did, started to give him some work to do for them, and also recommended him to others. His girlfriend, with whom he had been going out for almost two years, was caring and supportive and encouraged him to study for a degree in computer science. The course was beneficial not just to help him expand his interest and expertise in this area, but also for his self-esteem. Self-esteem had always been a problem, right from his early years. He was a shy and introverted person, did not have much self-confidence and this was particularly the case in social situations. He avoided going to parties where there were a lot of people and he did not like talking to people he did not know. Holding a conversation with people had always been a problem, as he felt that he needed to be interesting and to be able to come up with topics that would interest people. He monitored his performance and the behaviour of others he was talking to. If there were signs of him not meeting the standards he set himself or if others didn't seem to be interested in what he was saying, he would go quiet and withdrawn. His body just tensed up and he felt uncomfortable, his heart started pounding and he would eventually leave. However, he was determined to make a change for the better, as he knew avoidance and escape were not the way forward. His social circle was small, but he had a number of good friends and some outside interests such as swimming, walking, reading and tennis. He had been coping reasonably well since his discharge from hospital two years previously for the treatment of depression, low self-esteem and alcoholism. However, Christian had also struggled with the stigma of 'mental illness', both enacted and perceived stigma, for most of his life.

His parents divorced when he was 10 years old. He was so traumatised by this experience that it seemed to have negatively affected his self-confidence and self-esteem throughout his life. Not only did he blame himself for the divorce, believing that he was the cause of frequent rows between his parents, but he also believed that he was not good enough as a son. Following the divorce, he stayed with his mother and attended a local school, but his mother was diagnosed as suffering from depression, which made it difficult for her to care for him and his sister, Helen, who was two years younger. Christian said that his mother was 'a caring and supportive person with a nice personality and I love her'. She went downhill when she heard that her ex-husband was soon to be married as this dashed her hopes of their getting back together. The news hit her quite hard. She became quiet, tearful and withdrawn and found getting out of bed difficult. Sometimes she stayed in bed for days without going out of the house. She was diagnosed with depression and admitted to a psychiatric hospital as there were increasing concerns for her safety and that of her children. Christian did not have a close relationship with his father, who was described as a hard-working and successful businessman. However, he was also a cool and emotionally detached person who hardly spent any time with Christian and Helen. Christian believed he had been abandoned by his father and there must be something wrong with him. He was not good enough.

Helen went to stay with their father and stepmother and Christian was placed in a boarding school. Christian did not understand the reason for this and this made him believe even more that there must be something wrong with him: he was a reject. His experience at boarding school was painful and traumatic and he did not like it. He went to three different boarding schools, until he left when he was 18. He hated it and started to withdraw. He isolated himself from others and stayed in his room as much as he possibly could. The other children teased and bullied him and called him all sorts of names. In order to survive and try to be accepted he learnt to please others by conforming to their expectations. He smoked, drank and took drugs, as some in the school did, in the hope that he would be accepted and could become one of them. However, making friends was hard, as he found it difficult to get close to anyone and he didn't allow people to get too close to him, in case they found out something 'bad' about him. Rejection was always a fear and a problem that he found difficult to handle. Alcohol and drugs allowed him to escape from the pain of reality and they seemed to boost his confidence and improve his mood. He found it increasingly difficult to cope with life and turned to alcohol and drugs more and more. On hearing that his mother was going to marry again, his mood went down and he cried, saying, 'I am rejected again'. He was taken to a psychiatric hospital at the age of 16 and was diagnosed with depression with an addictive personality disorder. Since then, he had been in and out of hospital on many occasions. He was initially relieved to know the diagnoses, believing that drug treatments would 'cure' him in the same way medication does a physical illness. Despite being given a cocktail of drugs of various dosages over the years and a course of electro-convulsive therapy (ECT), his problems remained. He struggled with the stigmatising thoughts of 'I am insane, I am mental and I have a personality disorder', believing that there was no 'cure' for his 'mental illness'.

Since leaving school with six GCSE and two A levels, he had had a number of short-term low-paid jobs, as a labourer with construction firms, a filing clerk and a postman. With the support of his girlfriend and a therapist, his life was starting to improve, as was his relationship with his mother and his stepfather. He joined his mother's mail order company on a part-time basis as a web-designer. The company sold jewellery and employed four part-time staff. 'For the first time in my life, I started to feel that I had a future,' said Christian. He could not quite shake off the stigma of 'mental illness', however, and continued to encounter, from time to time, hurtful and offensive attitudes and behaviour. This impeded his recovery by adding stress and undermining his already fragile self-esteem.

Cognitive behaviour therapy approach to stigma

Stigma is due to an inaccurate belief that people with 'mental illness' are dangerous and unpredictable and are not in control of their mind and behaviour, thereby creating fear in the mind of the public. Violence and unpredictability are two stigmatising factors that have constantly emerged in attitude surveys since the 1950s. Such a belief is popularised by the unproven idea of 'mental illness' being 'a disease of the brain, genetic, or caused by chemical imbalances in the brain'. As such, there is little or nothing clients can do to change the way they feel (e.g. anger, depression or anxiety) or their behaviour (e.g. violence, aggression or unpredictability). The idea of drug treatment as the main mechanism in the treatment of 'mental illness' may not be helpful in combating stigma and in changing how mentally ill clients are perceived. In addition, clients may become passive in the treatment process (e.g. taking medication as prescribed) rather than being proactive in learning how to resolve their emotional difficulties or problems.

To reduce stigma, the CBT approach is to enrich clients with an understanding that feelings or moods (e.g. anger, guilt or depression) are closely related to the thinking process (e.g. 'I am no good', 'I will not get through the probation', or 'People think that I am stupid') and to the way in which emotional difficulties or problems are dealt with (e.g. procrastination, self-criticism or perfectionism). It is important for clients to understand that mental health problems (e.g. depression, anxiety disorders) are not the result of a biogenetic cause, but are due to a combination of interacting factors such as psychological, social, environmental and genetic. CBT empowers clients with a tool to handle these difficulties or problems in a different, more realistic and adaptive way. The idea is to give clients a feeling of being in control and the public a reassuring message that people with 'mental illness' are not mad and insane.

Technique: ABC model

Rationale and focus

Clients often believe that their feelings are beyond their control and there is nothing they can do about it. Some attribute it to external causes (e.g. 'People hurt me', or 'Doing a presentation makes me anxious and panicky') and the idea of 'mental illness' being a disease of the brain, genetic, or the result of chemical imbalances provides little incentive for them to learn to change their feelings and behaviour.

Introducing clients to the ABC model early in therapy helps clarify any misconceptions about the cause of their psychological and emotional

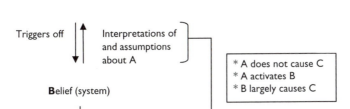

Activating event

Triggers off

Interpretations of
and assumptions
about A

* A does not cause C
* A activates B
* B largely causes C

Belief (system)

Causing

Consequences (emotional and behavioural)

Figure 1.1 The ABC model

problems and provides an understanding that it is the *interplay* among thought, emotion and behaviour that is central to or largely responsible for these problems. 'A' is known as an *A*ctivating event or the existence of a situation, 'C' is the emotional and behavioural *C*onsequence or reaction of the individual. According to cognitive behaviour therapy theory, A (the activating event) does not cause C (the emotional and behavioural consequence). It is *B*elief (the person's interpretation of, and assumptions about, A) that is largely responsible for C, the emotional and behavioural reactions. Figure 1.1 shows the relationship between A, B and C. For example, if a person experiences depression after a divorce, it may not be the divorce itself (at point A) that causes the depressive reactions (at point C) but the person's interpretations of and assumptions about the divorce: being a failure, being responsible for the cause of the divorce and being unable to find another partner.

When illustrating the concept of the ABC model, it is important to use a *relevant* example that the client can relate to. For example, an example of anxiety is used for anxious clients, an example of anger for clients with anger problems, and an example of guilt for clients with guilt problems. Christian, as described above, was anxious about going to social events. It makes sense knowing that it is not the social event that causes anxious reactions, but the interpretation of and assumptions made about the event. Otherwise, everybody in the same or a similar situation would have the same problem as Christian. Realising that anxiety is not caused by something being wrong with the brain not only motivates clients to stand back and question their (irrational or negative) thinking about the situation or event, but also may reduce the stigma and empower them to change their behaviour as a result.

Process

Therapist:	In CBT we use the ABC model to understand people's emotional reaction towards an event or a situation. Have you heard of this model before? [*Note that when teaching the ABC model it is best to use a pen and paper to illustrate the concept as this will help the client relate it better to his or her experiences/difficulties*]
Christian:	No.
Therapist:	'A' stands for an activating event such as going to a party or doing a presentation, 'B' for beliefs about the event, and 'C' for the emotional consequences such as anxiety, fear, avoidance or being withdrawn. Let me use an example to illustrate the relationship between A, B and C. Mark was anxious and worried about doing a presentation at work. About 100 people would be there, some of whom were senior people from the company. Ever since he had been asked to do it, he felt tense, experienced butterflies in his stomach, and had problems sleeping. Whenever he thought about it, his heart pounded and he shook.
Christian:	Oh. Well, I can relate to that myself. It is terrible.
Therapist:	Mark felt the same too. What was it that caused his anxiety and his bodily sensations?
Christian:	Doing the presentation, especially in front of so many people, I suppose.
Therapist:	What you are saying is that A (doing the presentation) causes C (anxiety and bodily sensations). Why do you think this is?
Christian:	Well. If he didn't have to do it, he wouldn't have felt the way he did.
Therapist:	It sounds logical. But do you think 100 people in a similar situation would have felt exactly the same? [*Note the use of 100 people technique here*]
Christian:	Oh. I have never thought of that. I suppose not.
Therapist:	If, as you believe, it is A causing C, one would expect that everybody in a similar or the same situation would experience the same consequences. The reality is that some people could be the same as Mark, some even worse, whereas some would not have any problem at all.
Christian:	It makes sense.
Therapist:	Could it be that something is wrong with his brain or with those of others in a similar position?
Christian:	Oh. Ah. I don't think so.

Therapist: Absolutely. Otherwise, everybody who experiences anxiety would have a brain problem. In CBT his anxiety was likely to do with his thoughts about it. What do you think his thinking was?

Christian: If he couldn't do it well, he was not good enough.

Therapist: This was what he said. What else?

Christian: This means that he was not as good as he thought he was. People would think less of him.

Therapist: Absolutely. He also said that he would be a failure and there would be no future for him, if the presentation did not go well. He thought about it a lot and about the consequences that it might have on his family. How helpful was it to think in this way?

Christian: Not helpful at all.

Therapist: Because of?

Christian: He put too much pressure on himself and this made his anxiety worse.

Therapist: If this is so, is it A causing C, or his thoughts (B) causing C?

Christian: I know what you mean. His thoughts (B) were the problem.

Therapist: Mark couldn't do the presentation as he was too anxious. Jack was asked to do it instead as he had been working with Mark on the project for some time. He was feeling excited as well as apprehensive about it. What do you think Jack was thinking about it that made him feel excited as well as apprehensive?

Christian: He might see it as an opportunity and a challenge.

Therapist: That's good. What else?

Christian: He could always learn from the experience.

Therapist: Jack also said that he would give it his best shot. He did not need to do it perfectly nor be able to answer every question well. Feedback (positive or negative) could help with the project they had been doing. Were his thoughts helpful or unhelpful?

Christian: Helpful.

Therapist: Because of?

Christian: He would be less anxious and worried about doing the presentation. This could help with his presentation.

Therapist: We can see that given the same situation or event, the consequences were different, as in the case of Mark and Jack. If A causes C, one would expect that everybody in the same situation/event would have experienced a similar level of anxiety, but it wasn't the case, as illustrated in this example. Do we have control and choice over the way we think and behave?

Christian: Yes. I think so.

Therapist: When people believe that their anxiety (or other emotional problems) is due to a brain disease or genetic factors, there is little or no incentive for them to learn a different, more realistic/adaptive way of thinking about things around them. The reality is that control and choice are always available.

Homework

Reducing the stigma of 'mental illness' is about giving clients *control* over their mood, which can be achieved through knowing that they do have a *choice* (helpful or unhelpful) over the way they think about and/or behave in certain situations. Christian was asked to keep a daily mood diary consisting of four columns for listing and describing situations, emotions, unhelpful thoughts and helpful thoughts.

In the first column, Christian described anxiety-provoking situations with the date and time on which they happened. In the next column he listed associated unhelpful thoughts and rated them (from 0 per cent to 100 per cent), according to how much he believed them. Next, he listed emotions associated with the situation and rated them for intensity (again, from 0 per cent to 100 per cent). Finally, Christian listed possible and believable helpful responses in relation to the unhelpful ones and rated his belief in those responses.

Through the use of the daily mood diary for two months, Christian now held a different, better informed perspective about the nature of mental health problems, and acknowledged that these problems were largely due to unhelpful thoughts and the way he coped. Knowing that mental health problems were not predominantly biological in nature (e.g. genetic, chemical imbalances) helped with stigma reduction, particularly the perceived stigma.

To build on the work of the daily mood diary, Christian was asked to read a number of chapters in a book called *Mind over mood* (Greenberger and Padesky 1995).

Other techniques

Other relevant techniques include 'The brain', 'Rewriting assumptions' and 'Cognitive continuum'.

Notes for therapists about stigma

- 'Mental illness' is a stigmatising term, whereas the term 'mental health problem' is relatively de-stigmatising.

- Helping clients to gain control over mood and exercise choices in the way they think and behave has the positive effect of reducing stigma.
- Mental health problems are the result of many interacting factors such as genetic, biological, environmental, psychological, emotional and behavioural, and are not predominantly due to biogenetic factors.
- A relevant example used in the teaching of the ABC model will help to shift the focus away from biogenetic causes to psychosocial explanations of mental health problems.

Chapter 2

Biological and genetic explanations of 'mental illness'

It has been suggested that stigmatisation of 'mental illness' is partly due to people being ignorant about the nature and causes of the illness. Biological and genetic explanations have been advocated as the likely causes of the 'illness', with the declared intention of reducing stigma, prejudice and discrimination. The idea of defining 'mental illness' as 'an illness like any other' is that individuals who suffer from it are no different from those with physical illnesses such as diabetes, epilepsy, Parkinson's disease, cardiovascular and lung diseases. They are 'victims' of inherited diseases. As such, they require psychiatric or psychological care, understanding, support and medication, not stigmatisation and discrimination.

Blaming the brain for mental health problems is assumed to have the effect of reducing the guilt, shame and blame in clients and their relatives. It also provides hope that these problems can be successfully treated in a way similar to that for physical illness. Physical illnesses, such as cancer, diabetes and heart disease, are either successfully treated medically or efficiently managed through nursing care and medical treatment. There is therefore no reason for clients, relatives, the public or professionals to view mental health problems any differently from physical ones and for these problems not to be treated in a similar way.

Some mental health professionals are keen to advocate the biological and genetic nature of 'mental illness'. This is particularly so with those clients who have a recurrent history of 'mental illness', display severe symptoms such as hearing voices, are difficult to treat, or are not amenable to drug treatment. The idea of 'mental illness' being a brain disease is deeply ingrained in the minds of the public, carers, relatives and clients and is often inaccurately and frequently reported as such by the media (Wahl 1995). People tend not to question the reliability and helpfulness of such explanations because of the powerful influence of the pharmaceutical industry (Ashton 2001) and of the support from some healthcare professionals, public organisations, contract-based medical research findings and political institutions. The identification of antipsychotic and antidepressant drugs lent credence to the notion of 'chemical imbalance' as the cause of mental health disorders and reinforced the view that biological pathogens were at work in mental health problems (Kinross-Wright 1955; Barsa and Kline 1956; Denber and Bird 1957). The 'biological' message is that depression is a flaw in chemistry not character; mental illness is due to an insufficient level or dysfunction of neurotransmitters; and depression is a physical illness like any other such as arthritis or diabetes (Double 2002; Moynihan et al. 2002).

It is therefore not surprising that clients are assessed for the presence of symptoms that correspond to a particular psychiatric diagnosis (e.g. schizophrenia, depression) and that a family history of 'mental illness' is often scrutinised for a genetic link to be established. The illness model persuades clients, relatives and the public (and some mental health professionals) to believe that medication is the main factor for recovery: 'Your problem (a diagnosis) is due to chemical imbalance or is genetic and you need to be on drug(s).' It implies that there is little or nothing clients can do to overcome their psychological and emotional distress through their own efforts, even with help and care. The following is what some professionals said about the causes of 'mental illness':

- 'This man suffers with a recurrent depressive disorder which may be biochemical in origin.'
- 'His father has not had treatment for depression but he does have a dysthymic personality.'
- 'I discussed the causation of his illness and the biochemical hypothesis must lie behind the recurrent nature of his illness.'
- 'There is clearly a positive family history in that his father, brother and elder son have all suffered from depression.'
- 'I think the most likely diagnosis is that he has a cyclothymic personality . . . with a view to seeing whether this man is treatable.'

Undoubtedly, clinicians' views of the cause of 'mental illness' can influence the way clients' problems are explained to them and their relatives. Whittle (1996) finds that clients' and relatives' beliefs become more biological after a first admission to hospital. These findings suggest that high exposure to psychiatric experts of a particular approach (biogenetic or psychosocial) can influence people's perception or belief about the nature and the causes of 'mental illness'.

Presenting 'mental illness' as a physical illness is assumed to have the positive effect of reducing stigma, prejudice and discrimination. It is therefore not surprising that clients (and relatives) want others to understand that 'mental illness' is a 'real' disease, not something imagined. They sought to have others recognise mental illnesses as real, because these illnesses are genetic or biological in nature. They compared their illnesses to other medical conditions and identified the brain as the afflicted organ. That 'mental illness' is a disease like any other disease has been portrayed in most de-stigmatising mental health educational programmes. Promoting psychiatric and psychological conditions as disease-based conditions has received support from organisations such as the United States National Institute for Mental Health (NIMH) and from some 'mental illness' advocacy groups including the National Alliance for the Mentally Ill (NAMI) and the National Mental Health Association (NMHA) in the United States and SANE and Depression Alliance in the UK (Mother Jones 2002; Moncrieff 2003). For example, the National Alliance on Mental Illness and many other campaign groups claim that:

- 'Mental illness' is a biologically based brain disorder. It cannot be overcome through 'will power'.
- It is a 'no-fault', inherited and genetic disease, just like the colour of your hair, the colour of your eyes and your body shape.
- It is not a choice, nor a weakness in a person's character or intelligence.
- 'Mental illness' is a chemical imbalance and brain disorder.
- It is not something in the imagination or something that happens because people are lazy or stupid.
- It is not a matter of thinking the right things and feeling the right way.

However, there is growing evidence that the biological view of mental health problems may not be as beneficial and helpful as it was hoped in modifying public attitudes (Read and Law 1999; Hinshaw and Cicchetti 2000; Phelan 2002). Stigmatising attitudes are found to have worsened in recent years (Sayce 2000). Research and clinical observations show that when clients subscribe to biological and genetic explanations, they tend to take a more passive role in the treatment process and to feel ashamed of having such conditions and/or to use the 'illness' to justify their irresponsible, antisocial and avoidance behaviour (e.g. 'I can't help it. I have no control over my addiction. My doctor said I have an addictive personality'). They are also pessimistic about their chances of recovery.

Research on causal explanations of mental health problems

Research evidence to date suggests that biological and genetic causal beliefs about mental health problems are related to negative attitudes in the general public, clients and mental health professionals. The most consistent findings are:

- 'Mental clients' are dangerous, antisocial and unpredictable (Nunnally 1950; Green et al. 1987; Riskind and Wahl 1992).

- Clients may take a more passive role with mental health professionals (Hill and Bale 1981).
- These biogenetic explanations may actually contribute to the continuing problem of stigmatisation of mental health problems (Crisp 1999; Sayce 2000; Read and Harre 2001; Walker and Read 2002).
- Mental health professionals are likely to take a more paternalistic role in treatment interventions.

What is not entirely clear is the extent to which different causal explanations (biogenetic versus psychosocial) could influence people's perceptions of 'mental illness' and of individuals who suffer from it. Do psychosocial explanations result in a different, less stigmatising attitude?

Experimental studies

A New Zealand study found that when a biogenetic explanation was given after participants had watched a video of a person describing his psychotic experiences (e.g. hearing voices and seeing things), ratings of dangerousness and unpredictability were significantly increased. However, a video explaining the same experiences in terms of adverse life events (psychosocial explanation) led to a slight improvement in attitudes (Walker and Read 2002).

Research shows that psychosocial explanations are significantly related to positive attitudes of treatment outcome and prognosis for clients suffering a range of mental health problems. We asked 110 community volunteers to rate clients suffering from a range of relatively common mental health problems such as anxiety disorders, eating disorders, psychosis, depression, substance misuse disorders and personality disorders (Lam et al. 2005). On each disorder, they were asked: 'How curable is mental illness?' 'How likely would they be to harm themselves?' 'How disabling is the condition to the client?' 'How much professional help does the client require?' 'Is hospitalisation essential?' Prior to the rating (completing a questionnaire), some participants were told that 'research suggests that these biologically based disorders may be the result of genetic factors', whereas others were told that 'research suggests that these psychologically based problems may be the result of stress factors'. A control group was told that 'research suggests that the causes of these disorders are not yet entirely clear'.

The participants, who understood (from research) that these problems were psychologically based, rated them as significantly less stigmatising than the other participants did. By contrast, the participants who were told that these problems were genetically based, rated them as more disabling, irrespective of the types of mental health problems such as panic disorder and schizophrenia. They also rated clients with these disorders as significantly

- less likely to be curable
- more likely to harm themselves
- more likely to require professional help and frequent hospitalisation.

Lam and Salkovskis (2007) investigated the extent to which causal accounts (biological and psychological) would influence clients' perception of a person with panic disorder. Participants in this study were anxious and depressed clients who did not suffer from panic disorder. Forty-nine participants suffering from depression and/or anxiety were played a ten-minute assessment video featuring a woman who suffered from panic attacks and agoraphobia. Crucially, before watching the video, some participants read an information sheet that explained that panic attacks are caused by psychological processes, whereas others read a version that said that panic is a biological condition caused by 'chemical imbalance' in the brain. A control group read that the causes of panic disorder are unknown. After watching the video, the participants rated the woman's chances for the future. Those who read that panic was a psychological condition rated the woman's chances of recovery as significantly better than the other participants did. By contrast, those who read that panic was a biological condition rated the woman as

- significantly less likely to make progress following treatment: medication and cognitive behaviour therapy
- requiring significantly longer period of treatment sessions
- significantly more likely to harm themselves and others
- significantly more likely to commit suicide.

The findings, in the context of previous publications, suggested that biological explanations of mental health problems may increase public, professional and client perception of harm (self-harm and harming others) and result in more negative predictions regarding prognosis and treatment outcome, while psychological accounts may have the opposite (de-stigmatising) effect. Biological arguments may in fact do more harm than good, increasing stigma, and causing clients to feel pessimistic about their chances of recovery. The results in these studies call into question the widely accepted practice of promoting biological or disease explanations of mental health problems (Lam et al. 2005; Lam and Salkovskis 2007; Lam and Salkovskis in press).

Why is focusing on biogenetic explanations of mental health problems a clinical issue?

Biological and genetic factors may be promoted (or over-promoted) as causal with little regard for the potential impact that such ideas may have

(Rimes and Salkovskis 1998). These accounts may have the unwanted effect of inducing pessimism regarding the likely treatment outcome in clients, their carers and the general public. This is particularly so with clients who do not respond to drug treatment or with clients with a series of relapses. There is now some suggestion that linking psychiatric or psychological problems with biological and genetic causes tends to lead to more paternalistic approaches to client care as mental health professionals tend to emphasise medication as a principal way to manage symptoms (Kent and Read 1998), instead of exploring the *cause* of these symptoms and the *mechanisms* involved in the continuation or worsening of these symptoms.

It has been suggested that labelling 'mental illness' as having a biological cause may bring about an element of shame to individuals (and their families) with mental health problems, adversely affecting their self-confidence, and their willingness to seek professional help (Kessler et al. 1996). Attributing mental health problems to brain disease additionally affects the extent to which sufferers are regarded as unpredictable, potentially antisocial or even dangerous by and to themselves and others. After all, the brain is commonly understood to be the organ of the mind and the 'seat of the self'. A diseased brain could mean a diseased mind and self, implying that these individuals do not have control over their mind and behaviour. As such, they are not responsible for their unpredictable, violent and aggressive behaviour. Note that unpredictability, violence and aggression are the most prominent factors associated with stigma, prejudice and discrimination.

The extent to which clients accept the notion of 'chemical imbalances' may therefore be linked to lower levels of perceived control, higher levels of depression and suicidal ideation. It also adversely affects their response and engagement in therapy. For example, one client said that his depression was due to 'chemical imbalance', as his psychiatrist suggested was the likely cause; this view was reinforced by his key worker. He did not put any effort or commitment into cognitive behaviour therapy and blamed his lack of progress and his mood problems on his 'diseased' brain.

The case of Caroline

'I was so pleased and relieved to know what was wrong with me. I now know that I suffer from depression. I did not know what was going on inside my head. I was fearful that I was insane or would go mad. I felt low, down, tired, and tearful and found it difficult to concentrate and get out of bed. I lost interest in going out to see people and socialise and could not go to work . . . It was terrible and scary,' said Caroline.

It is understandable that Caroline (and other clients) was relieved to know what was wrong with her. She now had a certainty in the form of a psychiatric diagnosis for these symptoms, although she did not know why these symptoms had developed and what made them worse. She was also hopeful that the drug treatment being prescribed would cure her depression, in a way similar to that for physical illness. Her psychiatrist told her that the cause of her depression was likely to be a chemical imbalance in her brain and also genetic, since her mother and her uncle also suffered from it, and that she was likely to take medication for a long time or even for the rest of her life. This was another 'bonus' for her as it indicated that her depression was not her fault and she was not psychologically weak. She was just the victim of an inherited disease.

Caroline was referred to cognitive behaviour therapy for depression and low self-esteem. 'I have been depressed all my life and medication hasn't been as helpful as I would have hoped for,' said Caroline. She was a 36-year-old mother of three young children, aged 10, 7 and 5. She had graduated with a first-class honours degree from a prestigious university, and then qualified as a chartered accountant. She was now a full-time mother. However, looking after her children was a struggle as she needed to be a perfect wife and mother. Her husband was a businessman and was supportive of her, but he couldn't understand her problem. He found it difficult to give her emotional support and did not understand depression and the nature of it, saying, 'We have everything we want in life: a big house, a holiday home, a yacht, cars, expensive holidays all over the world, and no financial worry.' 'What is she depressed about?' was the question he kept asking. He came to accept that depression was part of her and it was a genetic and biological condition. After all, her mother and an uncle suffered from depression and her psychiatrist and general practitioner all said that biological and genetic factors were the likely cause of her depression. In the last ten years or so, she had been hospitalised on three occasions, ranging from a couple of weeks to a month and had been on a range of drugs of various dosages. She was also given a course of electro-convulsive therapy (ECT) which had little or no long-term benefit.

Although she had the help of an au-pair, she just felt everything was on top of her. She had to organise and do everything perfectly. Otherwise, she would feel guilty and criticise herself for being lazy and useless. She had to be on the run or doing things all the time and found it difficult to relax. She admitted that she was a perfectionist and saw nothing wrong with needing to be perfect. 'I will feel guilty for not doing things. I can't just sit down and watch television, read the newspaper, or listen to music, even for a short time,' said Caroline. She saw this as being part of her personality, something that couldn't be changed: 'I was born like this and my mother was also that kind of person,' said

Caroline. Saying 'no' to requests from friends and relatives was particularly difficult for her, although she would have liked to have been able to do so in some circumstances. Not only did she need to be perfect in what she did, but she also needed people's approval and recognition. Otherwise, the fear of being disliked or rejected made her feel less worthy as a person. Admittedly, her self-worth was conditional on people liking and accepting her, and on not being criticised. She was a perfectionist as well as a workaholic, working hard to be a perfect wife and mother and to please people around her.

When Caroline was referred to CBT for the first time, she was not sure whether this type of therapy could help her depression, saying that 'it is not a matter of thinking the right things and feeling the right way and all will be well'. She was hoping that a 'right' drug or a combination of drugs could be found to cure her depression, despite having been on medication for a long time. Her previous experiences with psychotherapy had been disappointing. Biological and genetic explanations for her depression became more compelling as a result.

Slowly and surely, she started to respond to CBT and felt more optimistic about her recovery from depression. She could see that her perfectionism, self-criticism, approval-seeking behaviour (see Part III of this book), and fear of rejection and criticism (see Part IV) all contributed to the ups and downs of her moods, and to the development of her depression. However, the fear of the depression coming back was always at the back of her mind, despite the progress being made with CBT and a gradual reduction in her medication. 'While I am well now, I wonder how long it will last. I just feel that I do not have control over whether or not I am depressed or well,' said Caroline in an anxious and worried tone of voice. Her experience or feelings were not unusual as the idea of 'mental illness' being a disease of the brain had not only had a profound adverse effect on her (and other clients') fear, but also affected her confidence to reduce or stop taking medication. The desire to stop taking medication was there and not just because of its side effects; she said that she did not want to depend on it for the rest of her life. However, the notion of 'a diseased brain, chemical imbalance or genetic factor' was in the way of her taking a 'risk' and therefore making a full recovery: to be able to 'stay' better.

'My depression is coming back. Can I come to see you now?' Caroline phoned at eight one evening and was in a terrible state when she arrived. She was tearful and shaking, saying that she was fearful of the depression coming back. She couldn't go to sleep, despite feeling very tired. Not being able to go to sleep, to her, was a symptom of depression and was an indication of the imminent recurrence of her depression. This symptom was present prior to her becoming depressed in her last three bouts of depression. Another similar episode happened again a few months later. She called to say that her 'depression is coming back' with the same rationale as before. This time the symptoms were that she was feeling tired and drained and could not concentrate. Her psychiatrist warned her to watch out for these symptoms of depression.

She put her learning into practice at every available opportunity and started to have a better understanding of the way in which her emotional upset occurred (see Chapter 4 on 'CBT theory of emotional upset'). She accepted that her emotional upset had little or nothing to do with it being biological, and that it was more to do with the way she thought about the situation or other people and with her own reaction. As a result, she made steady progress in the two years of CBT therapy, which started with a weekly session for ten weeks, then once every month for three months, and then once every three months. On our final session, she said that she now had the confidence and a tool to deal with adversity. She also said that had she not been able to think in a more realistic and adaptive way, she would have gone down with depression a few times in the past two years. Her confidence had improved and her fear of the depression coming back was greatly reduced; this had changed her perception of 'mental illness' being a disease of the brain.

Cognitive behaviour therapy approach to causal explanations

Cognitive behaviour therapy takes the view that mental health problems are due to a range of interacting factors; these factors interact with one another in the development and continuation of the problems. Biological or genetic explanation is just one of them and should *not* be emphasised as the principal cause in de-stigmatisation programmes and/or in professionals' dissemination of information to both clients and the public. An integrative model of causality that focuses on psychological, social, biogenetic and environmental factors is believed to be an effective way of helping the public improve their perception of the nature of mental health problems (Figure 2.1). It also empowers clients to take responsibility for the management of their moods (e.g. anxiety, worry, anger, frustration, depression, guilt and shame) and their behaviour (e.g. procrastination, low self-esteem, self-criticism, avoidance, safety-seeking behaviour and approval-seeking behaviour). Blaming the mood and behavioural problems on 'a diseased brain' may in fact do more harm than good, increase stigma, and cause clients to feel pessimistic about their chances of recovery.

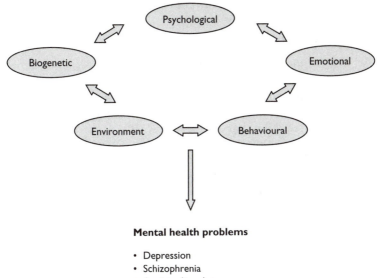

Figure 2.1 Integrated model of causality

CBT also takes the view that it is perhaps not the focus on biogenetic factors that is problematic, but rather the way in which the term 'brain disease and chemical imbalance' is being used to present these factors in the context of clients being portrayed as not having control over their mind and behaviour and therefore not being responsible for their actions. If so, this approach clearly does not empower clients to be proactive in the management of their mood and behaviour. These biogenetic factors could be presented in conjunction with the fact that many biochemical or physiological differences can be caused by psychosocial factors, including the 'abnormalities' found in people diagnosed as 'schizophrenic' or 'serotonin deficient' in people with depression and obsessive-compulsive disorder. After all, psychosocial factors are known to influence the way in which physical attributes develop or mature, including intelligence, temperament, body weight and height. Ironically, this is well accepted in illnesses such as cardiovascular disease, hypertension, diabetics and lung cancer. People with these conditions may have a choice and control over their conditions through changing lifestyle, for either better or worse. By the same token, mental health clients may be empowered to exercise a choice and control over their condition, once they understand that 'chemical imbalance or abnormality in the brain' can be caused by psychosocial factors. Sadly, this is not the case for mental health clients as they are portrayed as being victims of 'a brain disease', about which there is little or nothing they can do.

Technique: Developing an alternative explanation

Rationale and focus

Clients often do not look for reasons for their symptoms such as problems in sleeping, poor concentration, or tearfulness. The disease explanation often makes them believe that these symptoms are due to a 'chemical imbalance' in the brain. This can make them feel helpless and hopeless and may therefore increase the chance of a relapse. It is therefore not surprising that clients feel scared of the presence of these symptoms and become obsessed with the consequences as a result. They believe these symptoms are positively associated with the 'brain not working properly' and there is nothing they can do about it. One common observable fact is that while they are well clients often question how long they can be well.

Developing an alternative explanation not only helps clients seek less threatening reasons for these symptoms, but also questions the soundness of the disease explanation. Once an alternative explanation is established, the therapist can ask the client: 'Of the two possible explanations, which one is more believable and why?' In the case of Caroline described above, she believed that not being able to sleep (despite feeling really tired) was a symptom of depression and was an indication of depression returning.

Process

Therapist: How strongly do you believe that not being able to sleep means that depression is coming back?

Caroline: Quite high – 80 per cent.

Therapist: Because of?

Caroline: My psychiatrist said that a problem with sleeping is a symptom of depression and asked me to watch out for it. This symptom was there prior to my previous three episodes of depression.

Therapist: I can accept that this is a symptom of depression, but it could also be a symptom of other things. What else could it be?

Caroline: Oh. Ah. I don't know.

Therapist: Let's take the example of an individual winning the lottery, passing an examination, gaining a promotion, or getting married soon. Will the person have a problem getting to sleep?

Caroline: Yeah. I suppose so.

Therapist: Because of?

Caroline: They may be excited about it and there are a lot of things going through their head, making it difficult for them to get to sleep.

Therapist: True. Does it mean that they will suffer from depression?

Caroline: Oh. I don't think so.

Therapist: By the same token, people who are too emotionally tired may also have a problem sleeping, in anxious or worrying situations or events. In this case, there will be a lot of things going through their head, but it does not mean that they are *all* going to suffer from depression.

Caroline: Ah. I never thought of that.

Therapist: If people start to associate a problem in sleeping with depression or the return of depression, it can make things worse. This means that more and more things are going through their head. Don't forget that a sleeping problem is just one of the symptoms of depression, which does not lead to depression on its own. You need to have more symptoms in order to be sure about the possibility of having depression.

Caroline: It does make sense.

Therapist: What is going through your head?

Caroline: It's about this Christmas party that I am going to with my husband. I just don't always feel comfortable with parties and do not know what to say to people. I am anxious about people finding me boring or not liking me. This party is a company party and is important to my husband. I don't want to let him down.

Therapist: If your best friend was emotionally tired with all these things going through her head, would you expect her to be able to even sleep, let alone sleep well?

Caroline: Not really.

Therapist: Does it also mean that she was going to have depression?

Caroline: Yeah. I know what you mean. She will not.

Therapist: Of the two possible explanations, which one is more believable: a diseased brain or anxiety and worry about going to the party?

Caroline: Anxiety and worry about going to the party.

Homework

Caroline was asked to:

- Make a list of these thoughts in relation to going to the party and to change them into realistic alternative ones.
- Ask five of her friends whether they do or did have problems sleeping, in relation to either exciting things or worrying and anxiety-producing situations. If so, did they believe that the problem sleeping was about their developing depression?

- Read a chapter entitled 'You can change the way you feel' (Burns 1999). This chapter helped her understand that negative and irrational thoughts of magnification, fortune telling, black and white, mental filter, and/or mind reading about the Christmas party were the reasons for her problems in sleeping, not the 'diseased' brain.

Technique: Costs and benefits analysis

Rationale and focus

One way to weaken the power of the biological explanations is to discuss with the client what these explanations can offer and at what cost. As the process of the discussion goes on, it becomes clear to the client that such explanations may in fact do more harm than good not only in terms of treatment outcome, but also by adversely influencing their self-perception, self-image and self-esteem: a person with a 'diseased' brain.

Once the client realises that accepting the biological explanations is detrimental to their recovery and self-worth, it encourages them to give up the 'sick' role, which may be used for gaining unhealthy attention and support and for avoiding responsibility (e.g. 'I am sick and not well. I can't help it'). It also helps to motivate and empower them to adopt an alternative and effective approach in dealing with their emotional problems and coping with adversity. That alternative approach is cognitive behaviour therapy. Caroline (described above) realised that the biological explanations were not beneficial for her recovery from depression, despite having been on medication for a long time.

Process

Therapist: How strongly do you believe that your depression was the result of biological and/or genetic cause, on a scale of 1 to 100?

Caroline: It is much less now. It used to be 100 per cent.

Therapist: Good for you. What did you see as the benefits of accepting the biological explanations as the cause of your depression?

Caroline: I didn't really know. I was just relieved that it was not my fault I was suffering from depression. The problem was in my brain. Initially, it did help to reduce the guilt and shame.

Therapist: And?

Caroline: Not be stigmatised for having this condition.

Therapist: What else?

Caroline: That's all.

Therapist:	What are the costs?
Caroline:	Although it did help to reduce the guilt and shame of having depression, I somehow feel ashamed of being different from others and of being mental and insane. I also feel guilty for being a burden to my family and not working hard enough to pull myself together.
Therapist:	What else?
Caroline:	I feel vulnerable and do not feel that I am in control of my moods, despite being on medication.
Therapist:	It is not good to feel like this.
Caroline:	It is terrible.
Therapist:	It seems that believing that your depression is due to a 'diseased' brain has not been beneficial to your recovery, despite your being on medication. What conclusion can we draw?
Caroline:	It does not give me any hope and confidence about recovering as I feel there is nothing I can do about it. The only thing I can do is to take my medication regularly.

Homework

It is useful to keep a mood and behavioural diary in relation to upsetting events. The diary can show that our mood is largely the result of our thinking about the event and the way we react to it. It has nothing to do with a 'brain' disease. For example, an individual might feel low and down and upset for not doing well in a mock examination. The person was self-critical for not preparing well and for making so many mistakes and believed that it was unlikely they would pass the real examination. An alternative helpful thinking about the same event was that this result, however bad, was not the end of the world. It was actually a good learning experience, which would help with the preparation for the real examination. There was no need to be self-critical. Being able to engage in such realistic thinking about the event can motivate the person to become more resourceful in preparing for the examination.

Caroline was able to see that her moods (ups and downs) were not due to a 'diseased' brain. The evidence came from keeping a diary over a period of two months. As a result, her conviction that the cause of depression was biological and genetic was diminishing.

Other techniques

Other relevant techniques include the 'ABC model', 'The brain' and 'Prediction'.

Notes for therapists about causal explanations

- Biological explanations may do more harm than good, increasing stigma, and causing clients to feel pessimistic about their chances of recovery.
- An integrative causal model helps clients understand that a number of interacting factors are involved in the development and continuation of mental health problems.
- An emphasis on psychosocial causal factors may motivate and empower clients to work on their moods.
- One way to weaken the soundness of the biological and genetic explanation is to use an accumulation of evidence (e.g. keeping an emotional or thoughts diary) to show that emotional upset is largely due to our thinking and reaction, not because of a 'chemical imbalance' in the brain.
- It is important for therapists to examine their own causal attitude (biogenetic versus psychosocial) and what they say to clients in the light of research evidence. Their causal beliefs can influence clients' beliefs about the cause and nature of mental health problems, their working relationship with clients and treatment outcome.

Chapter 3

Prejudice, discrimination and 'mental illness'

When someone is rejected or will not be considered for a job for which he or she is qualified because of ethnic, racial, age or gender group, that is discrimination. Decisions to employ someone must, by law, be based on the prospective employee's ability, experience and qualification to do the job, not on his or her age, gender, race, and so forth. Discrimination happens because prejudices and stereotypes may influence employers' perceptions of an applicant and therefore their assessment of his or her ability to do the job, to get along with people and to work in a team setting. For example, an employer who believes that women are hormonally and emotionally unsuited to stressful corporate work may wrongly believe that a female applicant is indeed less able to cope with the demands of the job or less able to perform than a male applicant. The decision, based on prejudice and stereotypes, not to hire her is discrimination. Similarly, the decision not to hire female applicants because of a mistaken belief that women with families are more likely to take more days off over child care is also discrimination. An employer who does not hire African Americans because of a false belief that blacks are lazy and unreliable is discriminatory. An employer who does not hire older people because of an unfounded belief that older people are less productive and more likely to go off sick than young people is discriminatory.

The Disability Discrimination Act 1995 in the UK aims to end the discrimination that many people with disabilities face. This Act gives people with disabilities rights in the areas of employment, education, access to goods, facilities and services. The Americans with Disabilities Act 1990 (ADA) makes it clear that exclusion of qualified individuals based on disability is illegal. An employer who rejects someone in a wheelchair or someone with a visual or hearing impairment without regard to the person's ability and experience to do a specific job is discriminatory. If an employer denies a job to someone based on stereotypes of disabled individuals rather than on qualification, experience and ability, that is discrimination. By the same token, if an employer rejects an applicant with appropriate quali-fications, skills and ability because of his or her mental health status, or previous mental health status, or because he or she is on psychotropic medication, that is discrimination. Wahl (1999) reports that such discrimination is not uncommon towards individuals with mental health problems, once their mental health histories are revealed. The following is what some clients said:

- 'In job interviews, once they find out I'm on medication, I am usually dismissed. They don't give the reasons. But that's the reason.'
- 'A man who was recruiting me for a job called, and, when I told him [I had psychiatric problems] he got off the phone and he hasn't called me back.'

In another example of positive discrimination against individuals with mental health problems, Wahl (1999: 83) reported that one former client said: 'I was denied a job because I had circled the fact that I had a psychiatric disorder. But then I reapplied again . . . this time I did not put I was mentally ill or taking psychotropic medication. I got the job.' Discriminatory treatment in other aspects of clients' or former clients' lives is also reported in areas of housing, education, health insurance, voluntary work, immigration, parenting, driving licences and access to justice (Sayce 1998).

Psychiatric diagnosis often causes others to view individuals with mental health problems as less competent and less reliable; those on psychotropic drugs as having no control over mood and behaviour; and biological and genetic explanations suggest they have no control over their minds. These three factors may have contributed to the problems of prejudices and stereotypes, giving the public a *distorted* image of individuals with mental health problems as violent, criminal, dangerous, unpredictable and antisocial; and employers a false belief that they are less competent, less reliable and less able to deal with stress and to function at an interpersonal level. Negative and biased media input (e.g. films, television, novels and newspapers) often has the unwanted effect of maintaining the problems of prejudices and stereotypes and of contributing to discriminatory treatment against individuals with mental health problems (Wahl 1995).

Why is prejudice and discrimination a clinical issue?

Imagine that you were frustrated at failing to obtain employment because of your mental health history; that you were given a psychiatric diagnosis and were told that the problem was a 'diseased' brain; and that you needed to be on medication for the rest of your life or for a long time in order to restore the 'chemical balance' in the brain. How would this make you feel? It is quite demoralising, depressing and upsetting that prejudice, discrimination and stigmatisation are basically related to the issue of being 'mental': having no control over your mind and behaviour. Individuals in such circumstances may view themselves as being different from others, and believe that they are less acceptable to others or that others would reject or dislike them in a range of social and work situations, thereby adversely affecting their confidence to socialise and/or reintegrate into society. They may therefore behave in the way society expects them to in a self-fulfilling prophecy, thus worsening the problems of prejudice and discrimination and denting their chance of recovery.

Clients may dislike themselves for being 'mental', and be anxious and worried about rejection, about being disliked, about not being able to cope with work, or about reintegration into society. They may use the 'sick role' to avoid social contact, to act in a socially unacceptable manner (e.g. tantrums and attention-seeking behaviour), to stay in their 'shell' (e.g. not looking for a job), or to take a passive role in the treatment process. The problems associated with the 'sick role' and issues relating to prejudice and discrimination (by others and themselves) need to be addressed during the course of their treatment.

The case of Christian

As described previously, Christian could not quite shake off the stigma of 'mental illness' and continued to encounter, from time to time, hurtful and offensive attitudes and behaviour. (See the case of Christian in Chapter 1 for more information.) Christian's mother said:

> Christian, you should venture out into the real world and get a real job. I love having you working for me, but you don't have a future working here. You know that. You are talented and good at what you do. If you work for a company, you may be able to make a career and a future. All you need is self-confidence.

His mother was discussing Christian's future with him. Christian knew that. He also knew that his parents – and his mother in particular – could not be there for him for the rest of his life. At the age of 32, he should come out of his 'shell' and face the world in order to continue his recovery, to develop his confidence, career and future, and to overcome the problems of stigma, prejudice and discrimination. However, he felt uncomfortable and apprehensive about the uncertainty ahead: would he be able to cope? What if he couldn't cope? What if the stress became so great that he ended up drinking again or going back into hospital? Would he lose everything that he had achieved in the past two years since he left the hospital? He did not like having these thoughts, which bothered him quite a bit and undermined his self-confidence.

Although Christian knew in his heart that he was good at what he did, the thought of leaving his 'shell' was scary. He did not really look for a job and was frustrated over his procrastination. He was angry with himself for being a coward. He was highly critical of himself for not taking action to move on with his life. At the back of his mind, he was concerned about what others would think and how they would react, once his mental health history was revealed. His girlfriend was supportive and encouraging, saying:

> Christian, it's a good idea. You have nothing to lose. You should give yourself a chance. Avoidance or running away from reality will not give you the sort of confidence that you need for your recovery. You need to go out there to get experience, good or bad, in order to develop a career and a future.

His therapist agreed with his girlfriend.

With support from the people who were close to him and the benefit of CBT, Christian's view of himself slowly changed. He did not see himself as being different from others and/or stigmatised because of his previous mental health problems. He knew that his problems were *not* predominantly due to a 'chemical imbalance' in his brain, or to a genetic factor, or to a 'diseased' brain. His progress and the reduction in medication over the previous two years provided him with convincing evidence to reject the notion that his mental health problems were biogenetic in nature. It also gave him the confidence and hope to look for a different, better future.

He worked hard on his curriculum vitae, with the help of others, and sent out letters to companies. This was a big step for Christian, who never thought that he would be able to do that: to apply for a job. 'I have got an interview!' Christian was excited to be invited to go for a first-round interview with an international pharmaceutical company. He read the letter again and again to make sure that he had not misread it. 'I think I did well at the interview and I wasn't nervous and anxious,' said Christian, who was pleased with his performance and believed that he would get through to a second round. Two weeks after the first interview, a letter arrived, inviting him to attend a meeting with two senior people from the company. Although he was apprehensive about it, he was also excited and thankful for the opportunity and did a lot of research for it. After the second interview, one of the interviewers said:

> Christian, you did well at the interview. We have narrowed it down to two people (from twenty) who we think are suitable for the job. The

other candidate also performed well and was impressive. However, we are impressed not only by your confidence and knowledge in the field, but also by your articulation of ideas for web designs. We have decided to go for you. Congratulations.

Christian was over the moon and so were the people close to him. He was given a contract to sign and forms to fill in, one of which was a medication declaration. A week after returning the contract and the forms, he received a letter to say that the position was no longer available. This news was like a bombshell to him, shattering his hopes and damaging his self-confidence. He was tearful and confused and did not know the reasons for it. The only possible explanation was that he had indicated that he had suffered from depression, alcoholism and low self-esteem on the medication declaration form – but he no longer suffered from these problems. When he phoned to find out the reason, he wasn't given one. The position was not available was the reason given Christian said:

> What have I done to deserve this? It's not fair. I have worked so hard to change and now this has happened. The company makes drugs to help people. It's ironic that they have rejected me, probably because of my mental health history.

Christian was upset and tearful and in a state of bewilderment. His belief was that he would never be able to find a job.

Cognitive behaviour therapy approach to prejudice and discrimination

Changing the practice of prejudice and discrimination is a challenge and is not easy to do. However, it has been suggested that modifying people's perception of the nature and cause of 'mental illness' is a helpful and important step in working on such a challenge. There is growing evidence that an emphasis on mood problems (e.g. depression, anxiety, guilt, shame and anger) being basically related to the way in which a person thinks about and reacts to an adverse event (e.g. divorce, unemployment, argument, bereavement) can result in a less stigmatising attitude, which may in turn reduce the problems of prejudice and discrimination. Research shows that such an emphasis, in the form of describing mental health problems as being *stress-related*, is easier to understand and is more acceptable than the explanation of a 'diseased' brain. Some employers may even be able to relate it to their own personal circumstances or experiences.

For example, Nick was rejected for a job as a surveyor, once his depression was revealed on the medical form (or at the interview). However, he was successful in another interview, when he told the interviewer that he was depressed because of bereavement (his mother died) and his wife had just been diagnosed with cancer. Managing the family with two young children and caring for his wife was difficult and stressful, while he was grieving over the death of his mother (with whom he had a very close relationship) and doing a demanding job. However, he was no longer depressed and was not on medication. His wife had made a good recovery. Given such an explanation, an employer is more likely to focus on the applicant's suitability for the job based on ability, experience and qualification rather than the depression. Note that Nick declared his medical history at the interview and provided an explanation for it rather than leaving it to be found out on the medical form. Note also that in some countries, like the UK, it is illegal not to declare your health history when you are applying for a job, in the same way as when you take out medical insurance.

Helping clients improve their understanding of the nature and causes of mental health problems can have the effect of reducing self-stigma. It also helps them to explain their problems to others as stress-related, as most of these can be resolved with care, support, understanding and determination. A stress-related explanation may reduce the gravity of prejudice and discrimination.

Technique: Balloon

Rationale and focus

Many life events (e.g. a divorce, a job with long working hours, a mistake, an examination, a presentation, a row, or moving house) are potentially stressful, which can often be made worse (or better) by the way in which a person thinks about and/or reacts to the event. While the person may or may not be aware that he/she is stressed, an accumulation of stress can adversely affect the body's system, causing the person to feel increasingly frustrated, anxious, worried, hurt, resentful and guilty. Exhaustion, tiredness (emotional and physical), poor appetite, inability to concentrate and perform, declining social interests and sleeping problems can add more stress to the body's system. Ultimately, the system collapses or bursts, leading to the development of mental health problems such as depression, anxiety disorders, alcoholism, eating disorders or schizophrenia.

A balloon functions in a similar fashion to that of the body's system. Without a safety valve or allowing air to come out periodically, it will ultimately burst when the pressure inside the balloon reaches breaking point. An analogy like this is a good way to illustrate the cause of mental health problems and to correct the misguided views about individuals with these problems, thereby not only reducing self-stigma and self-prejudice, but also lessening the stigma, prejudice and discrimination that clients face. In using this technique, the therapist can work with the client to identify stressful events at different stages in his or her life and to evaluate what impact these could have on the body's system or on a balloon if stressful issues are not successfully resolved. In clinical practice, I often use a real balloon to maximise the impact of the concept.

Process

Therapist: A balloon is elastic. If we pump a bit of air into a balloon, what will happen to it?

Christian: It will get bigger.

Therapist: How about a bit more air?

Christian: Even bigger.

Therapist: Because it is elastic, it has a capacity to contain more air and becomes bigger and bigger. But if the air inside the balloon is more than its capacity, what will happen to it?

Christian: It will burst.

Therapist: Sure. Just before it bursts, it is still a 'functioning' balloon. A body is just like a balloon and is 'elastic', which means that it has the capacity to tolerate or cope with stress. However, if the stress levels have reached a critical point and beyond, what will happen to the body?

Christian: Oh. I suppose it will 'burst'.

Therapist: Meaning?

Christian: The body can't take any more stress.

Therapist: Meaning what in terms of health?

Christian: All sorts of health problems: physical and mental, I suppose.

Therapist: Absolutely. Physically, the person may develop high blood pressure, have a heart attack or a stroke. Mental health problems may include alcoholism, anxiety disorders and depression. Before it 'bursts', the body and the person can still function – just. For example, going to work or shopping, taking a holiday. They may not enjoy it or may struggle with daily living. Some people may not quite understand the reason for their depression or anxiety disorders. They think that it must be due to a brain disease, like a virus causing flu, or to a genetic condition like Parkinson's disease. The reality is that stress takes time, often months or years, to build before it causes damage to the body.

Christian: Oh. Ah. Is that what it is? It makes sense putting it in this way.

Therapist:	If you look back on your life, right from your early years, what sort of events did you find stressful?
Christian:	Well, I did not have a happy childhood. My parents argued a lot, often in front of us, and got divorced when my sister and I were young.
Therapist:	And?
Christian:	My mother was depressed and I felt responsible for her and for the divorce. I was sent to boarding school. I did not like it and was bullied. I was scared and frightened and did not know what to do. I avoided or tried to please people around me. I smoked and drank more and more alcohol to help me manage my anxiety and nervousness. It also helped me to feel better about myself, and to get accepted by other students at school.
Therapist:	Rather unpleasant, wasn't it?
Christian:	Yes. I felt rejected by my father as I had to go to a boarding school, whereas Helen, my younger sister, went to stay with him. I felt rejected by my mother when she remarried.
Therapist:	Had you not had these experiences, would you still have had the problems you had: depression, low self-esteem and drinking problems?
Christian:	I suppose not or it is highly unlikely.
Therapist:	Suppose these problems were due to a 'diseased' brain, how would such an explanation make you feel?
Christian:	Oh, yeah. I was told that my 'mental illness' was due to something wrong with my brain and that I have an 'addictive personality disorder' because of my drinking problem. I don't understand it and feel that I am different from other people. I am not normal.

Homework

Christian was asked to:

- Keep a stress diary, in which he would rate his stress levels using the scale of 1 to 100 in relation to a stressful event.
- Write down unhelpful and helpful ways of thinking and reactions towards the same event and then review the different stress levels afterwards. In the context of this book, the safety valve is the helpful thinking and constructive reactions.

Technique: Confirmation

Rationale and focus

Following a job rejection, Christian said that he would never be able to find a job. Another client said that she would never be able to find another partner after her divorce. These are examples of clients engaging in irrational thinking by over-generalisation, discounting the positive, magnification and mental filters (Burns 1999). These thoughts can adversely affect mood, motivation and confidence and therefore make it difficult for clients to change their present situation or reality. An unpleasant experience, however bad, is not confirmation that the situation or reality will always be the same in the future. However, not doing something in a proactive and constructive manner or giving up trying can have the unwanted effect of making the problem worse. In the case of Christian, his self-stigma and self-prejudice might get worse if he gave up trying and did not look at the job rejection as a learning experience.

The therapist can say: 'I had a bad experience of almost drowning in the sea when I was young. Does it mean that one such bad experience is confirmation that I will never be able to swim?'

Process

Therapist:	You said that you would never be able to find a job. How strongly do you believe that?
Christian:	My mental health history would go against me. I honestly do not think that I will be able to find a job. I will say 80 per cent.
Therapist:	80 per cent is quite high. It seems that one bad experience is confirmation to you that you will never be able to find a job.
Christian:	Yes.
Therapist:	Can you swim?
Christian:	Yes. I am quite good at it.
Therapist:	When I was young, I almost died in the sea. The experience was very scary and frightening. Does it mean that such an experience is confirmation that I will never be able to swim, no matter how hard I try?
Christian:	No. I don't think so.
Therapist:	Because of?
Christian:	You can always learn to overcome your fears and anxiety. Keep on trying and you will be able to swim.
Therapist:	If I don't?
Christian:	You won't be able to swim.

Therapist:	If you really believe that you will never be able to find a job and are not trying, then what?
Christian:	Yeah. Ah. I will never have a job.
Therapist:	You won't have a job. Is the problem due to you not trying or to your mental health problem?
Christian:	Oh. That's a difficult one to answer. I was rejected, most probably because of it.
Therapist:	That may be so. Does it mean that everybody who has/had a mental health problem will never be able to find a job?
Christian:	Ah. I suppose not.
Therapist:	Some individuals who have or have had mental health problems may experience problems in finding a job, but it is not confirmation that they will never be able to find one. We know for a fact that many of them are in employment. If you give up trying, then it is confirmation that you will never be able to have a job. Is it therefore confirmation that I will not be able to swim, just because of my early near-drowning experience?
Christian:	No. I know what you mean.
Therapist:	Is it confirmation that you will never be able to find a job, just because of one job rejection and/or of your mental health history?
Christian:	I need to keep on trying to overcome the stigma, prejudice and discrimination, in a way similar to you overcoming your fear and anxiety of drowning.

Homework

Christian was asked to:

- Write down a list of the costs of not trying to look for a job and a list of the benefits of trying.
- Talk to other clients or former clients, who were in employment, about their experiences (positive and negative) of seeking jobs. Christian would then know that although his mental health history might not be in his favour, it was not detrimental to job hunting. Furthermore, explaining his previous mental health problems in the context of their being stress-related could help.

Other techniques

Other relevant techniques include the 'ABC model', 'Developing an alternative explanation', 'Prediction' and 'The brain'.

Notes for therapists about prejudice and discrimination

- Prejudice and discrimination are a fact of life and happen to other disability groups. It is therefore important for the mentally ill to learn not to self-stigmatise and judge themselves in a negative way for having mental health problems.
- Clients' self-stigma and self-prejudice often pose a substantial threat to recovery and self-esteem and to achieving a better quality of life.
- Presenting the cause of mental health problems as stress-related is helpful to the public and clients in understanding the nature of mental health problems and to reduce the problems of stigma, prejudice and discrimination.
- Therapists' attitude towards mental health problems as biological in origin can exacerbate the problems of prejudice and discrimination for clients.

Part II

Therapist's perspective

A therapeutic framework

Chapter 4

Cognitive behaviour therapy theory of emotional upset

A few years ago, I was invited to give a lecture at a Buddhist temple in London on 'Emotional upset and mental health'. There were about ninety people there, of whom sixty-three were Chinese and the rest were mostly Europeans. I did a quick survey to find out their emotional experiences: 'Please tell me how many of you have ever experienced an emotion of . . .': the list ranged from anger, frustration, hurt, shame, worry, to anxiety. As expected, every one in the audience said 'yes' to all of these emotions. I am sure that if this survey was extended to a larger population or to people living in different parts of the world, from the United States to Africa, Canada and Australia to India, the response would still be the same. Everybody would say 'yes', irrespective of their culture, educational background, age, gender and social status. The results of this survey show that negative emotions are something we all experience and are part of being human.

I did another quick survey to find out what the audience would perceive as the cause(s) of emotional upset: 'What or who causes emotional upset?' The answers were not unexpected, ranging from people (e.g. 'She hurts me', 'He makes me angry') to external events (e.g. 'Doing a presentation makes me anxious and nervous', 'Divorce makes me depressed') as the causes of emotional upset. Their rationales were that if she did not reject me or if he did not criticise me, then I wouldn't have felt hurt or angry; and that if I did not have to do the presentation or *if* my spouse did not divorce me, I wouldn't have felt anxious, nervous or depressed. It may sound rational and logical to blame people or events for emotional upset, given the 'if' arguments. The reality is that we don't have control over what people say or do. By the same token, we may not be able to prevent bad things from happening, such as redundancy, criticism, rejection, higher tax, global warming, terrorism, war and bad weather.

Clients with mental health problems often believe that they do not have control over their moods and behaviour. Whether or not they feel all right depends on external forces. That is: everybody must be nice, supportive, helpful, fair, considerate, kind and generous; people should not be critical of me, dislike me or reject me; terrible, bad and upsetting things and events should not happen. Since they do not have control over external forces, what does it mean? It means that clients will continue to live a miserable, unhappy and struggling life, and that their mental health problems will continue or may even get worse.

There is a crucial difference between low and high levels of emotional upset. Many negative feelings, particularly at a low level, are normal and appropriate under the circumstances. For example, if you're having an argument with your parents, it is natural to feel angry and upset. If you fail an examination, you will probably feel sad and disappointed. If you go for an important interview, you will possibly feel anxious and nervous (see Chapter 13 on 'Healthy and unhealthy negative emotions'). In CBT terms, negative feelings in these circumstances are both normal and appropriate. It is often best to accept it. If clients believe that negative feelings are abnormal and blame external factors, these feelings can get worse. When clients are experiencing a high level of emotional upset, it often helps to question or challenge their (irrational) thoughts about the upsetting event. For example, 'Am I wasting my emotional energy over things that are outside my control?' 'What evidence do I have to support my emotional way of thinking?' One client said:

> I am feeling better and am more in control of my feelings. I accept that it is okay to feel a bit upset at times (e.g. low, down, irritable or frustrated) and nobody can be happy all the time. I am also learning to question my thinking and behaviour before I act.

Why is believing that external forces are the cause of emotional upset a clinical issue?

When clients are emotionally upset, they tend to blame others (e.g. 'She criticised me') or an event (e.g. redundancy or presentation) for their negative feelings (e.g. anger, hurt and resentment). They often dwell on some highly selective evidence (either factual or imaginary) to support their negative, biased thinking. For example, an 18-year-old student suffering from depression viewed herself as a failure, stupid and useless for not being able to get into a highly prestigious university. Alison obtained ten GCSEs at 'A' grades and four A levels, with two 'A' and two 'B' grades. Her school reports were excellent and the school's prediction was that she should be able to get the four A levels at 'A' grades, as required by the university. She blamed the university rejection as the cause (external) of her depression. Obviously, it did not make sense. But she was dwelling on the university rejection (factual evidence), on not being able to get the required grades in spite of working hard (factual evidence) and on her parents being disappointed in her (imaginary evidence) as evidence of her being a failure, stupid and useless. It was natural that her parents were disappointed in the results, but not in her as a daughter and as a person. After all, she was a bright girl.

While clients are emotionally upset, they tend to think about the event(s) over and over again. It is inevitable that they will find some more evidence to support their negative, biased thoughts, including evidence from the past, such as, 'I got low grades for my projects when I was 10 years old; I didn't get into a top primary school.' Worry about the future is also a source of evidence (imaginary) to clients. In the end there is overwhelming evidence from the present, the past and the future to justify their emotional upset (e.g. anger, hurt or anxiety) and to support their negative views about themselves, others and the world. What it means is that they can be stubbornly holding on to this evidence, and changing them can be difficult.

The case of John

John blamed redundancy for his depression. He said that *if* he did not lose the job, he would have been okay. He was a manager of a national IT company. With excellent academic records, diligence and flair, he had quickly achieved a promotion to become a sales managing director in the company at the age of 31. He was described as a single-minded person who was driven by success, social status and wealth. He enjoyed the success and recognition, and was accredited for his sales team being the most successful and efficient in the company. His company was taken over by another company two years after his promotion. He was made redundant, along with the whole management team from the old company.

His condition worsened and he was admitted to a psychiatric hospital because of concerns about his safety. He did not see the point of living as there wasn't much for him to live for. It was so difficult for him to get on with his life. He did not want to get out of bed to face the day, to see friends, or to look for a job. He was negative about everything and said:

> I'll never be able to find another job as good as the last one; there is no future for me, my friends think less of me; I am unemployed; I am a failure; I am not as good as I thought I was, nobody will employ a loser like me.

Cognitive behaviour therapy approach to emotional upset

Emotional upset is something that we all experience and will experience in the course of our lives. It is unavoidable. The CBT position is that emotional upset at a low level is normal and appropriate. It is often best to accept and tolerate these negative feelings. Otherwise, they may get worse. When emotional upset is at a high level, the problem is most likely to do with an individual's way of thinking about an upsetting event (e.g. redundancy). There are always two ways of looking at it. Helpful thinking means that the person may feel a bit upset about it, but he is able to get on with his life. For example, 'Redundancy is one of those things that happen in life. It is not the end of the world. I can always look for another job.' Whereas unhelpful thinking can cause even more emotional upset, making it difficult for the person to get on with life. For example, 'It is terrible to lose a job. I'll never be able to find another job like the previous one. I am a loser and a failure.'

In working with those clients, the CBT message is that:

- If an external event is the cause of emotional upset, then one would expect that everybody should experience the same level of emotional upset in the same or similar circumstances. But this is not the case in reality.
- Once they learn to think in a helpful way, they will experience less emotional upset.
- They can change the way they feel and be in control of their negative feelings.

Technique: 100 people – developing an objective point of view

Rationale and focus

Blaming external events or people for one's emotional upset is not uncommon and is often a habit. Because of clients' tendency to be selective in their search for supportive evidence for their negative thoughts and because of the way they are holding on to this evidence, it is difficult to alter their stubborn and strongly held beliefs. Lam (1997) suggests that it is best to help them to develop an 'objective' point of view in relation to an upsetting event before coming back to their negative views about themselves, others and the world.

Process

Therapist: How strongly do you believe that your depression is a result of losing your job, say on a scale of 1 to 100, with 100 being very strong?

John: 100. If I had not lost my job, I would have been okay.

Therapist: It sounds logical to think in this way, doesn't it? *Suppose* 100 people were in the same position as you: they all lost their jobs, which they enjoyed very much. Would they all end up with depression?

John:	Ah. Oh. I don't know.
Therapist:	Have a guess! Would they all become depressed like you?
John:	I suppose not.
Therapist:	Why not?
John:	We all are different.
Therapist:	Different!!! What do you mean by that?
John:	Well, we think differently and we behave differently. Our personalities and characters are different. Our expectations are different. Our intelligence is different.
Therapist:	Absolutely. But your logical argument is that redundancy causes depression. Why is it that logic does not apply to the 100 people, it only applies to you?
John:	Yeah. I see the point you make.
Therapist:	What?
John:	Redundancy does not cause depression. Otherwise, everybody would become depressed as a result of it.
Therapist:	I am glad that you are able to see this important point. What does it mean to you about losing your job?
John:	I am a failure, a loser and useless.
Therapist:	*Suppose* that it is the case: you are a failure, a loser and useless. How would you feel about being like that?
John:	It is terrible. I will be depressed and I am depressed.
Therapist:	Oh. If you truly believe that you are a failure, a loser and useless, then you feel depressed, is it right?
John:	Yes.
Therapist:	If so, is it redundancy or your belief that causes depression?
John:	I suppose it is my belief. But *if* I had not lost my job, I would have been okay. I still believe that.
Therapist:	Obviously, redundancy is an issue in your depression, but it is not the cause. It triggers the way you think. It is the way you think about redundancy that causes you to be depressed. When you truly believe that you are a failure, a loser and useless, it is depressing, isn't it, as you have said?
John:	It is true.
Therapist:	We just have to look at the extent to which your belief about yourself is true.

Homework

John was asked to:

- Write down evidence that supports or goes against his beliefs that he was a failure, a loser and useless.
- Ask five people he knew whether they saw him as such because of redundancy.
- Come up with helpful and realistic thinking about redundancy.
- Write down the costs and benefits of labelling himself with negative labels (e.g. 'I am a failure').
- Read Chapter 16 on 'Setback and relapse'.

Technique: 100 people – challenging negative labels

Rationale and focus

Despite knowing and accepting that negative or irrational beliefs contribute to mental health problems, some clients still believe the content of it (e.g. 'I am a failure'), and often use their feelings to justify it.

The therapist can say:

> Rather than using feelings to support your negative beliefs, we should use evidence instead. It is scientific, more reliable and believable. What would 100 people say about you as a person, if we present the evidence of your good and negative qualities?

Process

Therapist:	We have now established that the cause of your depression is not redundancy, but your beliefs about it. You label yourself a failure, a loser and useless because of redundancy. Is this correct?
John:	Yes.
Therapist:	How strongly do you believe that you are . . . on a scale of 1 to 100?
John:	Quite strongly, with the way I feel at the moment. I will say 95.
Therapist:	What do you see as your good qualities?
John:	Oh, I suppose I am hard-working, determined, intelligent and creative, with good people and communication skills. I used to consider myself a successful person, but it is not the case now.
Therapist:	You have all these good qualities. How about the negative qualities?
John:	Lazy, unmotivated and not having a job.
Therapist:	You have all these qualities as a person, positive as well as negative, but you see yourself a failure, a loser and useless. How logical is it?

John:	I know it is not logical. But I feel I am.
Therapist:	I understand that, but this is your feeling, which may or may not be true. It is best to base your judgement on the evidence. Does the evidence we have indicate that you are a failure, a loser and useless?
John:	I suppose not.
Therapist:	Suppose we take this evidence to 100 people and ask their opinion, will they say you are a failure, a loser and useless?
John:	Ah. Yeah. I suppose they will say no.
Therapist:	Because of?
John:	It does not make sense, obviously.
Therapist:	What will 100 people say, if we tell them that you feel that you must be?
John:	I suppose they will say that I am too harsh on myself and my expectation is not realistic.
Therapist:	Are you?
John:	I suppose I am.
Therapist:	How is it going to help you to get out of depression and move on with your life, if you continue to use your feelings to support your negative beliefs about yourself?
John:	It doesn't help. I will get worse.

Homework

John was asked to:

- Talk to five people and ask whether they see such a person (with positive and negative qualities) as a failure, a loser and useless.
- Write down the benefits and costs of basing negative beliefs on feelings, but not on evidence.
- Write a helpful and realistic statement as an alternative to the belief that 'I am a failure, a loser and useless for being made redundant'.

Other techniques

Other relevant techniques include 'Rewriting assumptions', 'Acceptance', 'Cognitive continuum', 'Daughter' and 'Judge'.

Notes for therapists about emotional upset

- Emotional upset is a fact of life and is the experience of all humans.
- You can't get rid of negative emotions. It would make the emotions worse.

- Not accepting and tolerating negative emotions is a waste of emotional energy and may cause or worsen mental health problems.
- Emotional upset is internally created, not caused by external forces.
- You can change the way you feel.

Chapter 5

Components in cognitive behaviour therapy

There are six essential components in contemporary cognitive behaviour therapy:

- collaborative therapeutic relationship
- cognitive case formulation
- structure
- socialisation
- cognitive behaviour techniques
- normalisation.

Collaborative therapeutic relationship

Success in developing a collaborative therapeutic relationship provides the foundation for all other aspects of treatment. It is therefore important that the therapist and the client are *equal partners* in the relationship, not the therapist being seen or promoted as the 'expert or rescuer' with all the resources to get rid of the client's problems and the client regarded as a 'helpless victim'. Otherwise, it may encourage a dependency culture, which is detrimental to the client's recovery. It does not encourage or give the client a chance to take responsibility for removing their 'roadblocks or obstacles' in order to arrive at the 'destination': to stay well. Note that clients are our 'teachers' and their problems are important and beneficial to our learning, thereby enhancing our therapeutic effectiveness. It is therefore important that we treat our 'teachers' with respect and with humanity.

In the treatment of mental health problems, changing our attitudes (e.g. negative) or frame of mind (e.g. 'I am the expert and know what is good for you') towards clients and their problems is essential. A genuine, respectful and trusting therapeutic relationship empowers and motivates the client to take responsibility for and become *proactive* in the management of his or her symptoms. To develop a successful collaborative therapeutic relationship, it is important for the therapist to be able to adapt skilfully to the client's circumstances (e.g. age, cultural background and educational attainment) and character (e.g. sensitivity), and to use the client's language to develop a close working relationship and as a bridge to get the 'CBT message' across. Note that the use of professional jargon can be a barrier to developing a healthy therapeutic relationship.

Cognitive case formulation

There are three stages in the cognitive case formulation. First, *assessment and data collection*, which involves:

- establishing a diagnostic profile
- conceptualising the client's past and current problems
- estimating the client's assets (strengths and limitations) for therapy
- identifying possible reasons for the failure of the client's previous treatment(s) or therapy
- investigating the family dynamics or relationships and the client's coping behaviour (past and current)
- determining the client's educational and achievement profiles
- assessing the client's perceived levels of self-esteem and self-worth.

Data for case conceptualisation can be usefully divided into six categories:

- background information
- presenting problems and current functioning
- psychiatric diagnoses
- family dynamics and relationship
- development profile
- cognitive profile.

First, some useful questions for assessment are: What do you see as your current problems? Which one of these problems concerns you most and why? How long have you had these problems? What could the reasons be? What did you learn from previous therapy? Why did it work? What is your relationship with your parents and siblings? Who (father or mother) do you think has the most impact (positive and negative) on you as a person and why? How did you deal with the difficulties? What could the rationale be for the way you cope (positively and negatively)? How would you describe yourself as a person? What would your best friend say about you as a person?

Second, the data collected in the initial assessment is used to *formulate hypotheses* about the client's current difficulties and to *predict* likely future problems, if changes are not made. Hypotheses not only tentatively provide the reasons (*why* did these problems develop in the first place?) for psychological and emotional distress or problems, but also identify the psychological and social mechanisms underlying these problems (what keeps these problems going and/or causes them to get worse). A clear, consistent and predictable pattern of the client's irrational thoughts and emotional reactions from the past to the present is therefore established and highlighted. This pattern is helpful in questioning the notion that mental health problems are predominantly caused by 'biological, genetic and disease' factors.

Third, hypotheses form the basis for a *shared understanding* between the therapist and the client about his or her current difficulties, and allow a prediction to be made about the likely outcomes of an alternative and helpful way of thinking and behaving relative to the outcome if the client does not make changes at both cognitive and behavioural levels. An agreed treatment plan can be developed to test and evaluate these hypotheses.

In short, cognitive case formulation is about data collection in order to formulate hypotheses for developing a shared understanding about the client's current problems. These hypotheses are then evaluated through a range of techniques and tests to see whether there is evidence to support or go against them. Cognitive case formulation is therefore a process of forming, testing and refining hypotheses about the psychological and social mechanisms underlying the client's problems, through data collected in the initial assessment and in subsequent sessions. A detailed discussion of cognitive case formulation can be found in various sources (Person 1989; J. S. Beck 1995; Clark 1999; Lam and Cheng 2001).

The case of Bryan: an example of cognition case formulation

Bryan, aged 30, was a manager of a national company. With excellent academic records, diligence and flair, he quickly achieved a senior position in the company. He had been happily married for about seven years, with a supportive wife and three children, aged 6, 4 and 1. He was referred for cognitive behaviour therapy because of attacks of severe epigastric pain and vomiting. The first attack occurred about five years earlier, while he was at work. Following investigations at a local hospital, doctors could not come up with any medical explanation for the pain and vomiting. The attacks increased in frequency, and this greatly affected his confidence at work. In the absence of medical explanations for the attacks, his general practitioner recommended psychodynamic psychotherapy. However, following two years of treatment, this therapy had not been found to be effective or beneficial.

Presenting problems

Despite intensive medical investigations and tests, there was nothing physical or medical that could explain the pain and vomiting. Bryan was convinced that it must be something to do with a virus or viruses that had yet to be identified.

The fact that psychological treatments had not been found to be beneficial had added to his conviction that the pain and vomiting could not be just in his mind or thoughts, as his general practitioner and psychiatrists had suggested. He reported that an attack could happen at any time, anywhere, and any day and that he did not have any control over it. Whenever he started having the pain, he was anxious about it and went to bed in the hope that it would go away. However, it always ended up with a series of vomiting episodes before he was able to get better. He could not identify anything that triggered the pain.

Bryan described himself as a dynamic and creative person, but he had a strong tendency towards perfectionism, particularly at work. He had very high expectations of himself and others. He became rather critical of himself and others if work failed to be perfect or to live up to his expectations. He believed that if he was not perfect or if he made mistakes in his work, he was a failure. This expectation of perfection thus created a high level of anxiety and worries not only in relation to the standard of his work, but also in relation to how others judged him, the standard of his work, and his ability. He believed that others would see him as weak and question his ability and competency if he disclosed his mental health history. He avoided going to meetings as soon as he started feeling anxious about not being able to stay well at meetings. He would go home and rest in bed, in the vain hope that the pain would go away and the vomiting would not start.

Cognitive case formulation

In the absence of physical or medical explanations for the pain and vomiting, the possibility of a relationship between the spiral of his rising anxiety and the negative meanings (e.g. 'Something is wrong with me') he placed on bodily sensations, particularly the pain, could be a plausible explanation. These two could reciprocally influence one another to induce an episode of vomiting. His avoidance and safety-seeking behaviours could play a role in the maintenance of his dysfunctional thoughts. These thoughts included: 'I must not be anxious. I must stay well. What if I can't stay well at meetings or presentations? People will think that I am weak with all these anxiety problems. I must be able to cope and be perfect or I am a failure.' His parents had very high expectations of him and expected him to be the best at whatever he did. The thought of not being able to cope, of not being perfect and competent in the eyes of others, made him anxious and worried about his job security and future. It also became a threat to his self-confidence and self-esteem, and this then fuelled his biological responses (the pain and vomiting) and led to the use of safety-seeking behaviours and avoidance as coping strategies.

Structure

The CBT treatment in the change process is based on a structural approach. Structure is essential to the development of therapeutic alliance, to provide a sense of direction and focus to both the therapist and the client. The structure of a CBT session consists of five essential elements:

- agenda setting
- identification of and dealing with problems
- periodic feedback
- homework assignments
- summary.

Each of the elements will now be briefly discussed.

Agenda setting

Agenda setting allows problems to be identified and prioritised, so that urgent and difficult issues can be given appropriate therapeutic attention. Agenda setting should be a collaborative approach and the agenda should be short (between two and six items).

Identification of and dealing with problems

This involves checking the mood and feeling of being in control of thoughts and behaviour. It also reviews homework assignments from a previous session. Questions for checking include: 'How has your mood been since the last session? How much control do you think you have over your thoughts and behaviour?' A rating scale should be used. For example, 'On a scale of 1 (very bad) to 100 (very good), what would you say?' Evidence should be looked for in support of the ratings (bad or good). If there are grave concerns in both the mood and feeling of being in control, these can be placed on the agenda for discussion. Reviewing homework can reveal the state of the client's progress. Any problems that emerge in the review can be placed on the agenda for further work.

Periodic feedback

It ensures that progress can be maintained and built on or that any misunderstanding can be sorted out as soon as possible. Questions for periodic feedback include: 'What conclusion can you draw from this? Is there anything so far that you don't feel comfortable about or are upset about?'

Homework assignments

The idea of homework is to deal with the client's immediate problems, to build on progress made, or to prepare new ground (e.g. read an article on criticism) for the next session (e.g. how to constructively deal with criticism). Homework should be formulated jointly. This gives the client a sense of control and responsibility in the change process (see Chapter 9 on 'Homework assignments').

Summary

Summary is a refresher of what is done in the session. It covers areas of discussion in the session, how these are related to the clients and/or what can be learnt or done to enable further progress or lessen problems. The responsibility of summarising can be given to the client as a way of consolidating the learning. The client is also encouraged to make brief notes of 'what I learnt in today's session' as 6–10 bullet points.

Introducing clients to the cognitive model

'People make me angry', 'She hurts me', 'Presentations make me anxious', 'Rejection makes me inferior', and 'Examination failure depresses me' are not uncommon beliefs. When individuals are anxious, hurt or angry, they tend to blame external events or other people for their emotional upset. Their 'logical' reason is that if these events had not happened, they wouldn't have felt the way they did. This 'logic' is clearly problematic and is part of the reason for them being stuck in an 'emotional maze'.

It is important to introduce clients to the contemporary cognitive-behavioural model early in therapy and this model is known as the ABC theory of emotional upset (Ellis 1962; Lam and Gale 2000). 'A' is known as an *A*ctivating event, 'C' is the emotional and behavioural *C*onsequence or reaction of the individual. According to the theory of cognitive behaviour therapy, A (the activating event) does not cause C (the emotional and behavioural consequence). It is the *B*elief (the person's interpretation of, and assumption about, A) that is largely responsible for C, the emotional and behavioural reactions. For example, in the statement 'People make me angry', it is not people (A) that make the person angry (C), but his interpretation of, and assumption (B) about, what people said (A). His interpretation and assumption could be that people were unfair to him, took him for granted, or did not respect him.

The ABC model helps clients better understand the reasons for their emotional and behavioural problems, encourages them to work on the irrational nature of their beliefs and thoughts, and develop a more adaptive and helpful approach to situations or people. The introduction of the model will be better perceived or understood after the completion of the cognitive case formulation or initial assessment. This helps clients to be more able to relate the concept of the model to their own lives and experiences. This understanding can instil hope in clients about the possibility of change, motivate them to take responsibility for their recovery, and encourage them to work collaboratively with therapists in the change process. Metaphors can be helpful to convey the key points.

Cognitive behaviour techniques

When a client is having emotional problems (e.g. anger, anxiety, guilt, shame or depression) and is struggling to cope with daily life and/or stressful events, techniques become an invaluable tool to bring about changes in the way the client thinks and reacts, thus helping to lessen emotional upset and improve the confidence and skills levels to cope with difficult and stressful events. A skilful use of a range of techniques can help the client to realise the immobilising and destructive nature of his or her irrational thoughts and reactions, to be more able to cope with adversity, and to develop a more realistic or adaptive way of perceiving self, others and the world.

A range of techniques is illustrated throughout this book to deal with the problems of stigmatisation and biological labelling of mental health problems (see Part I), self-prejudice and personal issues (see Part III), and self-prejudice and interpersonal difficulties (see Part IV). Whether or not a technique is skilfully and effectively used is closely related to the therapist's being able to understand the *rationale* and the *focus* of a technique, and the way in which it is used (the *process*). Each illustration in the book gives a description of a technique (the rationale and the focus) and an example of the way in which this technique is used (the process), followed by appropriate homework in support of the technique being used. Understanding the rationale, the focus and the process enables the therapist to apply a particular technique flexibly, not just to one particular problem, but to a range of problems. There are a number of excellent books on cognitive-behaviour techniques (A. T. Beck and Emery 1985; J. S. Beck 1995; McMullin 2000; Leahy 2003).

Normalisation

Normalisation is a process of reintegration of clients to society. There are two essential elements in the normalisation process: de-stigmatisation of the 'mentally ill' label and restoring positive experiences. De-stigmatisation involves identifying and discussing the (negative) meanings that clients might have about the 'mentally ill' label, and educating clients about the multifactorial nature of causal factors for mental health problems. This is a useful exercise to explore and rectify their self-schemas, personal worth and fear of others' opinions about mental illness. Useful questions for discussion include: How do you feel about the 'mentally ill' label? What do you see as the cause of your problems? Do you feel concerned about what people might think of you? How do you see yourself as a person? What do you think you can do to remove this stigmatising label?

Using the integrative model of causality can help clients to see that mental health problems are the result of the interplay of a range of interacting factors: psychological, social, genetic and environmental. It is suggested that when an emphasis is focused on mental health problems being a reaction to stress-related events, the stigmatising nature of the problems is likely to be lessened and clients are likely to be motivated to take responsibility for their recovery and to be proactive in the management of their symptoms.

Restoring positive experiences helps to shift clients away from spending too much time worrying about or being preoccupied with their problems and fosters a picture of reality about the importance of achieving a sense of balance and proportion in their lives. A fulfilling and satisfying experience of balanced life will have a positive influence on their thinking process, enable them to function or cope better in their environment, and reduce relapse episodes. This involves identifying and developing the positive experiences, such as personal interests and hobbies, and encouraging clients to attend to relationships. The latter is about repairing old relationships, reaching out for new ones, and working on current ones.

Chapter 6

A shared responsibility approach in the change process

Teamwork is important. The measure of a team is best judged by how much commitment and effort members are putting in or are prepared to put in, and by the way they work with and communicate with one another. It is true that a team will not be able to achieve and survive if members do not work together or are not supportive of one another. It is also true that when people are inconsistent in their commitment or some people do considerably more than others, conflict and resentment can break the spirit of a team and therefore the team. We all know that this is true. We accept it without question because it makes sense. The principle of division of responsibility is at the heart of and a guiding concept for a successful team. People in the team look at what expertise each member has, negotiate with one another to decide on what each can or will do, and then carry out their respective responsibilities in a consistent and committed manner in order to achieve the team goals. The spirit of a team approach can be observed in marriages, families, sports teams, organisations or governments.

An illustration of a successful team approach came from a television programme which reported how fifteen families decided to come together to self-build their own homes, with a bank providing a loan and help and support coming from local building experts. The families did not know each other prior to the project and they came from all walks of life, including teachers, a banker, a housewife, a lawyer, an accountant, a lorry driver, plumbers, an electrician and a bricklayer. A supervisor was appointed to coordinate, to draw up a contract based on the principle of division of responsibility for the group and for each member of the family, and to supervise the project. The spirit of the team approach prevailed and at the end of three years the project was successfully completed. The families were delighted at having their own homes at a price considerably cheaper than the market price. They were proud of their achievements and the sense of satisfaction was such that many families were prepared to go through the whole experience again. This inspiring and shining example illustrates that, for success to be achieved, a team approach is important.

By the same token, a team approach is crucial for the therapist and the client to work together in order to achieve the therapeutic goals or enable the client to 'stay' better (see Chapter 16 on 'Setback and relapse'). Working with clients to define what they consider as their responsibility and that of the therapist is a priority and should be done early in therapy. Useful questions are: What do you see as your responsibility in the change process? What do you see as my responsibility? What can *we* do in order to achieve the therapeutic goals? How can *we* ensure that our respective responsibilities can be achieved?

In CBT, learning to cope with difficult situations and people is as important as changing negative thinking, if not *more* important. Encouraging clients to review and modify their current coping strategies or behaviour and to practise new behaviour is an example of their responsibility. It is suggested that the therapist's responsibility is to help the clients understand the causes of their problems and the factors contributing to their continuing problems. Equally important is to provide clients with resources, confidence and the skills (e.g. role-play) to deal with these problems (e.g. self-criticism, others' criticism, conflicts, social situations and low self-esteem). The responsibility of clients is to put learning into practice in a variety of personal, social and interpersonal settings at every available opportunity, and to bring their experiences (positive and negative) into sessions, so that they can work at their problems in order to benefit from the experiences.

Why is clients' not taking responsibility a clinical issue?

When athletes refuse to work hard in training, it would be difficult for them to fulfil their potential and to win. By the same token, clients would not be able to benefit from therapy and recover from mental health problems if they refuse or are unwilling to take responsibility for their recovery.

When progress is not made or can't be made, therapists may feel frustrated with clients for not making an effort and may blame them for wasting time or even accuse them of attitudes such as laziness. Problems and conflicts may build up as a result, making recovery even more difficult to achieve. Similarly, clients may also feel frustrated with lack of progress and may experience feelings of guilt for letting people down. Not only would they feel anxious and worried about the future, but they might also believe that their problems are impossible to resolve, thus reinforcing a popular perception that psychiatric problems are due to a 'disease' in the brain.

The case of Bobby

Bobby had seen a number of therapists over the past fifteen years for the problems of depression, low self-esteem and anxiety. Unfortunately, he did not find 'talking' about his problems beneficial. Naturally, he was disappointed and frustrated at not being able to make progress, with so much money and time being invested in it, not to mention the suffering he had to endure all these years.

Bobby said in a frustrated tone of voice.:

> I just do not understand why they [therapists and counsellors] spent so much time going back to my past to talk about my childhood experiences, about my relationships with my parents, and about my schooling. To be honest, I do not remember much about these things and do not see how it is relevant to my current problems.

What Bobby wanted was to be able to cope in the present moment and to stop worrying about the future. What he wanted from the professionals was how to get rid of the anxiety, fear and worry, and to be happy. He found it difficult to cope with life, did not want to get out of bed in the morning, did not want to see friends or relatives, and was fearful about facing the day ahead. There were occasions that he would stay in bed for up to a week. He was pessimistic about his recovery and worried about his future.

'I do not understand why the psychiatrist referred me to cognitive behaviour therapy again. It did not work last time,' he said in a resentful tone of voice. The failures of psychotherapies had convinced him that drug treatments were the only way that could 'put chemicals right' in his brain, as he was told that his depression was due to 'chemical imbalances' in his brain. He accepted the biological explanation. Although drug treatments had not been successful so far, he was convinced that there must be a drug or a combination of drugs that would eventually work. However, the psychiatrist told him that the problems lay with his negative thinking and that he had to work hard at it, hence the second referral to CBT.

Bobby expected that the 'expert' would put his problems right (after all, he had paid for the service) and was not happy with the idea that homework was part of the CBT treatment. He said that he did not have time to do it. Doing homework reminded him of his schooldays, which he did not enjoy. In fact, he hated school. In the first five sessions, he did not put any effort into our work. No progress was made and he was disappointed, saying that 'with no disrespect, I just don't think coming to see you will help me to solve my problems'. My response to that was:

> The whole idea of CBT is for us to work together. You are right that I can't solve your problems, unless you are prepared to work hard with

me, as advised by your psychiatrist. It is no different from a boy going to school, and not being prepared to work hard and do his homework. There is no need for me to tell you what will happen to this boy. He will not do well and may even fail his examinations.

'Therapist, I feel that I am making progress. The important thing is that I feel different,' said Bobby. Not only did he complete his homework, putting in a lot of effort, but also he put learning into practice at every available opportunity, which is very important in CBT terms. For example, he made a complaint to a waiter in a restaurant about the food and asked for it to be changed. He was pleased with his approach, not aggressive or over-apologising, but assertive. This behaviour wasn't something that he would have carried out in the past, but being able to do it gave him confidence and therefore hope for the future. Bobby accepted that being able to make progress was about taking responsibility for changing his behaviour as well as his negative thinking for himself, with the support of and guidance of the therapist. He was the one who had to do all the hard work.

Cognitive behaviour therapy approach to shared responsibility

The concept of a collaborative partnership is a hallmark of the CBT approach. A functional partnership approach requires the therapist and the client to put in effort and commitment to their respective responsibilities in order to overcome the obstacles or problems in the pathway. The concept of the therapist being a 'rescuer or an expert' and the client being a 'helpless victim' is outdated as well as an obstacle to the success of a partnership approach. The therapist is more like a sports coach or an accountant (helping people to do better) than a doctor who cures diseases.

In working with clients, the CBT message is that sustainable therapeutic success requires both parties to work hard.

Technique: Education

Rationale and focus

The education system is a good illustration of a partnership approach, involving teachers, parents and students each taking their respective *responsibilities* in order to achieve the educational goals. In using this technique, the therapist can start with a general discussion with the client about the importance of *shared* responsibility for achieving students' educational potential and goals, and then go on to explore the importance of having the client's 'support and help' (i.e. commitment) for achieving the therapeutic goals.

Process

Therapist:	Do you have children?
Bobby:	Yes, two sons and a daughter.
Therapist:	Do they go to school?
Bobby:	Yes, my elder son is in his second year at university, my daughter is doing her A levels, and the younger son is taking his GCSEs this year.
Therapist:	Well, they all are grown-up children. How are they doing at university and school?
Bobby:	They are coping well, I think.
Therapist:	How important is it, to you, for them to do well?
Bobby:	It is very important. Education is not just about getting a qualification. It is a key to personality development, to intellectual stimulation, to a better quality of life and to wealth creation.
Therapist:	So it is very important. Who do you think is responsible for achieving your children's educational potential and therefore their educational goals?
Bobby:	Well, I suppose the educational establishment is very important. Parents' attitudes are also important.
Therapist:	How about your children?
Bobby:	They need to work hard and push themselves.
Therapist:	If they don't?
Bobby:	If they don't, it means that they will not be able to do well.
Therapist:	Absolutely. Educational success is based on a *shared* responsibility approach. No matter how good the school or university is and how supportive the parents are, the children have to take responsibility for their learning. Otherwise, we can all predict what the outcome would be, can't we?
Bobby:	Yes.
Therapist:	Coming back to you. Do you want to do well and feel in control of your mental health problems?
Bobby:	Yes.
Therapist:	Who do you think is responsible for achieving *our* therapeutic goals?
Bobby:	Yeah. Oh. I suppose it is me.
Therapist:	And me. We need to support each other and work hard at the problems, as the educational establishment, you and your wife,

	and your children do. In other words, we both need to accept our responsibility in order to achieve the goals. If you don't accept your responsibility, then what will happen?
Bobby:	I will not be able to do well and have control over my problems.
Therapist:	Can we predict what the outcome of your treatment will be?
Bobby:	Not good.
Therapist:	Not just that. You may become increasingly pessimistic in your beliefs about your problems and about your future. You may give up trying and believe that your problems are in your genes and there is nothing that you can do, which is depressing. Do you want to change?
Bobby:	Yes.
Therapist:	In light of our discussion, what is the best way to change?
Bobby:	Take responsibility and work hard with you.

Technique: An athlete and a sports coach

Rationale and focus

We know that an athlete and a sports coach are a fine example of teamwork. When both parties work hard, encourage and support each other, it motivates commitment, improves performance, and therefore enhances the chance of winning. Without the support of one or the other, or if one person in the team is not putting in enough effort, winning is almost out of reach. Even athletes with a disability can overcome obstacles to achieve their potential if they are determined and committed and with the support of a sports coach.

In using this technique, the therapist can say:

> We can be a 'winning' team, if we work hard together. Rather than blaming your brain for the problems, or believing the problems to be biological, you can give yourself a chance to work hard, like an athlete with or without a disability, to see what you can achieve. Rather than believing that there is nothing you can do, start with 'I am going to learn to do it.'

Process

Therapist:	In athletics, teamwork is important. It involves a sports coach and an athlete working closely together. Both parties need to work hard and be committed in order to win. This is true, isn't it?
Bobby:	Yeah.

Therapist:	Suppose the coach is really good in what he does and is committed to his work, but the athlete is not taking his responsibility seriously by training hard, what do you think will happen?
Bobby:	It is not going to get anywhere.
Therapist:	Meaning what?
Bobby:	There is no chance for the athlete to win anything. The coach will be disappointed and frustrated, or may even finish the partnership.
Therapist:	Does it mean that the athlete has no ability or potential?
Bobby:	Not at all. He does not give himself a chance to learn and make progress.
Therapist:	Absolutely. It is a pity that the coach is willing, committed, and is good at his job, but ending up with so much frustration. You are right to say that it does not mean that the athlete can't do it, or does not have the ability/potential to do well. The partnership is not working because the athlete does not take his responsibility seriously.
Bobby:	Yes. You are right.
Therapist:	By the same token, if you want to do well, what do you have to do?
Bobby:	Oh. I see what you mean.
Therapist:	What do I mean?
Bobby:	I need to take responsibility for my recovery and should not blame my problems on my brain.
Therapist:	You owe yourself a chance. Rather than blaming your brain for your problems or believing the problems are biological, why don't you give yourself the chance to find out whether or not you can do it?

Homework

Bobby was asked to:

- Make a list of his responsibilities for change and the rationale for each of them.
- Write down what he sees as the responsibility of the therapist and the reasons for it.
- Make a prediction about the outcome if both parties fulfil their respective responsibilities.
- Keep a responsibility diary to monitor his progress and to identify areas for further work.

Other techniques

Other relevant techniques include 'Daughter' and 'Education'.

Notes for therapists about the shared responsibility approach

- Two heads are better than one.
- A successful partnership prevents relapse.
- Being able to change is the responsibility of the therapist and the client.
- The therapist is like a sports coach helping clients improve and develop a stable self-esteem.

Chapter 7

Dealing with negative thoughts

Having negative thoughts in our head, particularly in uncertain situations, is not uncommon and is a fact of life for all humans. No matter how successful, intelligent or positive we are, negative thoughts can occasionally bother us, whether we like it or not. For example, it is natural to have negative thoughts in relation to an interview, an examination, a presentation, terrorism, a business deal, a social event, an appraisal or an illness. We tend not to pay too much attention to these thoughts, as we know in our hearts that these are just thoughts. They may or may not become a reality. Although it is rather unpleasant, it is not worth while wasting time on them, either worrying about or trying to get rid of them. The reality is that the more we try to get rid of these negative thoughts, the more powerful they become. For example, clients with obsessive-compulsive disorder (OCD) and post-traumatic stress disorder (PTSD) find their intrusive negative thoughts get stronger and more frequent, when they try hard to get rid of them. The harder they try, the worse it becomes.

At a press conference, a highly successful businessman, appointed to head an international corporation, was asked whether he had any doubts about being able to rescue the corporation. If so, how would he deal with the doubts? 'It is natural to have some doubtful thoughts, but I don't waste time on them. I just get on with what I need to do, and my credentials help to put the doubts into perspective.' A client said:

> I don't deal with negative thoughts when I am tired, feeling low and down, as it would only make the thoughts worse. I postpone dealing with them and allow myself to relax and recharge my body energy. When I feel fresh, I look at the problem either a few hours later or the next day, and the thoughts seem a lot less negative. The problem isn't that big after all.

These two examples illustrate that no human is immune to negative thoughts, whether they are a successful person or a client. How a negative thought is dealt with is the key to either good or poor mental health.

A negative thought can take the form of worry as in general anxiety disorder (GAD), anxiety as in panic disorder and health anxiety, intrusion as in obsessive-compulsive disorder and post-traumatic stress disorder, and depression as in depression. The frightening and authentic nature of a negative thought is such that clients often believe that the thought is a threat to their safety and/or their families or is real. One client said: 'I try to push it away and/or distract myself by keeping busy, so that I don't have to think, but the thought seems to be more powerful and comes more frequently.' Another client said: 'I engage with the thought a lot and seem to have found more evidence to support it. This makes me more and more anxious and depressed.' These coping strategies, as commonly used by clients to deal with a negative thought, are no different from putting 'fuel' on the fire, thus empowering the negative thought, creating more negative thoughts in the process, and causing more emotional misery (e.g. anxiety and worry).

CBT distinguishes three types of negative thoughts: automatic thoughts (e.g. 'She does not like me'), underlying assumptions (e.g. 'If I work really hard at work, I should be able to get a promotion' (positive); 'If I don't get the promotion, it means that I am a failure' (negative)) and core beliefs (e.g. 'I am a failure'). From experience, changing underlying assumptions is particularly important and is a priority in clinical terms. It not only helps with the mood, but also is beneficial in helping clients to develop healthy and effective coping strategies. An additional benefit is the change in core beliefs, which are regarded as part of the personality.

Why is underlying assumption a particular clinical issue?

Underlying assumptions are rules that are learnt early in life; are used to guide thinking, feeling and behaviour; and affect self-perception (e.g. 'I am successful and likeable' or 'I am a reject and a failure'). Rules can be positive as well as negative. In children, positive and negative rules are: 'If I work hard, am nice to people, and am a good girl, then my parents and teachers will like me'; 'If I don't do well at school, I am unlovable, stupid and useless'. Similar rules can be observed in adults. For example, 'If I work hard, am nice and friendly to and supportive of people, then people will like and accept me'; 'If I don't perform, am not perfect and competent, then I am a failure and useless'. It is not hard to see a predictable pattern of thoughts, feelings and behaviour in clients throughout their lives.

Underlying assumptions are just hypotheses (e.g. if . . . then), not the truth, whether they are positive or negative. When clients believe that assumptions are the truth, it means that the positive ones can cause perfectionism and encourage approval-seeking behaviour, and the negative ones procrastination and self-criticism. In the end, assumptions reinforce negative self-image and keep low self-esteem going. The dialogue below shows how assumptions can be identified.

Positive assumption

(If I am nice to and supportive of my friends, then they will be nice to me and see me as a good person.)

Client: I need to be nice to and supportive of my friends.
Therapist: Because of (or why)?
Client: They will be nice to me and see me as a good person.

Negative assumption

(If they are not nice to me and don't see me as a good person, then I am unlovable and a reject.)

Client: I need to be nice to and supportive of my friends.
Therapist: Because of?
Client: They will be nice to me and see me as a good person.
Therapist: If they don't, then how would you see yourself as a person?
Client: It will be terrible. I am unlovable and a reject.

The case of Alison

Alison was an 18-year-old student diagnosed as suffering from depression. She was depressed by not being able to go to a highly prestigious university to read medicine. She was tearful, quiet, withdrawn, tired, feeling drained and losing weight; she isolated herself from others, including her friends, brother, sisters and parents. Sleeping had been a problem, as her mind was so active with streams of negative thoughts, which depressed her even further. There was a concern about her safety as she said that there was no point in living and wished to die. Her family was very worried about her, and had taken her to see the family doctor and then a psychiatrist, who arranged an admission to hospital.

She was excited to receive a provisional offer from the university. Her assumptions were that if she worked really hard, she would be able to read medicine and be a doctor; if she read medicine, her family would be very proud of her and she would have a bright future. These assumptions were an incentive and a driving force to work hard. However, she failed to obtain four

A levels at 'A' grades as required, despite working hard and her school's positive prediction of what she should be able to get. Although other universities were happy with her two 'A' and two 'B' grades, she somehow believed that she was not as good as she thought she was. Despite her excellent school reports and ten 'A' grades in the GCSE examinations, she said that she was a failure, stupid and useless and had let her family down and that her friends would now think less of her.

Her father was a professor of medicine and her mother was a general practitioner. Her brother had a PhD and was a research chemist with an international pharmaceutical company, one sister was a diabetes specialist and the other sister had just completed her medical studies. Naturally, her family was disappointed in the examination results, but not in her as a person. After all, she was a bright girl. Her parents said that she had done her best and it was good enough. They encouraged her to go to one of the other universities to read another subject instead. She compared her own achievements with those of others in the family and believed that she was not good enough.

Cognitive behaviour therapy approach to negative thoughts

The CBT position is that emotional suffering is more to do with the ways in which negative thoughts are maintained, such as going over and over an upsetting event in the mind and actively engaging with it and looking for evidence that supports or seems to support negative thoughts. There is also a tendency to overlook, ignore or dismiss other evidence as irrelevant.

In working with clients with negative thoughts, the CBT message is that:

- Negative thoughts happen to all humans. It is not possible to eliminate these thoughts. A helpful way is to weaken the thoughts so that they are no longer believable.
- The ways in which negative thoughts are maintained are the cause of human emotional misery.
- Self-esteem can influence the ways in which negative thoughts are maintained.
- Negative thoughts should not be based on feeling, but on evidence.
- We need to examine *all* evidence (for or against) so as to decide on the reliability of a negative thought. Note that clients with low self-esteem also have high self-esteem, as shown by the fluctuation in their moods. Stable self-esteem is the goal of therapeutic intervention.

Technique: Judge

Rationale and focus

It is difficult to oppose a negative thought and to put things into perspective when the client is selective in what evidence to use or not to use in relation to a negative thought. Let the judge decide . . . is a powerful way to question the 'legality' of a negative thought. This technique encourages clients to review *all* evidence before deciding whether or not to believe a negative thought.

The therapist can say, 'Rather than be selective in the use of evidence, let a judge review *all* the evidence to decide whether or not he or she will support your (negative) thought or opinion.'

Process

Therapist: How strongly do you believe that you are a failure, stupid and useless, say on a scale of 1 to 100, with 100 the strongest belief?

Alison: I am. I am not as clever and able as my parents, brother and sisters.

Therapist: Your family has done well. But we don't know for sure whether or not you are less able or intelligent than them. The issue here is that how strongly you believe you are . . . ?

Alison: Quite strong, 90 per cent.

Therapist: 90 per cent is rather strong. What evidence do you have to support that?

Alison: I was rejected by the university; my hard work wasn't good enough; I did not get the top grades in two subjects.

Therapist: And?

Alison: Oh, I have no future.

Therapist: This is just a belief, not evidence. And?

Alison: Yeah. No more, but the evidence I have is enough to say that I am . . .

Therapist: What evidence do you have to say you are not . . . ?

Alison: Oh, I have ten GCSE at 'A' grades and my school reports have been excellent.

Therapist: How about A level results?

Alison: If I were able and intelligent, I would have got 'A' grades in all the subjects.

Therapist: Would you say your best friend is stupid and useless for getting only two 'A' grades and two 'B' grades?

Alison: Ah. I would not.

Therapist:	How logical is it your best friend is not and you are? Also, your school's prediction was positive about you being able to obtain the required grades.
Alison:	They were obviously wrong. I am not as good as they thought I was.
Therapist:	If you were the headteacher, would you make such a prediction, knowing that a pupil was stupid and useless?
Alison:	I suppose not.
Therapist:	So far, we have evidence that supports as well as goes against your negative thoughts. If we take all the evidence to a judge, what will the judge say about you being . . . ?
Alison:	Oh. I don't know. I suppose the judge will say that I am not.
Therapist:	I am not what?
Alison:	I am not a failure, stupid and useless.
Therapist:	Why does the judge make such a 'verdict'? What advice will the judge give you?
Alison:	The judge may say that all the evidence does not add up to indicate that I am a failure, stupid and useless. He may even say that I am quite a successful person, but I am too harsh on myself.

Homework

Alison was asked to:

- Ask five 'judges' (can be anybody) to review *all* the evidence and to make a note of their 'verdicts'.
- Write down what benefits there are in calling herself a failure, stupid and useless.
- Read and evaluate Chapter 14 on 'Fear of failure and procrastination'.

Technique: Law in the universe

Rationale and focus

Alison's assumptions were that: 'If I really work hard, I should be able to read medicine (positive); if I fail to read medicine, I am a failure, stupid and useless (negative).' There is no truth whatsoever in either the positive assumptions or the negative ones. It does not mean that working hard would logically result in her being able to read medicine, nor that failing to read medicine would render her a failure, stupid and useless.

There is no law in the universe to support underlying assumptions being the truth. These are just hypotheses and believing them can cause problems to one's mental and emotional health, and may even lead to the development of mental health problems.

Process

Therapist:	My friend, Christian, is an intelligent, dynamic and hard-working guy. He truly believed that if he worked really hard at his job, then he should be able to get a promotion. He knew that there was a promotion coming up soon. Was he right about his belief?
Alison:	Well. He would stand a chance to get it, but it wasn't definite.
Therapist:	He said that he should be able to . . . Is there a law in the universe to say that just because he worked really hard, then he should . . . ?
Alison:	I don't think so.
Therapist:	In fact, he didn't get it and he was very upset, believing that he was useless and not good enough for not getting the promotion.
Alison:	Oh.
Therapist:	Is there a law in the universe to say that if he did not get it (despite working so hard for it), he was useless and not good enough?
Alison:	No. There is no such law.
Therapist:	Absolutely. My lawyer friend confirms that there are no such laws. Assumptions are just hypotheses and are not the truth. Does it make sense?
Alison:	Oh, it does. It makes a lot of sense.
Therapist:	If you believe that assumptions are the truth, then what?
Alison:	A lot of upset, like Christian.
Therapist:	Is there a law in the universe to say that if you work really hard at your studies, you should be able to read medicine? Otherwise, you are a failure, stupid and useless?
Alison:	Ah, well. I know the point you are making. There is no law to say that.
Therapist:	If you believe such assumptions as the truth, then what?
Alison:	It would just make my life difficult.
Therapist:	You suffer from depression, are in the hospital and are seeing me. Can you see the problems in believing underlying assumptions as the truth?
Alison:	Yes.

Homework

Alison was asked to:

- Present her underlying assumptions (positive and negative) to five people and to make a note of what they said.
- Write helpful statements to replace these assumptions. For example, 'I will work really hard at my studies and it will be nice to be able to get into medicine as a result of that' to replace 'If I work really hard, I should be able to read medicine'.

Other techniques

Other relevant techniques include 'Rewriting assumptions', 'Cognitive continuum' and 'Read it out loud'.

Notes for therapists about negative thoughts

- It is natural to have negative thoughts in relation to anxious or worrying situations.
- Trying to get rid of or suppress negative thoughts can make them worse.
- Acceptance of these thoughts will diminish the frequency of the occurrence.
- Identifying and working on the underlying assumption helps to change both core beliefs and unhelpful behaviour.

Chapter 8

Dealing with unhelpful behaviour

Vince was anxious about doing a presentation, saying: 'It really makes me anxious and nervous to do the presentation in front of so many people, including the president of the company from the USA.' Juan was angry about the poor service at a restaurant. Mary was worried about a performance appraisal with her boss. These three examples show people tend to believe that external events are the cause of their emotional upset (e.g. anxiety, anger and worry), as in the presentation in the case of Vince, poor service in Juan's case, and appraisal in Mary's. It is sad that people believe that their feelings or moods are outside their control, and that they are at the mercy of external forces. If this were the case, one would expect that everybody would feel anxious about doing a presentation, be angry about poor service, and worried about an appraisal. Quite the opposite: not everybody would *think* exactly the same in these circumstances because people are different. They are different in their physical make-up, their personalities and their life experiences. With Vince, his thinking was: 'If I don't do the presentation well, people will think that I am not up to the job. There will be no future for me in the company. It is terrible. I am a failure.' Another person in the same circumstances could well have a different perspective: 'Well, it is going to be a challenge as well as an opportunity. I am going to enjoy it, to give it my best shot and to learn from the feedback. After all, I know my stuff well.' We can see what a difference different ways of thinking about the *same* event can make to the mood or feelings.

Clinically, there is an assumption that once clients accept that their negative thinking is the cause of emotional misery, their mental health problems (e.g. health anxiety, panic disorder, depression and obsessive-compulsive disorder) will be 'cured'. They will be on the way to recovery. Such an assumption is *incorrect*. First, clients often do not know how to change negative thinking. A few years ago, one depressed client was tearful and upset following a visit to a consultant psychiatrist, who was frustrated with her lack of progress. He said in a critical tone of voice: 'You know your problem is your negative thinking: change it to the positive one.' 'How?' asked the client. The psychiatrist became irritated and said: 'Just change it.' The client was then given a prescription to take more drugs. Another client acknowledged that her thinking was negative but did not know how to change, saying: 'Please give me something to hold on to before I give up my negative way of thinking. I don't know what to think.' It is often thought that positive thinking is an alternative; clients are encouraged to 'think positively'. For example, 'Everything will be all right. I will be able to cope. I am not going to make any more mistakes from now on.' However, the reality is that when clients are depressed, anxious or worried, positive thinking is unlikely to help or may not have a significant, long-lasting, positive impact on their mood. It is difficult to be positive while depression, worry or anxiety is so crushing.

If clients can believe what they think, then it may have a beneficial effect. Rational, logical and philosophical thinking is usually seen as an alternative, largely because it is believable and there is evidence to support this kind of thinking. For example, 'Doing things well is satisfying, but it is human to make and learn from mistakes' is a helpful and realistic alternative thought to 'I must not make any mistakes'. Believability is a key to generating alternative helpful thoughts. Clients need to be taught ways to develop these kinds of helpful thoughts.

Second, it is believed that changing unhelpful behaviour is as important as getting rid of negative thoughts, if not more so. Unhelpful behaviour is known to prolong emotional suffering and reinforce pessimism regarding the prospect of recovery. For example, we know that behaviour such as constantly seeking reassurance and avoidance are unhelpful in health anxiety and panic disorder; ritualistic checks in obsessive-compulsive behaviour; and perfectionism and procrastination in depression. There is evidence to show that unless clients are willing and committed to giving up unhelpful behaviour and developing a helpful alternative, progress can be difficult to make. Practical advice and skills training from therapists are important in giving clients the necessary confidence to change the way they behave.

Imagine that someone is learning plumbing, car mechanics or decorating, theories and concepts give them some idea of what to do, but they do not have the confidence to do it or to do it well, unless skills training and practical advice are also provided. Clients with mental health problems are no exception: they need more than knowing that their thinking is negative or irrational in order to make progress. For example, clients need to learn *how* to say 'no' to requests and to deal with criticism. They need to learn ways of preventing procrastination and perfectionism. Otherwise, their prospect of recovery is not that promising.

Why is not focusing on behavioural changing a clinical issue?

We know for sure that for progress to be made it is important for clients to put efforts into changing their (unhelpful) behaviour. Imagine someone who is anxious about cycling. He will not be able to enjoy the benefits of being able to cycle unless he is willing to get on the bike and to keep trying, despite falling off it. Persistence, despite setbacks, enables the secret of cycling to be learnt. By the same token, when clients are not willing or are not committed to putting any effort into changing their (unhelpful) behaviour, it is doubtful whether any meaningful progress can be made. For example, we know that avoidance, safety-seeking behaviour and reassurance are harmful to clients with health anxiety and panic disorder. This unhelpful behaviour needs to be given up first in order for clients to learn a helpful way to deal with anxiety and anxiety problems.

Otherwise, clients may feel frustrated and despair at the lack of progress. They may believe that their mental health problems are due to 'chemical imbalances in the brain or genetic', as is often suggested to be the reason for their problems. The biogenetic view is problematic: not only can it affect clients' self-image (e.g. I have a 'diseased' brain and I am mental), but it can also affect their response to and engagement with therapy.

The case of Christian

Christian was relieved and pleased to know that his panic attacks were not a biological condition, involving genetic factors and biochemical imbalances, which is often suggested to be the probable causes for the attacks. The ABC concept (see the teaching of the ABC model in Chapter 1, pp. 8–12) was beneficial to his understanding of his panic problem; he was feeling better as a result. He could relate the feeling of dizziness to irrational thinking (e.g. 'I am going to pass out', 'I am going to die') and to the use of the unhelpful behaviour of avoidance, reassurance and safety-seeking to prevent the likelihood of something bad happening to him.

His initial good feelings soon turned into frustration and despair, as he was still feeling anxious, tense and nervous about going into various anxiety-provoking situations, such as crowded places and lifts. In fact, he still avoided going to these places. He thought that he should be all right by now, knowing that his negative thinking was the problem, not the situation. Whenever he started feeling anxious about not being able to cope, avoidance was used and he stayed in his 'comfort zone or shell'. Whenever he felt dizzy and had difficulty breathing, he grasped a chair to sit down, or left the supermarket or crowded place immediately. Last year, he was on holiday with a couple of friends in Spain and was feeling unwell two days into the holiday. When the bodily sensations (e.g. heart pounding) became intense, 'something is wrong with me' was going through his mind over and over again. Inevitably, he experienced an escalated level of anxiety; it resulted in more bodily sensations being noticed, which seemed to get worse by the hour. He couldn't carry on with the holiday, believing something terrible would happen. He needed to go back to his 'comfort zone or shell'. Once he was on the next available plane back to the UK, the sense of relief immediately brought the anxiety down, and also the feared bodily sensations. He was angry with himself for spoiling the holiday and knew nothing would have happened had he stayed. After all, it was just anxiety.

Despite years of being on different types of drugs of various dosages, his panic attacks remained. It is not uncommon that drugs or psychotherapies may not be as effective as hoped for. This can be seen in clients with obsessive-compulsive disorder, health anxiety and depression, or with clients with chronic problems. Clients' willingness to give up engaging in unhelpful behaviour is therefore crucial. Christian realised that intellectual understanding was not enough if he wanted to take control of his panic problem. Through being exposed to a range of anxiety-provoking situations and with the help of a range of techniques, not only did his confidence start to pick up, but also his anxiety levels and the bodily sensations were subsiding.

Cognitive behaviour therapy approach to unhelpful behaviour

The idea that emotional misery could be reduced or even eliminated just by changing negative thinking is far from the truth. Intellectual understanding of the problem may be helpful in the short term, but it is certainly not the case for the long term. Changing unhelpful behaviour is seen as crucial. The CBT position is that it is the responsibility of the therapist to motivate and empower the client to work in this area. Practical advice and skills training (e.g. role-play and demonstration) are essential. Clients are expected and encouraged to work hard at a practical level.

Some clients may not be willing or may even refuse to give up the unhelpful behaviour, the CBT message is that:

- Learning how to deal with a realistically negative situation is just as important as learning how to rid yourself of distorted thoughts and feelings.
- Without commitment and efforts to work at the behaviour level, it is highly unlikely that their mental health problems can be 'cured'.
- The benefits from the behaviour change are considerable.

Technique: Swimming analogue

Rationale and focus

The idea that you can learn to swim through observation and/or understanding its theory is illogical. Mastering skills and developing confidence in any activities (e.g. swimming and cycling) or jobs (e.g. accountancy and plumbing) requires the person to learn and do it at a practical level. Relating the swimming analogue to mental health problems helps clients give up unhelpful behaviour, knowing that it is their responsibility (see Chapter 6 on 'A shared responsibility approach in the change process') to put theory and skills into practice in order to make progress. Therapists are there to guide, to advise and to support.

Process

Therapist: Can you swim?

Christian: Yes. I am quite a good swimmer.

Therapist: When I was young, I almost drowned in the sea. The experience was really scary and I have a fear of swimming. But I really would like to be able to swim, partly to overcome my fear.

Christian: Oh, I can understand that. I have problems going into crowded places or situations in which I do not have control, such as a lift or train.

Therapist: Yeah. Do you think I can learn to swim through observing how you swim? After all, you are a good swimmer.

Christian: I don't think so. You have to learn it in the pool.

Therapist: Oh. Can I overcome my fear, if I understand the theory or concept of swimming?

Christian: I don't think so.

Therapist: What do I need to do in order to overcome my fear and to be able to swim?

Christian: The only way to do it is to come to the pool.

Therapist: Oh. If this is the case, will you be able to overcome your fear and your panic attacks just by having a better understanding of your problems?

Christian: Oh. Ah. But I am quite anxious in those places or situations.

Therapist: Sure, I am quite anxious myself, when I am in the pool. Will you be able to overcome your fear and anxiety with your unhelpful behaviour, such as avoidance, safety-seeking behaviour or reassurance?

Christian: Well. I suppose not.

Therapist: What do I need to do in order to overcome my fear and to be able to swim?

Christian: Get into the water.

Therapist: What do you have to do in order to overcome your fear and your panic attacks?

Christian: Get into those places or situations and stop using unhelpful behaviour.

Homework

Christian was asked to:

- Identify a list of anxiety-provoking situations and rank the anxiety levels from the lowest to the highest in relation to these situations.
- Write down his negative thoughts in each of the situations and rewrite them with a helpful alternative.
- List the costs and benefits of unhelpful behaviour.
- Read an article on panic disorder.

Technique: Prediction

Rationale and focus

Getting the client to make a prediction of what would happen if he or she continues to engage unhelpful behaviour to cope with difficult or anxiety-provoking situations is an effective way to help the client realise that not only can progress not be made, but also that the mental health problem is likely to get worse as a result. Another prediction is find out what is likely to happen if a new 'set' of behaviour is used instead. For example, the therapist can say: 'Why don't we try a different way of dealing with the situation? If it doesn't work, you can always go back to your "old" behaviour. What have you got to lose?'

Process

Therapist: How long have you been suffering from panic attacks?

Christian: Quite a long time, about three years.

Therapist: Whenever you feel anxious or discomfort while you are in supermarkets, restaurants or cinemas, you would leave the place right away or avoid going to these places. Is that right?

Christian: Yes.

Therapist: Suppose you continue to use this (unhelpful) behaviour for the rest of your life, what is your prediction about what might happen?

Christian: I don't know. I suppose I won't be able to get better.

Therapist: You can be sure of that, and . . . ?

Christian: It may get worse.

Therapist: The chance of that happening is quite high. You may become depressed, losing hope of getting better and for the future. It will also have a more negative impact on your family life, affecting your

	relationships with your wife and your children. Besides, what sort of messages you are giving to your children?
Christian:	Oh, not good. They may learn from my behaviour.
Therapist:	Absolutely. What is your prediction, if you are determined and committed to change; is part of it to give up your unhelpful behaviour?
Christian:	I will be anxious in those situations and be afraid of not coping.
Therapist:	Sure. If you are able to manage your anxiety and fear better with a range of techniques and skills, what is your prediction about how you feel in these situations?
Christian:	Less anxious and fearful, I suppose.
Therapist:	And?
Christian:	Feeling more confident.
Therapist:	As a result of being less anxious and fearful and having more confidence, what is your prediction about your panic problem?
Christian:	I will be able to get better and to recover.
Therapist:	I agree with that prediction. What is your prediction, if you don't give yourself a chance to practise the skills and techniques?
Christian:	I won't be able to change.

Homework

Christian was asked to:

- Write down the costs and benefits of using helpful behaviour, such as exposure and imagery technique.
- Keep a diary of evidence of action.

Other techniques

Other relevant techniques include 'Rewriting assumptions', 'Cognitive continuum' and 'Read it out loud'.

Notes for therapists about unhelpful behaviour

- Clients should be encouraged to take responsibility for putting learning into practice and making changes at behavioural and emotional levels, not just changing their negative thinking.
- Treatment failure may occur, if emphasis is not placed on changing unhelpful behaviour.
- Emphasise the benefits of developing helpful behaviour, such as providing evidence either to support or refute negative thinking,

developing skills and confidence to deal with difficult situations and people, and having more emotional control.

- Positive thinking is not a helpful alternative to the negative one. Rational, logical and philosophical thinking is a better alternative.

Chapter 9

Homework assignments

'I am here to get treatment, not to do homework. It's only for kids,' a client said unhappily. Another client said, 'I don't like it. It reminds me of the bad times, when I was a kid.' These reactions are not uncommon, as the idea of homework in psychotherapy is fairly 'new'. Clients often do not expect it when they come for cognitive-behaviour therapy. However, homework is a core feature of the CBT process. In pragmatic terms, it represents the opportunity for clients to transfer the skills, concepts, theories and ideas from therapy to the everyday situations in which their problems actually occur, thereby enhancing their problem-solving and coping skills, preventing the likelihood of relapse, and increasing their self-confidence. If clients do not make use of the opportunity by putting effort and commitment into it, it would be difficult for them to 'stay' better. Recovery from mental health problems is not just about patients 'feeling or getting' better, but is about them being able to 'stay' better. (See the concept of 'feel, get and stay better' in Chapter 16 on 'Setback and relapse'.) Research shows that CBT involving homework assignments produces better outcomes than those from therapy consisting entirely of in-session work (Kazantzis et al. 2000). Treatment outcome is significantly enhanced when clients complete their homework assignments and are pro-active in putting learning into practice at every available opportunity.

The idea of doing homework is a familiar and well-accepted concept in education. It is hard to make progress and do well if pupils do not work hard at their homework. No matter how good a school or how prestigious a university is, success in their studies occurs only through hard work and commitment. Homework helps broaden the knowledge base of the subjects and leads to a deeper understanding of what is learnt in sessions. This gives them motivation and an interest in what they do and the confidence to do well. Many cultures see education as the key to prosperity, improving quality of life, and as a vehicle for crossing boundaries in a social class system. Parents ensure that their children develop the right and responsible attitude towards homework, through encouragement and support. In this respect, educational establishments (e.g. school or university), pupils (students) and parents work together as a team.

Clinically, homework is viewed as an important component in therapeutic success. However, therapists may find it difficult to motivate clients to take homework seriously. Problems in encouraging clients to do it are prevalent. From experiences of training and supervising students doing CBT training, motivating clients to do homework is a challenge as well as a problem. 'Do not have time, too busy, too tired, or forgot' are often given as reasons for not doing it. Some clients attempt to do it at the last moment, just before they come for the next CBT session. Benefit is likely to be negligible. Insufficient or lack of progress can be frustrating for both the therapist and the client. There may be a tendency for therapists to blame clients for being 'lazy' and 'unmotivated' and to question whether they really want to get better. Clients may even be labelled as trying to hold on to the benefits of being 'sick', or as suffering from 'personality disorders'.

Imagine that you, as a client, do not understand the reasons for being given a particular piece of homework and how relevant it is to your problems, that you do not understand the instructions, or that you do not know how to do it. Would you do it or feel motivated to do it? A few years ago, one client rightly questioned me on the point of doing his homework. I had not spent time reviewing what he had done and building on it. This was a good learning experience for me, helping me to realise that to motivate clients it is important to provide them with feedback. Equally, when clients are given too much work, without taking into consideration their family and work commitments or the time factor, their motivation and/or their ability to complete the task will be affected. In this respect, therapists need to take some responsibility for the problem and work with clients to identify any obstacles which would prevent them from completing their homework and how these obstacles can be resolved. Useful questions to ask at the end of the session are: 'Do you anticipate any problems in doing this homework? What do you think the reasons are for this particular homework?'

Homework can be conceptualised in terms of 'doing' and 'practising'. There is a crucial difference between the two. Imagine that a person is learning to drive: reading about driving and/or observing other people driving will provide the concepts and ideas of what to do (*doing* homework), but it does not mean that the person can drive. To be able to drive, it is essential to *practise* the ideas and concepts on the roads as much as possible in order to develop skills and confidence. By the same token, doing homework such as keeping a diary, reading articles, conducting a survey, or rewriting negative thoughts only shows that someone's thinking is indeed negative or unhelpful, but it does not mean that the client will have the confidence and skills to cope with adversity such as dealing with confrontational situations, saying 'no' to a request, or exposing themselves to anxiety-provoking situations. Persistently practising homework (e.g. ideas, concepts and theories) in everyday situations helps with developing the skills, confidence and understanding of these ideas, concepts and theories.

These are crucial to overcome anxiety as in obsessive-compulsive and panic disorders, to reduce worry as in general anxiety disorder, and to develop self-belief as in depression and in people with low self-esteem.

Practising homework is therefore a crucial therapeutic process, involving clients in learning to face anxiety-provoking situations, to deal with conflicts or social situations, to make requests assertively, to say 'no' to requests in an appropriate and adult manner, or to give up approval-seeking behaviour. Changing the way they behave in these situations gives them the confidence and conviction that they can do it. Imagine that for the first time in your life you are able to say 'no' to a request, to express your opinions, or not to run from a conflict- or anxiety-provoking situation. Isn't it a good feeling to have? Being able to change their unhelpful behaviours to the helpful ones (i.e. learning not to say 'yes' to every request) can provide them with evidence that there is really nothing to be anxious or worried about. This will not only give them confidence to continue their behavioural change, but help also to overcome their irrational fears or thoughts. Clients need to be empowered and entrusted with the responsibility to practise homework in everyday situations (see Chapter 6 on 'A shared responsibility approach in the change process'). In other words, to believe it – is good. To know it – is better (doing homework). To apply it – is best (practising homework).

Why is not putting effort and commitment into homework a clinical issue?

Imagine that a student did not do his college work or sufficiently prepare for his examinations; it would not be surprising if he did not do well or even failed his examinations. The problem may not have anything to do with his intelligence or ability; it is more to do with his commitment and effort. However, he may come to label himself as stupid and useless and become pessimistic about his future.

CBT is generally regarded as a 'talking' therapy. However, CBT considers that *action* is at least as important as talking, if not more so. In this respect, CBT is also regarded as an 'action' therapy. When clients are not 'practising' homework with effort and commitment and are not making progress, not only would they become pessimistic about their progress and their future, but also they may label themselves as failures and useless. This may have the unwanted effect of reinforcing the notion of mental health problems being caused by chemical imbalances in the brain and genetic factors. Bobby, as described here, said that 'there is something wrong in my brain' and believed that drug treatment was the only way to 'make it right'.

The case of Bobby

Bobby was doubtful about the idea of another referral to psychotherapy. He believed that drug treatment was the remedy for his anxiety and that his problems could not possibly be resolved through talking. Although he had been on a range of drugs of various dosages for most of his adult life, he just managed to stay 'above water'. His anxiety and associated bodily sensations were particularly bad in the mornings and there were no reasons for them. There must be something wrong with him physically. The idea of 'chemical imbalance' being the cause of his anxiety problem was appealing. It seemed reasonable to attribute his bodily sensations of anxiety to an insufficient level or dysfunction of neurotransmitters in the brain, like people suffering from Huntington disease or multiple sclerosis.

'I don't want to sound negative or pessimistic, but I don't think that it will work for me,' said Bobby, who was sceptical about a referral to CBT for the second time. 'Medication is the only way to help me to recover.' His consultant psychiatrist truly believed that his negative outlook was largely the problem and medication was an adjunct to CBT work. After five CBT sessions, there was little or no progress being made and he was both disappointed and frustrated. He did not see the relevance of doing homework (e.g. reading articles, reality testing) as a way of helping with his anxiety problem, although he did do it in a superficial manner.

The idea of homework is not just to get clients to read articles relevant to their mental health problems, to do reality testing to see whether there is evidence to support his negative thinking, or to change negative thinking to positive. Changing their unhelpful (or maladaptive) behaviour is as important, if not more so. For example, positive change comes about as a result of being able to express feelings, opinions and preferences, or to say 'no' reasonably and appropriately to requests, or to make a mistake and learn from it. Although *intellectually* understanding that it was the right thing to do, Bobby did not make any attempt to change any aspect of his unhelpful behaviour such as avoiding conflict, perfectionism, procrastination and self-criticism. It was therefore not surprising that he was both frustrated and disappointed with the lack of progress in his treatment.

I was equally disappointed and frustrated with his lack of progress and made it clear that 'there was no magic wand' to aid his recovery. It required hard work and commitment from both of us, particularly at the level of changing unhelpful behaviour. I said to Bobby that unless he was willing to take responsibility for his recovery and to work hard with me to achieve *our* objectives, continuing the therapeutic work at an intellectual level would accomplish little or nothing at all. When there is insufficient or lack of progress after five sessions, it is worth examining the possible reasons; not changing unhelpful behaviour is often a major contributor.

Bobby was pleased with himself for being appropriately assertive in his complaint about the standard of food in a restaurant and said that he wouldn't have done it in the past, for the same reason as that of his wife. His wife was anxious about the possibility of an angry reaction from the waiter and urged him not to make a fuss. In subsequent sessions, he reported the efforts being made to change his unhelpful behaviours at every available opportunity and learnt from the experiences of failure. As a result, his rising self-confidence had helped to bring down his anxiety level. His change is surely an inspiration to other clients with mental health problems. It also illustrates that the hard work put in to 'doing' and 'practising' homework is necessary. Positive change can't happen by chance.

Cognitive behaviour therapy approach to homework assignments

We know for sure that clients' attitudes will influence their commitment and effort to complete homework assignments, particularly those that involve a change of behaviour such as dealing with confrontational situations or saying 'no' to requests. Some clients may have had negative homework experiences in their early years and are therefore resistant to or anxious about homework. Changing their attitude is important. Various terms can be used instead of homework such as 'project', 'task' or 'challenge' and the use of a particular word is for the client to choose: 'Instead of calling it homework, is there any particular term or wording you would like to use?' This may help clients to feel more comfortable about it and therefore encourage them not only to be proactive in deciding on what needs to be done and how it can be done in relation to their problems, but also to practise homework in everyday situations.

The CBT message is that effort and commitment to homework is necessary to the recovery process and to clients gaining control over their lives and future.

Technique: Bricklaying

Rationale and focus

In CBT, clients often do not realise the importance of *practising* homework, although they don't have a problem understanding its concepts and theories. A technique that helps clients realise that if there are 'real' benefits to be gained there is no substitute for practising homework. The concept of bricklaying is a useful analogy as it is, in a way, similar to CBT concepts and theories. Ask anybody for their initial experiences of bricklaying: they will say it is difficult and frustrating. However, with persistence and despite setbacks (see Chapter 16 on 'Setback and relapse'), not only will they understand the secrets of the trade, but also they will become skilful and confident in the demonstration of the art. Practising CBT homework is no exception. Rewards in the form of skills and confidence cannot be achieved through 'talking', but gained from practising.

Process

Therapist: Have you seen a professional bricklayer working?

Bobby: Yes. I think so.

Therapist: Does it look easy when you see them doing it?

Bobby: They do it very fast and their work is good.

Therapist: They are skilful and confident, aren't they?

Bobby: Very much so.

Therapist: If we understand what needs to be done and how to do it, does it mean that we can all do it as well as a professional?

Bobby: No. I don't think so. To become skilful and confident requires a lot of hard work and practice.

Therapist: If someone who is keen and understands the concepts and theories of bricklaying, but does not put in the effort and commitment required, will they be able to be good at it?

Bobby: I don't think so.

Therapist: Absolutely. CBT homework is no exception. You may find it easy to understand its concepts and theories, like those of bricklaying, but if you do not take responsibility to practise it, will you be able to make progress?

Bobby: Oh. Ah. I see what you mean.

Homework

Bobby was asked to:

- Write down the costs and benefits of *not* practising homework.
- Write down the costs and benefits of practising homework.
- Talk to a bricklayer to find out what is required to be good at bricklaying.

Technique: Prediction

Rationale and focus

Prediction is often used as a technique to motivate clients to take responsibility for changing their unhelpful behaviour. For example, clients suffering from anxiety are asked to predict what may happen if they keep seeking reassurance and having tests and investigations done whenever they feel concern about their health, or if they reduce the frequency of these behaviours. The idea is to create two possible options for the client to choose, once they understand the consequences of each of the two options.

Getting the client to make such a prediction about practising or not practising homework is an effective way to encourage the client to take homework seriously (see Chapter 6 on 'A shared responsibility approach in the change process').

Process

Therapist: Clients coming to CBT may not be comfortable with the idea of homework as part of the therapy. The reality is that it is important and essential, which is no different from students attending schools and colleges.

Bobby: I see what you mean.

Therapist: Clients often have no problem understanding that homework is important and essential, but do not give it priority or take it seriously. What will be your prediction in terms of progress, if you do not put in the effort and commitment?

Bobby: Not good.

Therapist: Meaning?

Bobby: Feeling tense and anxious, more so in the morning. I just find it difficult to get up in the morning, to do anything or to face other people in social situations. I am also pessimistic about my progress and my future.

Therapist: It means that you are not going to make any progress. There is also the possibility that it is going to get worse, if you do not do anything about it in a positive and constructive manner. Is that what you want?

Bobby: No.

Therapist: Suppose you put in effort and commitment to homework, what will be your prediction?

Bobby: Well, I expect to get better.

Therapist: I am sure of that. It gives hope about your progress and your future, meaning less anxiety and tension. You will also have the confidence to cope in social situations. Is that what you want?

Bobby: Yes.

Therapist: Which option are you going to choose?

> *Bobby:* I am going to give doing the homework a go.
>
> *Therapist:* Good. Why don't we work together and support each other?

Other techniques

Other relevant techniques include 'Daughter', 'Education', 'Swimming analogue' and 'Costs and benefits analysis'.

Notes for therapists about homework assignments

- Practical advice and skills training are imperative to clients' confidence to put learning into practice. These increase the possibility of clients practising their homework.
- Identify possible reasons for not completing homework and ways to overcome the problems.
- Homework is a collaborative exercise, involving clients making a contribution to the type of homework that is relevant to their problems.
- Homework must be appropriate and relevant.
- Clients should be given credit for practising homework and for making progress.

Chapter 10

Drug treatments

Drug treatments are useful in the containment of some symptoms in mental health problems and are particularly beneficial to clients with severe and recurrent problems such as schizophrenia, bipolar disorder, recurrent depression and chronic anxiety problems. Medication has been found to be beneficial in relieving symptoms of emotional disorders and in improving the concentration, memory and mood of clients, whereas CBT has been established as the treatment of choice for a range of mental health problems because it is cost-effective, has a low dropout and relapse rate in comparison to other forms of psychotherapy and drug treatment (Roth and Fonagy 2005; National Institute for Health and Clinical Excellence, available online at www.nice.org.uk). Drug treatments and CBT are usually seen as an effective combination in the treatment of mental health problems, with drugs being used to stabilise or lift the mood in order for the client to learn to develop effective personal coping resources or strategies through CBT. There is a suggestion or recommendation that 'talking therapy', and CBT in particular, should be offered to clients in the first instance.

However, drug treatments are often promoted as the main factor for recovery: 'Your problem [a diagnosis] is due to "chemical imbalances" or is genetic and you need to be on drugs.' The endorsement reinforces a narrow biological conception of the nature of mental health problems and powerfully sponsors medication as central in restoring the balance of chemistry in a 'diseased' brain. As such, it may imply there is little or nothing clients can do to overcome their psychological and emotional distress through their own devices, even with help and care. In the event of the failure of drug treatments or that medication has not been beneficial, clients may feel that the problem in their 'diseased' brain is so bad that even medication is unable to help, thereby creating feelings of helplessness and hopelessness. There is mounting evidence that focusing on biological, genetic and 'disease' concepts, with drug treatments being actively promoted as a cure for 'mental illness', can worsen the problems of stigmatisation for mental health sufferers, resulting in their experiencing prejudice and being discriminated against. Clients also stigmatise themselves for being 'mental and insane' because of a 'diseased' brain. The biogenetic endorsement does not encourage clients to be proactive in the management of their symptoms and to take responsibility for their recovery (see Chapter 6 on 'A shared responsibility approach in the change process').

Moncrieff (2003) cautions against overemphasising the role of drug treatments, about drugs being prescribed for overly long periods and in excessive doses, and about the unwanted effects of drugs on reducing personal coping strategies, reducing self-confidence, and creating fearful and anxious beliefs about being on medication (e.g. I am weak, I am inadequate, I will never be able to come off the medication). Side-effects are a particular concern as there is some evidence of drugs being linked to suicide and self-harm (Moncrieff and Pommerleau 2000; Van Praag 2002; Moncrieff 2003; Whittington et al. 2004) and to severe obesity, diabetes and impotence (Koro et al. 2002). Drug treatments have also been associated with adverse cardiac events (Hennessy et al. 2002).

There is a crucial difference between 'feeling/getting' better and 'staying' better. Although drug treatments are helpful in relieving symptoms and in improving the concentration, memory and mood of clients, they do not deal with the cause or root of mental health problems. Clients may 'feel and/or get' better in the short term but they may not be able to 'stay' better in the longer term, unless the cause or root of the problems is addressed (see Chapter 16 on 'Setback and relapse'). According to CBT theory, the root or cause of emotional misery (e.g. envy, shame, anger, frustration and depression) lies in the ways in which an individual perceives others or the world. How individuals perceive the world or others is closely related to the way they see themselves: their self-worth and self-esteem (see Figure 10.1). Developing stable self-esteem is therefore important in CBT terms (Fennell 1999).

Why is the perception of drug treatments being the main factor for recovery a clinical issue?

When drug treatments are perceived as the main factor for recovery, it reinforces the social stigma of clients being different, insane and not having control over their mind and behaviour. Clients may also stigmatise themselves for having mental health problems and for not being able to do anything that could make a difference, apart from punctually taking medication.

Believing drug treatments are the only way to get better, together with the problems of stigmatisation, can affect their response to and engagement with therapy. When recovery can't be achieved in spite of being on drugs treatment, clients may develop feelings of helplessness and hopelessness and

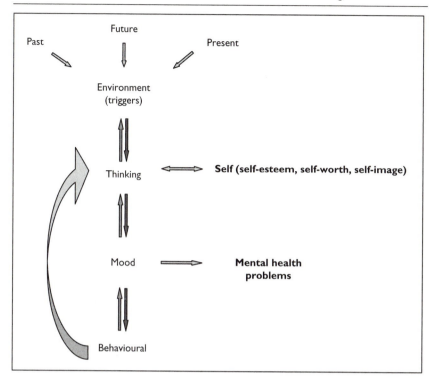

Figure 10.1 Perception and self-esteem

start to see themselves as different from other people. In other words, they have a 'disease' in the brain. Such a belief also affects their self-esteem and self-confidence and can cause pessimism regarding treatment outcome.

The case of Caroline

'I'll never be able to come off the medication,' said Caroline, when she came for the first CBT session for her depression and low self-esteem. The idea of taking drugs for the rest of her life got her down, but at the same time she was fearful of not taking them in case she relapsed into depression again. She said that she had been depressed all her life, for as long as she could remember: it was so terrible to be depressed – again. The reality was that, despite being on a cocktail of drugs, she had had three major episodes of depression. The relapses greatly affected her self-confidence and the way she perceived herself as a person (e.g. 'I am a failure, inadequate and weak'). Each relapse led to an admission to hospital because of concerns about her safety.

While she was depressed, she was troubled by a stream of negative and suicidal thoughts (e.g. 'What is the point in living? You will never be able to get better. You might as well kill yourself and not be a burden to your family'), which scared and paralysed her. She said that these thoughts were just too powerful to ignore. The harder she tried to resist, the more frequent and powerful they became, which made her condition even worse.

'Your depression is most likely to be genetic and/or biochemical imbalances in your brain. You probably need to take drugs for the rest of your life,' said the psychiatrist who had been treating her for years. Her general practitioner was in agreement with the psychiatric diagnosis and drugs being seen as the main factor in containing the depressive symptoms. Her mother was also diagnosed with endogenous depression and one of her uncles killed himself with an overdose. He too suffered from depression. There seemed to be overwhelming evidence to support the diagnosis that her condition was biogenetic in nature. It was not surprising that Caroline came to accept the medical judgement as the truth and to believe that she would never be able to come off drugs.

She was responding well to CBT treatment. However, the fear of the return of her depression persisted. Caroline was tearful and upset when she phoned to ask for an urgent appointment, saying that 'her depression was coming back because she was tired and forgetful, and she had also forgotten to take her medication for two days'. Another similar occasion on which she believed that her depression was coming back was that she had problems sleeping well. She lived on an edge of fear that depression could hit her any time (even with the help of medication) and that she did not have any control over it. She said that these 'symptoms' were there prior to each of the three previous episodes of depression that she had had. However, she soon realised that tiredness, forgetfulness and not being able to sleep well could be some symptoms of depression, but they could also be symptoms of other things (e.g. overexcitement and doing too much). Her 'daily activities of living' showed that she had been running around like a 'headless chicken' for family, friends and relatives, leaving little time to rest and relax. She also felt guilty about relaxing and not doing things. She accepted that it was her irrational fear and over-reaction that made these 'symptoms' seem to be worse than they actually were. On both occasions, she did not end up with depression.

Over the course of nine months of CBT work, her confidence was starting to improve and she believed that she was in control of her mood. This led to a gradual reduction of her medication. After two years, her medication was stopped.

Cognitive behaviour therapy approach to drug treatments

CBT takes the view that medication may be necessary, particularly for clients with severe and recurrent mental health problems. However, when clients believe that drugs treatments are central to restoring the balance of chemistry in a 'diseased' brain; that their mental health problems will get worse without medication; that taking medication is a sign of personal weakness (e.g. 'I am weak and inadequate'); or that medication is harmful (e.g. 'I'll end up taking an overdose'), it may affect their response to and engagement with therapy.

In working with clients with a set of irrational beliefs about drug treatments, the CBT message is that:

- There is insufficient scientific evidence to indicate that emotional misery is due to a 'diseased' brain.
- Emotional misery primarily lies with dysfunctional thinking and maladaptive behaviour, something that can be put right through a course of CBT.
- The balance or imbalance of chemistry in the brain is closely related to the way we think about and react to adversity.
- Taking medication is not an indication of personal weakness or of medication being harmful, certainly not in the short term.
- Medication can be reduced and stopped once clients are more in control of their thoughts and behaviour and have developed effective personal coping strategies.

Technique: The brain

Rationale and focus

The idea of a 'diseased' brain and chemical imbalances as the cause(s) of mental health problems is often a puzzle to mentally ill clients, like nuclear physics to the general public. It is hard for them (or even for some professionals) to understand what it means. As a result of not knowing what to do that could make a difference to their problems, they may develop feelings of helplessness and hopelessness, which can worsen their mental health problems.

They often 'forget' that the brain can function as a centre for processing information or data and not just as a 'complex factory' for making chemicals which are essential to a range of human activities, such as reasoning, analysing and muscular coordination. There is evidence to support the view that the way in which information is processed (positively or negatively; accurately or inaccurately) by the brain (e.g. the way we analyse information

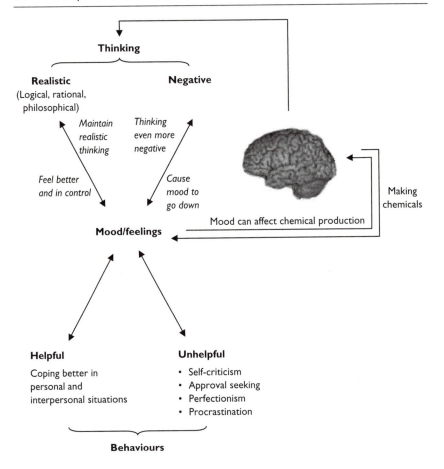

Figure 10.2 The brain

or data) can affect the mood (good or bad), which can in turn affect how the brain works: processing information and making chemicals. It means that there is a reciprocal relationship between mood and the ways in which the brain works. In CBT terms, we have a choice of what to think (positive or negative; helpful or unhelpful) and that choice comes about because we have *control* over the way we think about things. Once clients understand that they have that choice too and learn to *choose* a more helpful or realistic way to perceive self, others and the world, it would surely have a beneficial effect on how the brain works: making chemicals (Figure 10.2).

In using this technique, the therapist and the client can talk about the concept of choice in general, and then relate this concept to thinking, behaviour and mood. For example, do we have a choice of what to think and how to behave?

Process

Therapist:	We all have a brain, including animals. Isn't it true?
Caroline:	Of course.
Therapist:	How long have you been suffering from depression?
Caroline:	Almost all my life. I have had three major episodes of depression. My mother also suffered from it, as did my uncle.
Therapist:	How do you feel about it?
Caroline:	I don't like it. In fact, I am frightened of it and hope that I will never have it again. But I just don't feel that I have control over it.
Therapist:	It is not good to suffer from it, especially when you feel that you do not have control over it. I can understand that feeling. Coming back to the brain, we all have one. What do you think the brain is for?
Caroline:	Oh. I don't really know. I know it is very important. Without it, we will die. My doctors said to me that my depression is due to chemical imbalances in the brain. It worries me and I don't know what it is and what I can do. I just feel so helpless.
Therapist:	So the brain makes chemicals that are important to our mood – such as your depression, isn't that so?
Caroline:	True.
Therapist:	What else is the brain for?
Caroline:	I don't know.
Therapist:	How about thinking? Can we think?
Caroline:	We do, of course.
Therapist:	Would you say that the brain is also for thinking, helping us to process information/data? For example, we look up a map to decide how to go from A to B, or we read instructions on how to operate a computer, a television or a washing machine.
Caroline:	True.
Therapist:	What would you say the brain is for?
Caroline:	Making chemicals and thinking.
Therapist:	Absolutely. Do we have control over the quantity of chemicals the brain makes?
Caroline:	No, I wish I had.
Therapist:	Do we have control in the way we think about things?
Caroline:	Yeah. Oh. I suppose we have. Yes, we do have.
Therapist:	Does it also mean that we also have choice in what we do?
Caroline:	Yes.
Therapist:	Ask yourself: Do you have a choice about what to wear, where to go on holiday, what to buy in a supermarket, who you want to be friends with?

Caroline:　Yes, sure.

Therapist:　By the same token, we do have a choice in what we think and how we behave, don't we?

Caroline:　Yes.

Therapist:　In CBT terms, the way we think (positively or negatively; rationally or irrationally) can affect our mood, which in turn affects the functions of the brain. The brain is responsible for making chemicals and for thinking.

Caroline:　Oh. I can see that my mood can be affected by my negative and irrational thinking. My doctors and family have been telling me this for years. But I did not know that the mood can also affect the way in which the brain works.

Therapist:　Of course it does. For example, when you feel bad, how does it affect your thinking (or the way your brain works)?

Caroline:　Even more negative and irrational.

Therapist:　How about when you feel good and that you are on top of the world?

Caroline:　Great, I feel more confident and my thinking is good.

Therapist:　It is true that we do not have control over the quantity of chemicals the brain makes, but we do have control and choice over the way we think and behave. This means that we also have a choice over the way we feel. Logically, what does that imply about the amount of chemicals being made in the brain, when we feel good?

Caroline:　It means that more chemicals can be made in the brain which in turn helps with the mood.

Homework

Caroline was asked to:

- Keep a diary for a month on her mood relative to her thinking to see if there was a relationship between thinking and mood.
- Write a conclusion on the functions of the brain.

Other techniques

Other relevant techniques include 'Rewriting assumptions', 'Daughter', 'Acceptance' and 'Read it out loud'.

Notes for therapists about drug treatments

- One of the objectives of the CBT approach is to reduce or stop medication. However, long-term medication may be necessary for clients with severe or recurrent mental health problems such as personality disorders, schizophrenia or depression.
- Taking medication is not a sign of personal weakness or personality defects.
- Medication may be necessary for clients to get benefits from the CBT approach.

Part III

Client's perspective

Self-prejudice and personal issues

Chapter 11

Approval and approval-seeking behaviour

Isn't it comforting to be approved of by others, particularly those who are close and important to us? When we talk about approval, we talk about it in terms of recognition, acceptance, praise, love and affection. Just ask your friends, your colleagues and anybody you know whether they like to be recognised, accepted, praised, loved or given affection. It would be hard to find anyone who does not like any of these. Even animals such as dogs or cats enjoy a bit of love, attention and affection.

Humans are no exception. We would not be happy and contented just to have something to eat to fill up our stomachs and a roof over our heads. Once these physical needs are met, we look for human contact for psychological and emotional reasons, involving receiving and giving love, acceptance, recognition and praise. When you do well in an examination, in a project or in a presentation, it is good to get recognition and praise for your hard work. When you dress well for an occasion, it is pleasant to receive compliments for the way you look. In other words, it is gratifying to be loved, praised and accepted by those around you. Wanting approval is part of human nature. It's a fact of life that you feel good about getting approval. There is nothing wrong with that; it is natural and healthy and is good for your mental health.

However, it is well recognised that not everybody will approve of you all the time, no matter how charming, wealthy or loving you are. If you are honest with yourself, you know that even those who love you, such as your parents or your partner, would still disapprove of things you do or say at times. Therefore, it is a fact that people do feel bitter and upset about disapproval. For example, Christian said that he 'did not like being disapproved of by others, it made him feeling anxious, hurt and angry'. This is human and understandable. However, the reality was that he criticised people and did not like some people himself. Ask yourself: Did you ever disagree with a friend or a colleague's opinion? Did you ever snap at a loved one when you were feeling irritable or tired? Did you ever criticise someone whose behaviour was unacceptable to you? There is no law in the universe to say that Christian (or you) could do it to others, whereas others couldn't disapprove of him (or you).

When approval is viewed as *desirable* and is not related to one's self-worth or self-esteem, people in general would have no problem with disapproval, even from those who are close and significant to them. They know that it is a fact of life even though they may get upset over it for a while. In fact, some people may think that it is not worth while to get upset over it. The important thing is not so much about disapproval itself; it is about how to deal with it. More importantly, they would not see themselves as 'I am a reject or I am unlovable' because they know their self-worth and self-esteem is not or should not be based on it.

When approval is seen as a *need*, it becomes problematic for people's mental health as they tend to believe that approval and disapproval is the proper and ultimate yardstick with which to measure their self-worth and self-esteem. These people are likely to subscribe to a set of unhelpful beliefs or assumptions about it (e.g. it is terrible to be criticised or rejected) and therefore engage in a range of approval-seeking behaviour to get it. Joseph said that he was good at saying what people want to hear because he needed people to like and accept him. Carol said that she would ask herself what others would like her to wear whenever she went out with people. Christian said that he had a range of masks to use for different social and work situations because he needed to be liked and to be the centre of attention. Tim insisted on paying for meals and drinks for his friends because he needed them to see him as a likeable and generous person. Lisa was anxious and worried about saying 'no' to requests because she did not want to offend anyone. All these examples illustrate that needing approval causes individuals to be extremely vulnerable to what other people think about them, and to how these people behave towards them. Others will be able to use this vulnerability to manipulate them. These clients will have to give in to their demands more often than they want to because of the fear of being rejected or being looked down upon. These clients set themselves up for emotional blackmail.

Some clients believe that they were born with approval-seeking traits. It is in their genes and there is nothing they can do about it. Others argue that the problem is so deeply ingrained that it would be difficult to change. Where did this approval problem come from in the first place? We can only speculate that it may lie with their interactions with people who were important to them when they were children. As a small child, you might have a parent who had high expectations of achievements and was unduly critical when you misbehaved or did not live up to their expectations. Your teachers might be critical of your behaviour, saying, 'You were bad for doing that or for behaving like that!' Similarly, when praise and recognition were given for acceptable behaviour, you would work even harder to get more of it. Emma (in the case example given below) said that as a small child her spirit, mood and confidence were affected by her parents' behaviour and by what her teachers said. She recalled that her parents were so proud of her in her primary school reports, constantly praising her for being a 'good' girl. She *needed* to be a good girl.

As a child, you probably saw your parents and/or teachers as infallible or gods and accepted that everything they said was true. If your teacher said, 'Never talk to a stranger or go with a stranger, it is dangerous,' or if your mother said, 'You only cross the road when the crossing light is green,' this was literally true. Most children might have assumed that nearly everything their parents or teachers said was true. So when they said that you're no good, you'll never learn, they didn't like you, or you're lazy, you tended to believe it, without asking whether it was true. You were too young to be able to reason and didn't have the emotional maturity to put things into perspective. No wonder that as an adult you have developed the bad habit of automatically looking down on yourself (e.g. 'I am not good enough') every time someone disapproves of you and view disapproval as terrible. Blaming the genes or personality traits does not resolve the problem; it can only make the problem worse. But changing the thoughts and beliefs about approval and disapproval does.

Why is needing approval a clinical issue?

The price the client pays for needing approval will be an extreme vulnerability to the opinions of others and a wide fluctuation of moods. Disapproval poses a threat to his ego, to the treatment process and outcome, or to recovery from mental health problems. It also contributes to the problem of relapse into another episode of depression and/or into other mental health problems. The moment someone who is important to him expresses disapproval, he will crash painfully, just like a junkie who can no longer get his 'stuff'.

The case of Emma

Emma had been a sales executive for an international drug company for five years. My first impression of her was that she was a nice, friendly and good-looking person. However, she was also anxious at our first meeting. She said that she was worried about what I thought of her and that how people saw her was important to her. It would affect her mood and how she felt about herself. She wanted to be seen as a nice, friendly and intelligent person and would do anything that she could to get people's approval. She was referred to CBT for her problems of alcoholism, depression and low self-esteem.

When she came to one of our sessions, she was so happy and excited, saying that her presentation to a group of 100 people was well received. She felt she had done well and at the end of the presentation many people came to congratulate her for an excellent performance. She was well pleased with the recognition and praise that she had received. Naturally, I added my voice to the congratulations.

She was tearful, upset and depressed when she came for the next session, saying that she had done another presentation after the last successful one. But hardly any people went to her to say anything nice about what she did. She said that she had put a lot of effort into it and felt that it had gone well. Not getting the recognition and praise that she craved for had driven her mood down, so much so that she did not go out or do anything except drink heavily over the weekend and feel sorry for herself.

Her unhelpful assumption about approval was that 'If people did not come to congratulate me or appreciate my work, this meant that I was not good enough and I couldn't feel good about myself as a person'.

Cognitive behaviour therapy approach to approval and approval-seeking behaviour

In CBT terms, not getting people's approval is not the cause of emotional upset. It doesn't make sense, as not everybody in a similar situation would end up feeling upset, tearful or depressed. Some would feel upset (e.g., hurt, anxious or worried), whereas others would feel fine with it. We are all different and therefore our responses to it are likely to be different. Not getting approval is just a situation (the A of the ABC, see the ABC model in Chapter 1, pp. 8–12), in a way that is similar to not getting a job following an interview or not being invited to a wedding. The underlying problem really lies with the person's thoughts and beliefs about approval and disapproval and with the way he or she copes with disapproval.

The client often overlooks the fact that it is only his thoughts and beliefs which have the power either to lift up or lower his spirits. Another person's approval or disapproval has no control over his mood unless the client believes what the other person says is valid (e.g. you are no good). If the client believes the compliment is well earned, it is his belief which makes him feel good. Similarly, if the client believes the disapproval is terrible, it is his belief which makes him feel bad.

In working with the client on the issue of approval, the CBT message is that:

- It is pleasant to have other people's approval or recognition, but it is not a necessity.
- Self-approval or self-acceptance is the key to developing a *stable* self-esteem.
- It is the client's thoughts and beliefs about approval and disapproval which largely determine his or her spirits.

- It is the client's approval-seeking behaviour that causes him or her to be extremely vulnerable to people's opinions.
- Self-worth does not depend on approval and disapproval.

Technique: Assumption

Rationale and focus

Clients often do not question the assumptions they make about approval and their need for approval. Their assumption is that they will be 'all right' as a person if they are loved, accepted, praised and recognised. Such an assumption is problematic on the grounds that nobody can be liked, accepted, loved or recognised all the time and by everybody, irrespective of their wealth and social status. By the same token, nobody can be disliked, rejected, unloved or unrecognised all the time and by everybody.

Such an assumption can be challenged with another 'assumption', the therapist can say: '*assuming* that you have the approval of everybody today, what about tomorrow, the day after, next week, next month . . . ?'

Process

Therapist:	How important is it to be approved of by people in terms of acceptance, love and recognition, on a scale of 1 to 100?
Emma:	Very important. I will say 95.
Therapist:	Because of?
Emma:	Oh, I don't know. I suppose it is about rejection: not good enough and unlovable.
Therapist:	So you assume that if people approve of you, you are okay as a person.
Emma:	Yes, in a way.
Therapist:	So your self-worth and self-esteem are dependent on people's approval.
Emma:	Oh, yeah.
Therapist:	Assuming that you are approved by practically everybody *today*, how much effort do you have to make in order to get their approval?
Emma:	A lot. I please people all the time and say what they want to hear. I often feel tired and exhausted afterwards. It's hard work.
Therapist:	Suppose you do not mind putting in the hard work. What guarantee do you have that you will still have their approval tomorrow, next week, next month, next year, and for the rest of your life?

Emma: Oh, I never thought of that. There is no guarantee at all.

Therapist: If you do not have their approval tomorrow, this means you have to work even harder to get it, assuming you could get it. How about the day after, next week and next year . . . ?

Emma: Yeah. It is really a waste of time and effort, isn't it?

Therapist: Absolutely. The question is: should your self-worth and self-esteem be based on people's approval? If so, then you give away control of your happiness or life, yet there is no guarantee that you will get it all the time and from everybody, no matter how hard you try.

Emma: You are right.

Homework

Emma was asked to:

- Ask five of her friends whether approval should be regarded as a need or as desirable and whether one's self-worth and self-esteem should depend on it.
- Write down the costs and benefits of needing approval. Write down her negative thoughts relating to not getting approval.
- Make a list of her approval-seeking behaviour.
- Read an article entitled 'You don't need their approval' (Dyer 1996).

Technique: Rewriting assumptions

Rationale and focus

It is often thought that once an assumption is proven to be unhelpful or harmful, the client will be able to come up with a helpful and adaptive alternative. This is not true. Clients are often reluctant to abandon their unhelpful assumption unless they can come up with an alternative assumption that works better for them. Having challenged and rejected an assumption, the therapist can assist the client in developing a new, more flexible and realistic one. For example, the client might replace 'I should be competent in everything I do. Otherwise I am not good enough' with a more adaptive one such as

> I will do the best I can; it is not realistic to expect myself to be competent in everything I do. Doing things well is satisfying, but it is human to make and learn from mistakes. Not doing things well has nothing to do with not being good enough.

To assist the client to develop skills and confidence in rewriting an assumption, the therapist can ask whether the new one:

- *challenges* the content of the 'old' one
- is *believable*
- has *positive impact* on the mood.

The example given in the above has met the three criteria and therefore should work better for the client than the 'old' one.

Process

Therapist:	Approval was so important to you. As a result, your self-esteem and self-worth were really affected by how much approval you could get. You do not seem to have control over your mood, which fluctuates quite a bit. Not only that, it could also be a factor that makes recovery from your mental health problems more difficult and for you to learn to be yourself. Your assumption was that 'I must be loved, accepted and recognised by everybody. Otherwise I am not good enough and unlovable'. Obviously, you do not have control over what people think and how they behave. Is that true?
Emma:	My assumption that 'I should get the approval of everyone' was obviously not realistic.
Therapist:	This assumption is hard to live up to and makes life difficult for you. Let's find a new and helpful one that can empower you by giving you a sense of control and self-acceptance.
Emma:	I guess I could say that I am worthwhile regardless of what others think of me.
Therapist:	That is good. What else can you say?
Emma:	Well, it is nice to have others' approval of me and of what I do, but it is not essential. I don't need approval in order to be a worthwhile person or to respect myself.
Therapist:	How does that sound to you?
Emma:	It sounds good. It takes the pressure off: I *feel* good about it.
Therapist:	Does it *challenge* the old way of thinking?
Emma:	It does.
Therapist:	Do you *believe* in what you have said just now?
Emma:	Yes, I do. I can learn to believe in myself and accept the person I am, rather than relying on people to make me feel good about myself. This way of thinking is realistic and gives me control of my life.

Homework

Emma was asked to:

- Rewrite other unhelpful assumptions. Any assumptions that come up will be changed accordingly.
- Work on her approval-seeking behaviour and keep a diary about it.

Other techniques

Other relevant techniques include 'Best friend', 'Costs and benefits analysis', 'Daughter' and 'Survey'.

Notes for therapists about approval and approval-seeking behaviour

- Approval is desirable, but it is not essential. It is natural and healthy to feel good about approval. Similarly, disapproval usually tastes bitter and unpleasant, but it doesn't last for ever.
- Needing others' approval will set you up for emotional blackmail, allowing others to use this vulnerability to manipulate you, thereby creating a great deal of misery and frustration in your life.
- It is impossible to go through life without incurring a great deal of disapproval. It is the way of humanity, something that simply cannot be avoided.
- When you need others' approval, it simply means that 'You don't trust yourself – check it out with someone else first.' It also means that your self-worth and self-esteem are determined by others.
- Experiences of dealing with disapproval are invaluable to human growth and development.

Chapter 12

Perfectionism and competitiveness

Jeremy was a keen table tennis player and the best at his club until another man joined who was better than he was. He became preoccupied with his own performance and his need to be better. He was intensely self-critical if his performance was not better than that of the new member. He no longer enjoyed the game because he was not the best. In the end he stopped going to the club. Sara studied hard for her examinations and got reasonable grades but not all top marks. She felt guilty and ashamed for letting people down and wished that she could have tried harder even though she had studied many hours a day. Peter was anxious about information technology being increasingly used in the company and in his job. Although he was very competent in his job, the thought of not being able to understand IT and use it competently made him anxious and tense, thereby actively avoiding having anything to do with it. His thoughts were, 'I will never be able to be good at it; I would never be as good as those young people; people would think that I am not as good as they thought I was; I am a failure/stupid.' He was angry that the company expected too much of him and did not give him enough support in his work. He complained that he did not have time to learn this 'new' thing and that he had too much to do. These examples illustrate features of individuals needing to be perfect, or of perfectionist styles in individuals. These people probably have problems with low self-esteem, which can become a driving force for perfectionism and competitiveness. These people need to be seen as special, unique and/or superior in order to feel good about themselves as people. Their self-worth seems to be conditional on their being able to be perfect or to be as good as, if not better than, the person they are being compared to. As a result, their mood fluctuates up and down and is subject to external forces. For example, when things are going well and/or people are nice and supportive, they feel good. Otherwise, they feel low, down, anxious, worried, frustrated and depressed. Some clients believe that they do not have control over their mood because there is something wrong with their brain (e.g. chemical imbalances). They may use medication to help them to feel better, which obviously is not a long-term solution. The problem partly lies with the need to be perfect and competitive.

People are all different in the way they define perfection, which is undoubtedly influenced by their personal values, cultural background and life experience. Because of the variation in these qualities, it is therefore difficult to be precise about what perfection is, in the same way as the problem with defining intelligence. Some people may even question whether there is such thing as perfection or the best. Take Ian as an example. His garden was perfect as far as he was concerned; he devoted a lot of time, effort and money to it and was pleased with it. An old man walking past with a dog said: 'I don't like it. It is too much and too colourful.' Ian was upset by these comments, but he then came to a realisation that what was perfect to him was not necessarily the case for other people. Needing to be perfect is therefore a case of wasting emotional energy and of preventing people achieving their potential. People may even procrastinate because they can't be perfect or be the best. We can agree that 2 plus 2 is 4. But it is a lot more difficult to agree on what is perfect or what constitutes perfection, let alone being able to achieve it. If this is the case, why do people like Jeremy, Sara and Peter need to be perfect? Perfectionist and competitive people find it tough to cope with failure and are terrified by it or even by the thought of it. The idea of failure is terrifying to them, and can trigger and reinforce an unhelpful belief that they are not 'good enough, useless and incompetent'. They do not want to be or to be seen as a failure (see Chapter 14 on 'Fear of failure and procrastination').

As much in our society concentrates on succeeding and achieving things we have actually become incompetent at failing. One client recalled that he deliberately lost balance in a school race, knowing that he was not able to be first to cross the line. He sabotaged his effort to avoid failure. Another client was frustrated and angry with her procrastination, as the need to achieve high standards in everything became a barrier to getting things done; this dented her self-confidence and motivation. Procrastination could be seen as a mechanism to avoid failure. The focus on high standards and the need to be perfect means that, when people fall short of these standards, they can become highly self-critical and experience a lot of frustration and anger; and that when other people do not come up to their expectations, they can become angry with them and tend to focus on their shortcomings or what they did wrong rather than their positive qualities or how good they are. In social situations, perfectionist and competitive people believe that others expect them to be really interesting and fun to be with and that they will be rejected and ignored if they don't come up to those expected standards. So they continually monitor their performance and others' behaviour to see if they are interested in them and in what they say. This increases their anxiety and the bodily sensations of anxiety (e.g. racing heart, butterflies in the stomach) and makes conversation more difficult and less enjoyable. Research and clinical experience show that perfectionists and competitive people don't have a good time, do not enjoy what they do, and may have marital and family problems. They put all their eggs in one basket: being perfect, often at the expense of their mental health and family happiness. They tend to experience a great deal of worry, guilt, shame and suffer from various mental health problems such as depression, anxiety disorders, eating disorders and alcoholism.

There is a crucial difference between 'be the best' and 'try your best'. When a person demands 'to be the best' in everything he does, he will never be happy or contented with the results and appreciate the effort he has put in. Sara, as described above, was upset (e.g. feeling guilt, shame and anger) by not being able to get top grades in all the subjects, despite the hours of effort put into her studies. She was angry with herself for not working harder and putting in more effort. The problem is: how much effort? Another problem with these people is that they judge themselves and others only by the results and not the effort. No effort is good enough if it does not produce the expected results. Later in life, these people may well have problems in judging what reasonable and acceptable effort is and what is not. They may have a problem prioritising their effort according to the circumstances and to the importance of their work. They may eventually give up trying in the end.

'Do your best' is a healthy approach to learning and life. People with such an attitude are not terrified of failure, do not judge their self-worth on the results, and are more able to appreciate their effort. Another important aspect is that they do not undermine their self-confidence, regard themselves as less worthy, or feel inferior, when they do not perform well or as well as others. They know that they have done their best, which is good enough. In this respect, not only will they be more able to learn from their setbacks and mistakes and succeed, but also they are more relaxed in the learning process (see Chapter 16 on 'Setback and relapse').

Why is perfectionism and competitiveness a clinical issue?

Perfectionism and competitiveness are often mistakenly viewed as protective mechanisms against failure. In addition, there is a false belief that being 'perfect or the best' is good for one's self-worth, self-image and self-confidence. Not being the best or perfect means that they are just average and mediocre, something they are anxious and worried about. As long as clients hold these *assumed* benefits, they are unlikely to agree to give up being 'perfect or the best' or see any reasons for changing. This may get in the way of positive therapeutic change and therefore prolong or even worsen their mental suffering and emotional health.

Some clients may believe that perfectionism and competitiveness are part of their personality, like mental 'illness'. One client said: 'There is nothing I can do. It is in my genes to be competitive.'

The case of Michael

Michael was a perfectionist. He worked long hours, including some weekends, to ensure that he did everything perfectly well. Although he did very well in his job and rose rapidly in seniority in the company, he no longer enjoyed what he did. He said that he was relieved when a difficult project was successfully completed or he did not make any mistakes. The pressure to perform and to live up to what he believed to be people's expectation was such that he was constantly feeling tired and exhausted and sleep was a problem. While he was lying in bed, his mind became hyperactive, making sleeping even more difficult. He found it difficult to relax and would feel guilty for not doing anything or resting. He even took his laptop with him when he went away on holiday.

Both his parents, his father in particular, were a big influence on him as a person and on his attitude towards work. 'What would people think of you if you were average or mediocre at work? Average and mediocre is not good enough and you need to be the best at whatever you do,' as his father used to say to him. This had a profound impact on him, right from his early years. His father was a hard-working and successful lawyer. His brother was a doctor and became a consultant at a young age; his sister was a successful and talented interior designer. Michael was terrified of not being as good as his brother and sister and would feel bad for not living up to his father's expectations. There was a culture of competitiveness and jealousy in the family; Michael worked very hard to gain first-class honours from a prestigious university and his first job was working in the City. His father and the rest of the family were naturally very proud of him when he was promoted to managing director of an international company. Such recognition and rewards from a highly paid job strengthened his belief that perfectionism and competitiveness were the key to a promising future. However, it was also edging him towards developing mental health problems.

The competitiveness culture was even more intense in the City and this put him under even more pressure to keep up with the others; it was tough going. In the first CBT session, he said that he 'needed to be as good as others, if not better'. He was preoccupied with what others were doing and felt that 'if other people can do this and can do it well, so can I'. In recent months, he had become easily irritated and frustrated, and lost interest in recreational activities such as tennis, swimming and socialising. On returning from a two-week holiday, the thought of going back to work on Monday brought his mood down. He became tearful and cried on the plane, saying that he could not cope with the pressure. He was diagnosed as suffering from depression due to a high level of stress at work.

Cognitive behaviour therapy approach to perfectionism and competitiveness

Clients often do not question the idea of perfectionism and the values of being competitive. It never occurs to them that there is a need to do so, even though these cost them their mental and emotional health.

The CBT approach explores what being perfect is and how this can be achieved. More importantly, are there benefits in being perfect? If not, what could be a realistic and adaptive alternative that works?

Technique: Define the term

Rationale and focus

Perfection is difficult to define. In order to define the term one needs to identify the criteria the client uses to define perfection. There are two ways in which the technique can be used. The therapist can ask, 'What is perfection?' or 'What do you have to do in order to believe that you are perfect?'. 'What is perfect?' has the effect of encouraging the client to develop an awareness of the (unhelpful) way in which he or she defines perfection and whether it is possible to achieve it in reality. The second way is to get the client to say what criteria to use and how to achieve perfection. In the process, the client will come to realise that being perfect is an elusive concept, which is difficult to define and/or impossible to achieve.

Process

Therapist:	You are a perfectionist, aren't you?
Michael:	I am working on it.
Therapist:	Okay. You are working on it. So what do you have to do in order to believe that you are a perfect person?
Michael:	Oh. I don't really think about it. I just want to be perfect.
Therapist:	To be perfect means what?
Michael:	It means that I have to do everything right.
Therapist:	And?
Michael:	I don't make mistakes.
Therapist:	What else?
Michael:	To get praise and recognition from others in what I do.
Therapist:	Suppose you can't get everything right and you make some mistakes and people do not always give you praise and recognition, then what?
Michael:	Ah. I feel like a failure.

Therapist:	Let me see if I understand you correctly. To be perfect means that you need . . . otherwise you are a failure.
Michael:	Yes.
Therapist:	Do you know one person who is able to meet your criteria of being perfect?
Michael:	Oh. Ah. I don't think so. I can't think of one.
Therapist:	Do you think such a person exists in this world?
Michael:	I don't know. I don't think so.
Therapist:	Why do you think no such person exists in this world?
Michael:	I suppose it is difficult to get everything right all the time and not to make mistakes. In fact, it is impossible. Besides, whether or not people give praise and recognition is outside our control.
Therapist:	Absolutely. Does it mean everybody, including members of your family, is a failure, since they are not perfect?
Michael:	Oh. Ah. They are not. I know what you mean.

Homework

Michael was asked to:

- Talk to five people to find out how they would define 'perfection'. If there is such thing as perfection, what could they do to achieve it? If there is no such thing as perfection, what could be reasons for it? The idea of this homework is for him to see that there is a mismatch between his definition and that of the others.
- Read Chapter 12 on 'Perfectionism and competitiveness'.

Technique: Benefits of being fallible and infallible

Rationale and focus

Clients often assume that there are benefits in being perfect and push hard to achieve such a goal, without realising that this can be detrimental to their mental and emotional health and cause depression, anxiety disorders and drinking problems. A technique that challenges such an assumption about the benefits of being infallible (perfect or the best) may encourage clients to accept their fallibility as part of being human. They will make mistakes, have setbacks and experience failure, but these are opportunities for learning and growth. The therapist can say: 'Perfectionism and competitiveness are often thought to be a good thing, but you have to ask yourself why you want to be perfect and the best? Have you been able to achieve it so far? Why are you here for therapy?'

Process

Therapist:	People often assume that there are benefits in being a perfectionist and competitive. This is just the perception, not the fact. What could the benefits of being infallible (perfect or the best) be?
Michael:	You can feel good about yourself, motivated to achieve more, and get recognition and praise from others.
Therapist:	All the time!
Michael:	Well. I suppose not. But if I can truly be perfect and the best, then it is possible.
Therapist:	How long have you been trying to be like that: perfect and the best?
Michael:	A long time, almost all my life. I am now 45.
Therapist:	How much longer do you need in order to achieve what you need?
Michael:	Oh. Yeah.
Therapist:	Suppose you try for another forty-five years, what guarantee do you have that you will be able to achieve your goal?
Michael:	I don't have it.
Therapist:	Since you don't have any guarantee for it, no matter how hard you try and you are suffering, what is the point of being perfect?
Michael:	Ah. I never thought about it in this way. I thought being perfect is a good thing.
Therapist:	I can say at this point that it is highly unlikely you will. One of the reasons why people need to be perfect is that they do not want to be a failure or be seen as a failure. Another reason is that their good feelings and self-worth often depend on what others perceive of them. That's why they need to be infallible.
Michael:	Oh. That's me.
Therapist:	If there are benefits in being infallible, there's no need for you to come here for therapy.
Michael:	You are right.
Therapist:	What could be the alternative to being infallible?
Michael:	Be a fallible human, I suppose.
Therapist:	What could the benefits be?
Michael:	Take the pressure off and enable me to relax and sleep better.
Therapist:	And your performance?
Michael:	I suppose that I will not have the fear of making mistakes and will be able to learn from setbacks and failures. If this is the case, I will perform better.
Therapist:	Good. There are two options to choose from: being a fallible or infallible person. Make a right choice!

Homework

Michael was asked to:

- Make a list of his perfectionisms, rank them from the least to the most difficult one to change, and work from the least to the most difficult. For example, he would spend less time tidying up his office (least difficult).

Other techniques

Other relevant techniques include 'Daughter', 'Acceptance', 'Seeing the event from the other side' and 'Cognitive continuum'.

Notes for therapists about perfectionism and competitiveness

- Do your best rather than trying to be the best or perfect.
- Judge yourself on effort and not on results.
- Doing well is satisfying, but it is human to make and learn from mistakes.
- The secret of success is the ability to fail.
- If you want to do well at any task or problem, learn to welcome your mistakes and errors, rather than becoming horrified by them.
- Ask yourself, 'What is the worst thing that can happen if you can't be perfect?' Could it be as bad as losing your limb(s) or your eyesight or . . . ?

Chapter 13

Healthy and unhealthy negative emotions

Adam regarded feeling low and down as an indication that something terrible would happen and was anxious about having these feelings. 'It is terrible to have these feelings,' said Adam. 'I would hate to be depressed again.' Adam had just recovered from depression. His doctor advised him that doing too much and not having enough rest could cause his mood to go down, which might contribute to another bout of depression. He therefore assumed that a low mood (or negative emotions) could be a symptom and a cause of depression. Angela had suffered from panic attacks over the previous two years and medication had not been as effective as she had hoped. She noticed that prior to having a panic attack, not only did she experience some uncomfortable bodily sensations (e.g. breathing very fast, pounding heart, feeling faint), but also she experienced feelings of anxiety. She developed a fear of anxiety and came to view anxiety as a threat which could trigger panic attacks. 'I mustn't be anxious. I must control my anxiety. It is terrible to be anxious' were her views about anxiety. These examples illustrate that negative emotions (e.g. low, down, sadness, frustration, anxiety) tend to be seen as 'abnormal'. One client said that he 'needs to get rid of negative emotions and wants to be happy all the time'. He, like many other clients, wanted to have an 'emotion switch' that could switch off negative emotions and switch on the positive ones, in a way that is similar to a light switch. Some clients wrongly believe that positive emotions are normal, whereas negative ones are not. In their view there must be something wrong with them or with their brain for having negative feelings.

Negative emotions or feelings can be either healthy or unhealthy depending on the circumstances, the duration and the level of these feelings. If the circumstance is appropriate, expressing your negative feelings is viewed as healthy. For example, it is natural to feel:

- Anxious at an interview, at a presentation, or in an examination.
- Worried while you are waiting for examination results or if the company you work for is planning to make some people redundant.

- Frustrated when things (or a project) have not gone well despite a lot of effort being put in.
- Disappointed if you fail to get a promotion or an examination.
- Angry and upset if you have an argument with your parents.
- Sad if your loved one has passed away.

An expression of these emotions in the above circumstances is not only healthy but also necessary. For example, it is necessary for a safety valve of a central heating system to release the built-up pressure in order to keep the system healthy or running properly. Burns (1999) believes that many negative emotions, particularly at *low* levels and for a *short* period of time, are normal and appropriate under the circumstances. It is often best to accept these negative feelings. Being able to accept them can lead to a constructive way of coping with those situations and prevent the feelings from escalating to higher levels. At such levels, these emotions are unhealthy, in the sense that they are destructive and immobilising and can cause clients to be more negative, irrational or pessimistic about themselves, others, events and the future. In this context, negative emotions or feelings, like the positive emotions of joy and happiness, are an essential part of human experiences which are important to learning, growth and maturity.

Leahy (2002) makes an important distinction between clients' viewing negative emotions (e.g., sadness, disappointment, frustration and anxiety) as either normal or abnormal and discusses how these attitudes influence their coping strategies. If clients believe that negative emotions or feelings are abnormal, they will try to avoid having these feelings through the use of unhelpful behaviours such as avoiding anxiety-provoking situations, giving up tasks that are either difficult or frustrating, taking drugs and alcohol to help them feel better, pleasing others to avoid criticism or rejection, or being particularly sensitive to their occurrence. These behaviours can play a decisive role in the continuation of mental health problems, thereby reinforcing the incorrect view about negative emotions being abnormal (Lam 2005). This distinction is clinically important, especially to those clients who have anxiety about anxiety, worry about worry, anger about anger or clients who have low frustration tolerance. It is therefore important for therapists to use therapeutic techniques that promote the acceptance of negative emotions (Jacobson 1994; Leahy 2002). This will lead to better and more effective management of negative emotions (Linehan 1993).

Why is believing negative emotions are abnormal a clinical issue?

The problem with believing that negative emotions or feelings are abnormal is that it may lead to clients stigmatising themselves for having such feelings. Prior to suffering from an anxiety problem himself, Peter always regarded people with anxiety as being weak and believed they would have a problem coping with stress. They were therefore less able to perform in demanding jobs. He said: 'I would not consider giving these people a job in my team.' When he subsequently developed an anxiety problem, he saw himself as weak and useless and was highly critical of himself for not being able to control or get rid of his anxiety. Worrying about how other people would perceive him not only caused him to feel ashamed of having this problem, but also he tried to hide his anxiety from others rather than confronting it.

Self-stigmatising, self-critical and avoidance behaviours are also evident in clients with other types of mental health problems. When clients are anxious about having negative emotions, this can lead to the problem of 'anxiety about anxiety' as in panic disorder, 'worry about worry' in general anxiety disorder, and 'anxiety about feeling low, down and sad' in depression. The belief about negative emotions being abnormal is therefore a clinical problem as it can adversely affect how they view themselves, their self-esteem and their response to treatment.

The case of Adam

Adam was a 42-year-old managing director of a haulage company. He worked hard to become the youngest director in the company and attributed his success to hard work and to being a perfectionist. When people fell short of his standards or were not up to the mark, he became upset and experienced a lot of frustration and anger. Instead of expressing his feelings and/or asking them to do the work again, he took on the work himself. 'I don't want all these hassles to confront them. In any case, it doesn't take me long to get the jobs done myself. I can do them better and faster,' said Adam. 'It is not nice to tell people off.' Adam needed to be seen as successful, competent, efficient and a nice and supportive guy.

His focus on high standards, eagerness to please people and the need to be perfect was taking its toll on him: not only did he find it increasingly frustrating not being able to meet his expectations, but his relationship with his wife and children were also affected. This in turn affected his confidence, his concentration at work and his moods. His father died unexpectedly of a heart attack at the age of 65 and the sadness over the loss of a loved one had a crushing impact on him and on his moods. He found it difficult to cope, was tearful, didn't want to get out of bed or go out, and was socially withdrawn. He was diagnosed with depression, hospitalised for two weeks and referred to cognitive behaviour therapy. His doctor advised him to have plenty of rest and not to do so much as these were important to his recovery and his moods. Adam didn't like having these negative feelings as he thought that low moods and sadness could have something to do with his depression.

His neighbour died at the age of 68. Both Adam and his wife were very fond of this neighbour as they had been living next door to each other for almost twenty years. Although the death was not unexpected, he was dreading being depressed again because of the sadness and low moods associated with death.

Cognitive behaviour therapy approach to healthy and unhealthy negative emotions

If the circumstances are appropriate, it is natural to feel sad, down, low, frustrated, anxious, guilty or angry. There is nothing wrong with having these emotions or feelings. Cognitive behaviour therapy takes the view that the problem is due to the clients' perception of negative emotions being abnormal. Such a perception affects their ability or willingness to tolerate these feelings, however low-level. Low tolerance has the paradoxical effect of not only worsening the symptoms of mental health problems, but also escalating these feelings to higher and more harmful levels, thus reinforcing their incorrect view about negative feelings.

An effective approach to changing the incorrect view about negative feelings is to help clients see that these feelings (e.g. low, down, sadness, frustration, anxiety) are very common experiences for everyone and to understand that most people do not perceive them as abnormal and it is all right to experience these feelings when the circumstances are appropriate. When negative emotions are no longer perceived as abnormal, it gives clients confidence to tolerate them. The more they learn to tolerate, the faster these feelings will diminish and the less discomfort they will feel.

Technique: Survey

Rationale and focus

Surveying is a powerful technique to illustrate that there is a discrepancy between the client's perception of negative emotions and those of the majority of society. All humans experience negative emotions which are often regarded as a normal and essential part of a reaction (e.g. language) to different situations or circumstances. Knowing about such a discrepancy helps the client realise that having negative feelings is not the problem. The problem is due to his or her belief about negative emotions being abnormal. In using this technique, the focus in the therapeutic process is to use the survey's information to highlight the existence of such a discrepancy, to question the benefits of avoiding having these negative feelings and to find ways of handling these feelings.

Together, we came up with a list of specific questions to be used in the survey. Note that negative emotions in this survey referred to feeling low, down and sad, as these feelings were particularly troublesome to Adam. The questions are as follows:

1 Do you know just *one* person who never experiences any negative emotions (e.g. low, down and sadness)?
2 Did you experience negative emotions before?
3 Will you ever experience any negative emotions in future?
4 Is it normal or abnormal to have these emotions?
5 Did you suffer from depression because of these negative emotions?
6 If the answer to Question 3 is 'yes', why?
7 If the answer to Question 3 is 'no', why?
8 Is it normal and appropriate to feel sad when you lose a loved one?
9 Is it normal and appropriate to feel low and down after a funeral?
10 What will be a helpful way to deal with negative emotions?

Note that responses of either 'yes' or 'no' to the quantitative questions (1, 2, 3, 4, 5, 8 and 9) would show the extent of the discrepancy between Adam's view about negative emotions and the views of the five people he was going to do the survey with. Their replies to the qualitative questions (6, 7 and 10) not only would help to generate a more realistic view about negative emotions, but would also provide some useful ideas on how to deal with these emotions.

Process: before the survey

Therapist: You believe that there must be something wrong with feeling low, down and sad.

Adam: Yes.

Therapist: Because of?

Adam: I just want to be happy. I don't want to have all these negative feelings.

Therapist: It is nice to feel happy. Why do you think that there is something wrong with having these feelings?

Adam: It is not normal. I should be happy, not feeling low, down and sad.

Therapist: Oh. Is it possible to be happy, if you fail to get a promotion?

Adam: No.

Therapist: What should the feeling be?

Adam: Disappointment, I suppose.

Therapist: Is it possible to be happy, if the company you work for is planning to make some people redundant?

Adam: Ah. No.

Therapist: What should the feeling be?

Adam: Worry and anxiety, I suppose.

Therapist: It is natural to feel disappointed, worried and anxious under these circumstances. Why is it not normal to feel low, down and sad?

Adam: Oh. I don't know. After my father's funeral, I was feeling low, down and sad, and then I was depressed. I have a fear that it may happen again after my neighbour's funeral, because I know that I will feel low, down and sad.

Therapist: Is it possible to be happy after the funeral?

Adam: I suppose not.

Therapist: What should the feeling be?

Adam: Oh, yeah. Low, down and sad, I suppose.

Therapist: It is natural to feel low, down and sad over the loss of a loved one. We all feel the same. These feelings are healthy and have nothing to do with depression. Otherwise, we will all end up with depression.

Adam: Well, it makes sense. I was already feeling stressed before he died. His death made it a lot worse for me. I didn't sleep well, was tired physically and emotionally, and found it difficult to get on with my work.

Therapist: Would you say that these feelings have something to do with your last depression?

Adam: No.

Therapist: Let's do a survey and ask five people their views about negative feelings.

Process: after the survey

Therapist: Who did you talk to?

Adam: I talked to five people: a neighbour, two friends, a colleague and my wife.

Therapist: Good. Did any one of the five people know just one person who had never experienced any of these negative emotions? [Question 1 in the survey]

Adam: No.

Therapist: Had they experienced any of these negative emotions before? [Question 2]

Adam: They all said yes.

Therapist: Will they all experience these emotions in future? [Question 3]

Adam: One said that she didn't know and the rest said yes.

Therapist:	Do they see having these emotions as normal or abnormal? [Question 4]
Adam:	Normal.
Therapist:	Oh. It seems that their views about negative emotions are different from yours.
Adam:	Yes.
Therapist:	They had all experienced these emotions before. Did they all end up with depression? [Question 5]
Adam:	No.
Therapist:	What conclusion can we draw?
Adam:	These feelings are normal and have nothing to do with depression, I guess.
Therapist:	Absolutely. You view them as abnormal probably because you linked your previous depression to these feelings. It is not surprising that you are anxious about having these feelings again after your neighbour's funeral. You simply do not want to be depressed again.
Adam:	You're right.
Therapist:	What did the other four people say, when they said 'yes' to Question 3? [Question 6]
Adam:	Because it is inevitable. One person said that you will get upset if you fail an examination or have an argument with somebody. Another said you will feel angry if you're unfairly criticised. They all said that you couldn't control external forces like people or events.
Therapist:	Did they say that it is normal and appropriate to feel sad over the loss of a loved one? [Question 8]
Adam:	Yes.
Therapist:	How about Question 9?
Adam:	Again yes. They all said that it is normal and appropriate to feel low and down after a funeral.
Therapist:	What conclusion can we draw?
Adam:	It is okay to feel low, down and sad.
Therapist:	When we believe that these feelings are abnormal, it may have the unwanted effect of causing us to feel anxious or even fearful about having these feelings. The thought of 'there must be something wrong' will keep coming into our minds which, in turn, can cause more of these feelings, thus creating a vicious circle.
Adam:	I can relate to that.
Therapist:	How did they deal with these negative emotions? [Question 10]

Adam: Two people said that they would just put up with it and it would diminish after a while. One person said that she would accept these feelings as normal and not dwell on them. The other two said that if you keep going on normally, these feelings would not be as bad.

Knowing that there was nothing wrong with having these feelings brought a sense of relief to Adam. These feelings were indeed natural under the circumstances. He therefore accepted rather than reacted to these feelings and two days after the funeral he started to feel better. 'I did feel low, down and sad after the funeral,' said Adam. 'But knowing that it is okay to have these feelings enabled me to tolerate them and carry on life as usual. It has helped.'

Homework

Adam was asked to:

* Keep an emotional diary in which he would record what emotions he experienced (e.g. anxiety, worry or frustration) at different events (e.g. interview, party), rate his emotional levels on a scale of 1 to 10, and indicate whether the expressed emotion(s) was appropriate.

Technique: Sun and rain

Rationale and focus

Clients with mental health problems are anxious or fearful of having negative emotions. Not only are these emotions perceived as abnormal, but they also believe that having them means that something terrible will happen such as a panic attack or another form of depression. They therefore need to have an 'emotion switch' to get rid of these emotions, which is impossible, in the same way that we can't switch off bad weather and have sunny days every day. The focus in the therapeutic process is to help clients understand that it is natural to have negative feelings and that the best way to manage them is to accept and tolerate them. If we can't switch off bad weather, we can't switch off negative emotions. By refusing to accept this as a fact of life, they will intensify their negative emotions, thus turning their fear into reality, causing them to have a panic attack or depression.

Process

Therapist: Is it possible to have sunny days every day?
Adam: Of course not.

Therapist:	Because of?
Adam:	Even in some countries with really hot weather like Australia or Dubai, they can't have sunny days every day.
Therapist:	Because of?
Adam:	It is the weather and we have four seasons a year. Different seasons have different kinds of weather.
Therapist:	Is it possible to have rain every day?
Adam:	Of course not.
Therapist:	Absolutely. Do we have control over the weather?
Adam:	No.
Therapist:	When it is a sunny day, what can we do?
Adam:	I suppose we should make the most of it and enjoy it, while we can.
Therapist:	And bad weather?
Adam:	Nothing we can do to change the weather, so we need to accept it and get on with doing things indoors.
Therapist:	If we can't change the bad weather and refuse to accept it – 'The weather shouldn't be like this. It is terrible' – will it help with our mood?
Adam:	No.
Therapist:	It is something we can't change as it is out of our control, so it is better to accept it, like the weather. It is natural to have good and bad weather throughout the year.
Adam:	True.
Therapist:	Is it possible to be happy all the time?
Adam:	No.
Therapist:	Is it possible to get an 'emotion switch' that can switch off negative feelings such as worry, frustration or anxiety?
Adam:	No.
Therapist:	Why can't we switch off negative feelings?
Adam:	I know what you mean. It is like the weather, we can't have sunny days every day. It is natural to feel low, down and sad after a funeral.
Therapist:	Good. You're able to make this connection. However, if you believe that it is abnormal to have these feelings after a funeral, how helpful will such a belief help you?
Adam:	It doesn't, I suppose.
Therapist:	Because of?
Adam:	When I feel that there must be something wrong with me, it would get me even lower, going down more and make me sadder. It did last time, when my father died.

Therapist: In a way, it might have even contributed to your last depression.

Adam: Oh.

Therapist: When you have these and other negative feelings, what would be a helpful way to manage these feelings?

Adam: Like the bad weather, it is best to accept and tolerate and get on with doing things. It can take your mind off these feelings.

Homework

Adam was asked to:

- List the costs of not accepting and the benefits of accepting negative emotions.

Other techniques

Other relevant techniques include 'Daughter', 'Best friend', '100 people' and 'Cognitive continuum'.

Notes for therapists about healthy and unhealthy negative emotions

- Negative feelings at low levels are healthy and normal, if the circumstances are appropriate.
- There is no 'emotion switch' that can turn off negative emotions.
- Negative emotion at low levels is also actually beneficial as it helps the person to be more alert in what they do. For example, a bit of anxiety improves performance.
- Acceptance and tolerance of negative emotions will result in having fewer of these emotions.
- Negative emotions at high levels are unhealthy as they are destructive and immobilising in nature and adversely affect performance.

Chapter 14

Fear of failure and procrastination

'Unless I can be 120 per cent sure that going for another job will work out, it is not worth taking a risk,' said Terry. 'I don't want to fail.' While Terry was eager to move on from the job that he had been doing for the past fifteen years since he left university, he was also anxious about leaving his 'secure' job to face the unknown in a different working environment. He knew that there was little or no prospect for him in terms of career development and promotion working for his present company as it employed only fifteen staff, although he had ability and was good at his job. He was frustrated and angry with himself for being indecisive and for not having the courage to step out of his 'comfort zone'. Louise was devastated to have lost her well-paid job. It was a big blow to her already fragile self-esteem, causing her moods to go down and adversely affecting her self-confidence. She was quiet, avoided social contacts and withdrew into her 'comfort zone'. Conversation with her tended to be difficult as she avoided talking about herself, her feelings or the future with anyone. Not only was it difficult for anybody to understand her behaviour and support her, but also staying in the 'comfort zone' was also detrimental to her mental and emotional health. As a result, she became depressed and was subsequently put on medication. Although she started to get better, she put off looking for another job. 'I am ill,' said Louise, who tried to justify her procrastination. 'I am still on medication.'

These examples illustrate features of individuals who procrastinate for different reasons. Procrastinators often say: 'I know I should be doing it, but I'll get around to it later; I hope things will work out; I wish things were better; or maybe it'll be okay.' By postponing or staying in the 'comfort zone', not only will they be unable to live their lives in a fulfilling and meaningful way and to achieve their potential, but also their emotional turmoil (e.g. anxiety, frustration, shame, anger and worry) can have the unwanted effect of self-stigmatisation (e.g. 'I am a loser') which, in turn, can affect their self-esteem and self-confidence. Low self-esteem is a symptom and a cause of mental health problems such as anxiety disorders, depression, eating disorders, bipolar disorders and schizophrenia.

One major reason for procrastination is the fear of failure. 'I know I must do that, but I'm really afraid that I might not do it well/perfectly,' said Mark, who was a perfectionist and a people pleaser. 'I don't want to make mistakes and people to think less of me.' What Mark said was not unusual for individuals who use procrastination to reduce their fear of failure. They take the attitude that 'If I wait and do nothing, maybe it'll work itself out.' This sort of attitude never works, as things never work themselves out. They remain precisely as they are. At best, things change, but they don't get better. Things themselves (circumstances, situations, events or people) will not improve on their own. If your life is better and you feel more in control, it is because you have done something constructive to make it better. In the case of Terry, Louise and Mark, when they believed that things were unlikely to be done perfectly, that mistakes were likely to be made or that there was a possibility of being rejected for a job, they procrastinated because it hurt to be a failure.

After Thomas Edison's seven hundredth unsuccessful attempt to invent the electric light, he was asked: 'How does it feel to have failed 700 times?' The great inventor responded with a classic example of a positive and realistic perspective: 'I have not failed 700 times,' he replied. 'I have not failed once. I have succeeded in proving that those 700 ways will not work. When I have eliminated all the ways that will not work, I will find the way that will work.' This inspiring story illustrates that there are two perspectives in viewing the experience of failure: helpful and unhelpful. An unhelpful perspective will perceive that such an experience is terrible and is a reflection of one's lack of self-worth and competency. A helpful perspective is that failure can be a positive experience as it is the highway to success. Every fresh experience points out some form of error or mistake which we shall carefully avoid in the future.

If you have made some mistakes, even serious ones, there is always another chance for you. Failure is part of the process of becoming success-ful and you always pass failure on the way to success. Winston Churchill rightly said, 'Success is the ability to go from one failure to another with no loss of enthusiasm.' In this context, failure, however unpleasant, is an invaluable learning opportunity to grow and develop. It is not about you being a failure as a person, if you do something less than perfect, make mistakes, or are rejected for a job, what it means is you're a fallible human. This helpful way of thinking can help to diminish the fear of failure and the problem of procrastination.

Why is fear of failure and procrastination a clinical issue?

Procrastination is often used to avoid not just the fear of failure, but also the belief that 'I am a failure'. The 'I'll wait, it'll get better or I'll get around to it later' attitude hardly works. Anxiety, frustration, worry, guilt and anger that go with this attitude can not only cause clients to lose self-respect, but can also undermine their self-confidence and motivation. Procrastination is therefore a symptom and a cause of mental health problems.

The case of Hannah

'I should get down to writing the book, but I just don't feel like doing it,' said Hannah, who was highly critical of herself for being so lazy. Hannah had been successful in her fashion business, but decided to give it up to pursue her dream of becoming a novelist. She had sold her business ten years earlier and lived in a big house with her husband and son. Her family was supportive of her decision, believing that she would be as successful in her new venture as in the fashion business.

Hannah, aged 55, was intelligent and bright and had graduated from a prestigious university with a first-class honours degree in English Literature. She put her success down to hard work and to being a perfectionist. Her focus on high standards and the need to be the best had taken a toll on her health. She recalled that she had to delay her final year's study at university because of anxiety attacks and depression, for which she was prescribed some medication. Her anxiety was due to her thoughts about not being able to do well in the examinations and the consequences of that on her future. She thought about it over and over again in her head, thus creating a fear of failure and a rise in her anxiety levels. Not only was she unable to sleep, concentrate or study, but also she felt panicky over bodily sensations such as a pounding heart, dizziness, breathlessness and feelings of unreality. She did not know what these were. Neither did she understand why she had these feelings and sensations. She thought she was 'mad', which drove her into a panic attack. On the advice of her general practitioner and a college counsellor, her studies were postponed for a year. 'I feel like a failure,' said Hannah, who was depressed over the postponement of the studies.

She was successful in the fashion business and made a name for herself in the field. 'It was tough going and was very competitive,' said Hannah, who was having some doubts as to whether she would be able to keep the success going. She was advised to take a break from running the business as there were concerns about her mental health. 'Taking a break' was interpreted as an indication of her failing again, which meant that she was 'a failure'. The fear of failure emerged again in her mind, which created considerable pressure on her to continue to do well in order to avoid failure. Inevitably, the combination of constant tiredness, problems in sleeping, poor concentration and long hours of work not only adversely affected her work and performance, but also pushed her down the path of depression. 'I am a failure,' said Hannah.

She was overjoyed by an offer for her business as she knew that there would be no financial worries for her and her family. It was also an opportunity to pursue her dream of becoming a novelist, in addition to the added benefit of having a relaxing lifestyle. When she finished her first book after many months of hard work, she was so pleased and proud. However, the book did not sell as well as she had hoped, which was a huge disappointment for her. She compared herself with other successful and established novelists and felt so inferior, believing that she would never be as successful. The fear of failure came back to hit her once again and badly affected her self-confidence and motivation. She had been working on her second book for many months, but had elicited no interest from publishers so far. 'My first book is not selling well. This means I am not good enough. Because I am not good enough, no publishers will ever be interested in my work. I am a failure,' said Hannah, who was unhappy with her procrastination.

Cognitive behaviour therapy approach to fear of failure and procrastination

Cognitive behaviour therapy takes the view that failure is not a problem, no matter how bad or serious the failure is. A failure can become an invaluable learning opportunity to grow and develop. The problem is due to clients perceiving themselves a failure for making mistakes and for failing, or not doing well, at certain tasks. The combination of the fear of failure and procrastination can prevent them from developing a realistic view about self, others and the future and, therefore, recovering from mental health problems.

Over-concern with achievement can result in your being fearful of taking chances, of making mistakes and of failing at certain tasks. These fears, in turn, tend to sabotage the achievement for which you are striving, thus leading to lack of enjoyment of the task and a propensity to fail at it. 'You haven't done it well. You have made mistakes' is often taken by the person as meaning 'You are a failure'. People with low self-esteem or those who are worried about what others think of them and their work tend to make such an assumption, which inevitably serves to maintain the fear of failure.

Once it is shown that there is no evidence to support this assumption and that procrastination is unhelpful, rather than helpful, in diminishing the fear, not only will the assumption and the fear be put into perspective, but also the client is likely to build up the confidence and motivation to work on the procrastination. A helpful way to overcome procrastination is to refuse to base your self-worth on the result, outcome or success of what you do, to end comparing yourself enviously and resentfully to other individuals who do achieve, to stop trying to be better than them (or to be perfect) or to stop pleasing others trying to gain acceptance and recognition. Instead, try to focus on enjoying the process of what you do. When you try to do it well, try to do so for your own sake rather than mainly to please others or to be better than others. Success is the ability not just to go from one failure to another, but also to learn from the experience of failure.

Technique: Define the term

Rationale and focus

In working with clients who have a fear of failure, getting them to define the meaning of failure will help to clarify that there is a real difference between experiences of failure and failure as a person. There is often an incorrect assumption that not being able to be perfect in what you do, making mistakes, a rejection (e.g. job), or being criticised means that you're a failure as a person. How logical is this assumption that just because of . . . you are a failure? In the eyes of clients, this assumption is accurate and they never question it because of errors in their way of thinking such as discounting the positive, mental filter, black and white thinking and magnification. For example, Hannah (described above) not only discounted her achievements (e.g. a first-class honours degree, business success, having a book published and a happy family), but also magnified the 'not so good things' through the use of 'mental filter' and 'black and white' thinking (Burns 1999), such as the fact that her first book was not selling well and no publishers had taken an interest in her second book.

Failure as a person is therefore a target for intervention rather than the fear of failure. The therapeutic focus is to examine the difference between experiences of failure and failure as a person. Not only does it show that there is no logical connection between the two of them, but it also illustrates that, paradoxically, success often comes from experiences of failure. In using 'Define the term', the therapist can ask, 'What is failure to you? How will you define failure? What do you have to achieve in order not to see yourself as a failure?'

Process

Therapist:	You seem to have a problem with failure!
Hannah:	Yes.
Therapist:	Because of?
Hannah:	I don't want to fail.
Therapist:	Because of?
Hannah:	If I fail, it means that I am a failure.

Therapist:	Let me see if I understand you correctly. Your assumption is that if you fail at certain tasks, you're a failure as a person. It hurts to be a failure.
Hannah:	Yes.
Therapist:	How would you define failure?
Hannah:	Oh. Failure is about not being able to be perfect in my work and making mistakes. It is terrible to be rejected by publishers or criticised by others.
Therapist:	What do you have to do in order to avoid failure?
Hannah:	Everything must go well: be perfect, no mistakes, no rejection and criticism.
Therapist:	All the time?
Hannah:	Yes. Otherwise, I feel like a failure.
Therapist:	When you do things, do you work hard?
Hannah:	Yes.
Therapist:	When you do things, do you put in the effort?
Hannah:	Yes.
Therapist:	If you have worked hard and put in the effort in your work, but the result is not good or does not meet your expectation, you will see yourself a failure.
Hannah:	Yes.
Therapist:	Do you have children? [Note: 'Daughter's' technique is used in conjunction with 'Define the term']
Hannah:	A son.
Therapist:	Do you love him?
Hannah:	Very much so.
Therapist:	Suppose he was feeling low, down and tearful for not being able to present a project well at work. He saw himself as a failure, even though he had worked hard and put a lot of effort in. Would he be a failure?
Hannah:	Of course not.
Therapist:	Because of?
Hannah:	It was not nice that the presentation had not gone well. You don't expect everything to go well in life all the time. The important thing was that he worked hard for it and put in a lot of effort.
Therapist:	Hang on. He should be a failure according to the way you define failure.
Hannah:	Oh. Ah. But he is not.
Therapist:	How is it logical that he is not, but you are?
Hannah:	It is not logical. I suppose that I expect a lot of myself.

Therapist:	Will it be helpful or unhelpful to have an unrealistic expectation?
Hannah:	Not helpful.
Therapist:	Because of?
Hannah:	I am fearful for not being able to do well and tend to procrastinate.
Therapist:	Such a fear of failure can not only affect your self-confidence and performance, but can also make the procrastination even worse. Is this what you want?
Hannah:	Oh. No. I can see the point you have made. Failure to do things well does not mean I am a failure.
Therapist:	Absolutely. Otherwise, every human is a failure. How will you define failure now?
Hannah:	Failure can be a positive experience. I may be disappointed if I fail, but I am certain to fail if I don't try.

Homework

Hannah was asked to:

- Talk to five people about their perception of failure (see the Survey technique in Chapter 13 on 'Healthy and unhealthy negative emotions').
- List the benefits of focusing on the effort and process and the costs of focusing on the result or outcome.

Technique: Cognitive continuum

Rationale and focus

This technique is useful to modify a belief that failure is terrible or dreadful. In the case of Hannah, not being able to find publishers interested in her work (the second book) was not the end of the world. It was disappointing, but not terrible when it is compared with other things in life such as illness, divorce or redundancy. The therapeutic focus is to repeatedly compare how terrible a particular failure is with other things or events that are generally perceived as worse on a continuum scale. The objective of the comparison is to put the belief into perspective and to show that although failure is disappointing and may be unpleasant, it is not the worst thing. In using the 'Cognitive continuum', the therapist can say: 'How terrible is it when compared with . . . ?'

Process

Therapist:	How bad is it that no publishers are interested in your book?
Hannah:	Very bad. I need to do well.

Therapist:	On a scale of 1 to 10, what would you say?
Hannah:	10.
Therapist:	Suppose your house was destroyed in a fire and everything you and your family had were lost. Is it bad?
Hannah:	It is terrible. It is really bad.
Therapist:	How bad it is, on a scale of 1 to 10?
Hannah:	10.
Therapist:	Does it mean that not having publishers interested in your book is as bad as the loss of the house and all the possessions?
Hannah:	Oh. I suppose not. It can't be.
Therapist:	Of course, it doesn't make sense. Which one is worse?
Hannah:	The house and possessions.
Therapist:	Put things into proportion. How bad is it that no publishers are interested in your book compared to the loss of the house and possessions?
Hannah:	It is not as bad.
Therapist:	The house and possessions is 10, what about the 'book'?
Hannah:	6.
Therapist:	You have a son, who lives with you and your husband. Do you love him?
Hannah:	Very much so.
Therapist:	Suppose he was unconscious and critically ill in intensive care because of the fire. Is it bad?
Hannah:	It is terrible.
Therapist:	It is. How terrible is it compared with the 'house and possessions'?
Hannah:	There is no comparison.
Therapist:	I agree. On a scale of 1 to 10, what will you say?
Hannah:	10.
Therapist:	Does it mean that the loss of the house and possessions is as bad as your son being unconscious and critically ill in intensive care?
Hannah:	Of course not. My son is a lot more important.
Therapist:	Absolutely. He is 10, what about the 'house and possessions'?
Hannah:	I suppose 7.
Therapist:	How about the 'book'? It was 6 before.
Hannah:	Now you have put the whole thing into perspective, not having any publishers interested in my book doesn't sound that important any more.
Therapist:	I agree. The rating was 6 before, what is it now?
Hannah:	2 or 3. It would be nice to get another book published, but it is not the end of the world.

Therapist: It is always nice to have another book published. Not having publishers interested in your book now is not confirmation that your book can never be published. If you continue with your procrastination, your book will never be finished, let alone go into publication. If you stop the procrastination and try to enjoy the process of writing, it will make a difference.

Homework

Hannah was asked to:

- Keep a 'failure' diary for a month. She would rate each failure on a scale of 1 to 100, and then ask, 'Is this the worst? How does this compare with . . . ? What would be a more helpful way of thinking about this?'

Other techniques

Other relevant techniques are 'Acceptance', 'Seeing the event from the other side', '100 people', 'Prediction' and 'Best friend'.

Notes for therapists about fear of failure and procrastination

- Experience of failure is unpleasant and disappointing, but it is not an indication of someone being a failure as a person.
- Failure is a perception and a belief, not an outcome and a fact.
- Success isn't permanent and failure isn't fatal.
- Failure is the highway to success.

Chapter 15

Self-criticism

Being self-critical is usually seen as a tool to promote development and growth. The idea is that you have to be critical of yourself for making mistakes in order to learn and to make progress. Many cultures see self-criticism as a good and helpful thing. People always say: 'Talking about yourself and your achievements gives an impression that you are boasting and are big-headed. Being modest is the key.' Parents want their children to keep their feet firmly on the ground and do not want them to get too big-headed and become complacent. Some children are encouraged to work harder, achieve more and behave better, but they often receive little or no praise or recognition for successes or efforts. Adults (e.g. parents, teachers) tend to place more emphasis on pointing out faults to help learning, instead of building on what children have done right. One client said:

> My father never gave me any praise or recognition for working hard or doing well. He often pointed out what I did wrong, although it was not intended to be critical. But I somehow perceived it as such, which made me feel stupid and not good enough and that I should have tried harder and better. I became a perfectionist and beat myself up a lot for little things. I compare myself with others, such as my sister, my brother and friends. Jealousy and envy seem to be the features in my character.

Another client said: 'My parents always focused on what I did wrong, but they did not tell me how I could learn or improve. I felt so inadequate.' Both clients acknowledged that their parents' intentions were good. Parents often do not realise the unpleasant impact of such an approach (e.g. pointing out faults, giving no praise or recognition, or no clues on how to improve) on their children's self-confidence and self-esteem. This could be the way they were brought up as children. As parents, they are just passing on cultural values, without realising that some of these values may no longer be appropriate, or may even be regarded as harmful. But their children have developed a habit of self-criticism.

Just imagine someone following you around and pointing out every little mistake you make, or telling you what you have done is all very well, but you could have been done it better, faster or more effectively. How would you feel about it? How would it affect your confidence in your ability to cope and succeed in life? How would it influence your ability to make decisions and take initiatives? More importantly, what impact would it have on your self-confidence and self-esteem? In the end, you would believe that you are not good enough, feel that you will never achieve anything worth while, and criticise yourself for failing or for not doing things better, faster or more effectively. Self-critical beliefs or behaviours are often learned early in life and become a habit and a knee-jerk reaction, which people may not even be fully aware of.

There is a crucial difference between being critical of your mistakes and criticising yourself for the mistakes. When you are being critical of a mistake, it is helpful because the focus is on the mistake, not on you as a person. You are not harsh on yourself and don't waste emotional energy, but you are able to learn from it. You don't like making a mistake but acknowledge it and accept it as a learning experience. You ask yourself: 'Why did I make it? What can I learn from it? What could I do differently in future?' You can see things more clearly when you look back and your new insight would enable you to learn from your experience. If a similar situation happened again, you would have a different, better perspective on how to deal with it.

When clients attack themselves for a mistake, it is harmful because the focus is on them as a person, not on the mistake. It makes them feel bad as a person and paralyses them. It won't help them think more clearly and do better next time. It also prevents them from thinking clearly about themselves and their lives, and from changing those aspects of themselves that they want to change. Clinically, when clients criticise themselves for their problems or difficulties, it does not help to resolve them. It can make problems even worse, including worsening mental health problems. One client noticed that he was feeling better and more energetic, when he started to be less critical of himself for making mistakes. 'Learn from it and don't waste emotional energy,' he said.

Why is self-criticism a clinical issue?

When clients repeatedly beat themselves up for small mistakes, failures or errors of judgement, for not being confident or assertive, or for being anxious or depressed, it has the unwanted effect of wasting emotional energy, of damaging emotional and mental health, and of demolishing self-confidence. Imagine if somebody repeatedly kicks you when you are down; it is hard to stand up again. It is hard to recover from mental health problems or to build up self-confidence, when you are repeatedly kicking yourself with self-criticisms.

As a result, it is not surprising that clients label themselves as being 'mental' and criticise themselves for being 'different' from others, or tell themselves that they are 'a failure, useless, stupid, or pathetic'. They may even believe that their mental health problem is due to a 'disease' in the brain because they can't control their moods and tantrums. However, they know in their hearts this is not true. Some clients even engage in the 'sick role' to their advantage, thereby getting unhealthy attention (e.g. negative attention is better than no attention), getting what they demand, and/or avoiding responsibility. When the 'sick role' is being reinforced (e.g. a psychiatric diagnosis), it is hard to make changes. Clients become pessimistic about their prognosis, recovery and future.

The case of Clare

'I know I could have done it better, if I had pushed myself harder,' said Clare. She was one of those clients who was unable to appreciate her effort in working hard or being successful. She did not praise herself for the success and was embarrassed to talk about herself and her achievements. She often beat herself up for small mistakes or for not performing to what she believed to be people's expectation of her. She was harsh on herself for not performing better, faster or more effectively and was terrified about letting people down.

She was promoted to manager after working as a temp for twelve months, but resigned within three months because she believed that she was not up to the job. She said that she had let people down, particularly the person who promoted her. She was very critical of herself for being so useless and a failure, and started to worry about her future. She went to her general practitioner because she was tearful, feeling tired and unable to concentrate. Getting out of bed was difficult for her. She woke up every morning feeling anxious and tense, and was not looking forward to the day ahead. She beat herself up for being weak and lazy. Depression and anxiety disorder were diagnosed.

> I know my parents were supportive and caring. They didn't put any pressure on me when I was young. They always said that doing my best was good enough. But the way they talked and behaved were strange and different. I don't know how to put it.

Her parents were really pleased when she came home from school with a good report, she did well in an examination, or she was well behaved.

Otherwise, they did not say much. 'Just learn from it,' was their response. To her, they were disappointed in her as a daughter and it was a sign of disapproval of her as a person. The thoughts were painful and terrifying to Clare. Although they did not say anything bad or criticise her, she thought that she had let her parents down. In order to make them happy, she must work hard, be successful and never disappoint them. She became a perfectionist. Her unhelpful thoughts of should/must, magnification, discounting the positive, mind reading, fortune telling, and mental filters were there right from her early years. There was a recognisable and predictable pattern in her self-critical beliefs/behaviour throughout her life.

Cognitive behaviour therapy approach to self-criticism

It is absurd for clients to believe that beating themselves up for small mistakes, failures, or errors of judgement, for not being confident or assertive, or for being anxious is a helpful and constructive way of self-improvement or growth as there is no scientific proof to support it.

The CBT approach is to help clients to understand that self-criticism is a drain on emotional energy, affects motivation and concentration, and can be a contributing factor to mental health problems. In working with self-critical clients, the CBT message is that:

- Self-criticism contributes to keeping low self-esteem going.
- It prevents them from viewing and accepting themselves as a whole person with strengths as well as weaknesses or flaws.
- It makes them feel bad as people and paralyses them so that they cannot learn.
- It prevents them from working constructively on aspects of themselves that they wish to change.
- It triggers feelings like guilt, shame, anger and frustration.
- It encourages procrastination.

Technique: Read it out loud

Rationale and focus

Self-criticism has become a habit and a knee-jerk reaction and clients are often not fully aware of the problems it causes. Once they realise that it makes their feelings worse, is harmful to self-confidence, and does not help with learning, less of it will be used.

In using this technique, clients are asked to write down a list of the self-critical beliefs that they have (e.g. 'I am useless; I am a failure'), then observe how they feel while the list is being read out *loud* a few times.

Process

Therapist:	How often do you beat yourself up?
Clare:	I don't really know. I tend to be quite negative about myself.
Therapist:	Negative about yourself?
Clare:	Yes, I expect a lot of myself. I don't like to be mediocre or to make mistakes.
Therapist:	When you do, then what?
Clare:	I am critical of myself and call myself all sorts of names.
Therapist:	Such as?
Clare:	I am pathetic, useless or stupid.
Therapist:	You don't like to be mediocre or to make mistakes. Otherwise, you are harsh on yourself and call yourself all sorts of names. Is that right?
Clare:	Yes.
Therapist:	Suppose you read out loud a list of all the negative things you say about yourself: 'I am stupid, useless, pathetic . . .' How would this make you feel?
Clare:	Yeah, not good. I suppose.
Therapist:	How about you read it out loud at least twenty times a day for a month, a year or even the rest of your life?
Clare:	It would be terrible, making me feel really bad as a person. It depresses me.
Therapist:	Absolutely. Criticising yourself all the time (for whatever reasons) will make you feel bad as a person and destroy your self-confidence, almost like having a parrot on your shoulder constantly telling you in your ear that you are stupid, useless and pathetic. How would it help you to learn and improve and not to be mediocre?
Clare:	It doesn't. It makes me feel worse.

Homework

Clare was asked to:

- Carry out an experiment, which was to read out loud a list of self-criticism (e.g. 'I am a failure') twenty times a day for five days and note her feelings afterwards.
- Do another experiment after the first five days, which was to rewrite all her self-criticisms and turn them into something helpful and realistic.
- Read it out loud twenty times a day for the next five days, and note her feelings afterwards.
- Draw a conclusion about the experiment.

Technique: Follow your son around

Rationale and focus

Clare's self-criticism was not just directed at her mistakes or errors of judgement; she also demanded her work to be perfect and better. Remember that she was a perfectionist and was never happy with the standard of her work. To other people, the work could well be reasonable and acceptable. 'I did not make mistakes; it does not mean that my work is good enough. I could or should have done it better (or faster or more effectively)' was what she always said. Constant self-criticism has the unwanted effects of affecting motivation to work, of making it harder to recover from mental health problems, and of encouraging procrastination.

The idea of this technique is that if the client does not constantly criticise her son or demand that he is perfect, why do it to herself?

Process

Therapist:	You do beat yourself up quite a lot, don't you?
Clare:	Yes.
Therapist:	What can you gain from doing it?
Clare:	I suppose, it can help to stop myself from being lazy and not getting on with things. I want to motivate myself to do things better.
Therapist:	So you believe that constant self-criticism is helpful.
Clare:	Yeah.
Therapist:	Has it been helpful so far?
Clare:	I don't know. I thought that this is something I should do.
Therapist:	If it is helpful, why are you here to see me?
Clare:	Ah. Oh, well. I see the point you make.
Therapist:	Do you have a son?
Clare:	A young boy, who is 5 years old.
Therapist:	Do you love him?
Clare:	Very much so.
Therapist:	Suppose you follow your son around all the time and keep telling him what he has done wrong and never give him any praise for what he has done right or his efforts, or that he could have done the work better, would it help him to get on with things and to motivate him to do things better?
Clare:	No. I don't think so.
Therapist:	How do you think that your constant nagging (or criticism) would make him feel?

Clare:	He won't like it.
Therapist:	I am sure. How would it make him feel?
Clare:	I imagine that he would be frustrated, angry, hurt and resentful.
Therapist:	Can you blame him for these feelings?
Clare:	No.
Therapist:	What do think the impact would be on his confidence and motivation?
Clare:	Not good at all.
Therapist:	Absolutely. It can destroy his self-confidence and make him feel inferior and inadequate. Would you follow your son around all the time and tell him that what he has done is all right, but he could have done it better?
Clare:	No, I would not.
Therapist:	Would you follow your son around all the time and pick faults with what he does?
Clare:	No, I would not.
Therapist:	Why not?
Clare:	It won't help him. It would make him feel worse as a person, destroy his self-confidence and affect his motivation to get on with doing things.
Therapist:	If you won't do it to your son, why do you do it to yourself? What is the logic in that? It is almost like having a parrot following you around all the time and sitting on your shoulder constantly nagging at you.
Clare:	Oh.

Homework

Clare was asked to:

- Make a list of advantages and disadvantages of self-criticism and then draw a conclusion after that.
- Keep a self-criticism diary for two months to help her to be more aware of her self-critical behaviour and the circumstances in which she criticised herself.
- Turn these self-critical beliefs into something that was helpful and believable. For example, 'I am stupid to make mistakes' to 'Making mistakes has got nothing to do with being stupid. Doing well is satisfying, but it is human to make and learn from mistakes'.
- Read the chapter on 'Combating self-criticism' in *Overcoming low self-esteem* (Fennell 1999).

Other techniques

Other relevant techniques include 'Rewriting assumptions', 'Cognitive continuum' and 'Daughter'.

Notes for therapists about self-criticism

- It simply points you in the direction of what you did wrong, but it does not give you any clues as to how to do better next time.
- It reinforces the strength of negative labels of being a bad, stupid or incompetent person, or a failure, and prevents you viewing yourself as a whole person with strengths and limitations.
- It does not give you credit for your assets, strengths, qualities and talent.
- It is a waste of emotional energy, causing you to feel tired, with poor concentration and affects your motivation to get on with things.
- Remember that you do have a *choice* between being critical of your mistake or criticising yourself for the mistake. Make the right choice!

Chapter 16

Setback and relapse

Life is about ups and downs and we all know that. The crucial point is about how the 'down' is being dealt with, not just knowing. The measure of a person is best judged by how they cope with adversity and whether they benefit from it. Whether or not they can pick themselves up and how quickly are closely related to their mental attitude. Confucius said: 'Our greatest glory is *not* in never falling, but in rising every time we fall.' It is true that no human being can be on top all the time and it is also true that we can't have sunny days every day. We all know that this is the truth. We accept it without question, because it makes sense. We tell ourselves, our friends, our families and our children about setbacks being a fact of life. After all, the 'fall' will help toughen up our personality, develop adult thinking, mature us psychologically and emotionally, and enable us to be more creative and imaginative in our work. In other words, the list of benefits from the 'fall' can go on and on, but only if we have the right mental attitude.

When a highly successful fund manager in the city was asked by a national newspaper about the secret of his success, he pondered for a while and then said that he owed his success to the unpleasant, painful at times, experiences of the falls in his early career. His attitude was that he just learnt from it and got on with life, rather than worrying about it. There was no need to make the experience worse than it actually was, he said. Another inspiring story came from a television interview with someone who talked about his experience of the 'fall' from a very highly successful catering business to nothing and how he coped with life in general. He said, 'That's life. There is no point in looking back, just accept it and do whatever I can for a better future. I am not currently doing well but this doesn't mean that it will always be the case.' These two examples illustrate that a setback or 'fall' is not only a fact of life for all humans; it is usually seen as an opportunity for personal and professional development or growth and business success.

By the same token, setbacks are an important and necessary part of a successful and sustainable recovery from mental health problems. When clients are recovering, it means that they 'feel' and 'get' better. When clients have recovered, it means that they are able to 'stay' better. 'Staying' better is therefore a therapeutic goal. It requires setbacks to enrich experiences and to build the confidence to cope with adversity, thereby reducing the probability of relapse.

One client was horrified about her recent setback, saying: 'I have gone backward by one step and am losing control.' Clearly, her unhelpful beliefs of magnification, mental filter, discounting the positive, and black and white thinking (Burns 1999) were the cause of her terrifying emotions and caused her to be over-reactive, rather than the setback itself. She expected that her progress would be a smooth one, without any turbulence in the recovery process. This was unrealistic and could have made her mental health problems worse. It did. She was depressed for two days until she started to question her mental attitude towards it, using her CBT learning.

Setback and relapse are different in clinical terms, but are often perceived, unfortunately and inaccurately, as the same by clients and carers and possibly by some mental health professionals. With a setback, it is often mistakenly taken as strong evidence of an impending relapse (e.g. 'I am depressed again'). Quite the opposite: setbacks help to identify difficulties for further work to be done in order to achieve the goal of 'staying' better. The therapeutic reality is that the therapist cannot prepare the client for every eventuality or setback in the course of the treatment. Clients' acceptance of setback is therefore important to a successful and sustainable mental health recovery and can be strongly influenced by the professionals' views. An undue concern about a setback may reinforce the fear of a setback, thus causing an increase in the levels of guilt, worry and anxiety, which can in turn trigger even more setbacks.

Why is the fear of setback a clinical issue?

When clients perceive a setback as a terrifying experience and seek to avoid it, they develop a fear of a setback, which could lead to even more setbacks. This fear affects their response to and engagement with therapy. Pessimistic about their future and treatment progress may lead to their believing that their mental health problems are biological and genetic in nature.

The case of Anne

Anne made good progress after fourteen sessions of cognitive behaviour therapy for her depression and low self-esteem. She said:

> I am now feeling better about myself and feel more in control of my thoughts and mood. I am coping better and don't get upset as easily as I used to. Some of my friends are also noticing the change in me, which is

good. My family is so pleased with the change I have made and has started to enjoy my company.

Not only did she better understand the nature of her depression and low self-esteem, but she also felt that she now had a tool to cope with the life ahead. Anne was feeling positive about the change and was optimistic about her progress and future.

Medication had not been as beneficial as she, and her doctors, had hoped, despite years of being on different types of drugs of various dosages. With the help of medication, she was, at best, feeling just above water without being overwhelmed by the feeling of 'dark and thick clouds' over her head. Psychotherapy with a number of therapists over the years had not been very helpful either. She was quite right to be sceptical about another referral to psychotherapy, this time to cognitive behaviour therapy. She said in the first session: 'I don't see "talking therapy" can help me, with no disrespect. I just want to be honest.' Her scepticism soon turned into hope as she was able to relate her problems and experience to the work of CBT.

'Danny, I am losing control and have gone back two steps. It is terrible. I have done so well since I came to you,' said Anne in an anxious tone of voice, with tears streaming from her eyes. She was upset about it and criticised herself for losing control. She was fearful of being depressed again and was highly anxious that things were falling apart. She thought that she had a tool (CBT) to cope with the life ahead, should be happy and in control all the time, and should not have a setback. Her family said: 'You'd better go to see the doctor, you have a setback and are not coping.' The fear of a setback was reinforced.

She was greatly disturbed by a stream of negative thoughts about it, including: 'I am a failure, I have let everybody down. I will be completely stuck in my miserable life and have to take medication for the rest of my life. I will never be happy again. I am mental.' These thoughts undermined her self-confidence and lowered her self-esteem, causing a spiral of anxiety and worry and problems in sleeping. She believed that there was nothing she could do about her mental health problem. The problem was biological and was in her genes.

Cognitive behaviour therapy approach to setback and relapse

Setback is a fact of life. It is *not* the cause of clients suffering a relapse, probably with another depression or mental health problem. According to CBT, it is an important and necessary ingredient for a sustainable recovery or for clients being able to stay better. The problem lies with clients' unhelpful thoughts and beliefs about it and with the way in which it is being dealt with.

In working with clients with fear of a setback, the CBT message is that:

- A setback is a fact of life and is unavoidable.
- Everybody has setbacks in the course of their lives.
- It is not the same as a relapse.
- Irrational thoughts or beliefs about it would make it worse than it actually is and could lead to a relapse as a result.
- Accepting and learning from it will result in a faster, better and sustainable recovery.

Technique: Acceptance

Rationale and focus

We learn to accept a lot of things in life. If you live in India in the summer, you learn to accept the hot and humid weather. If you live in Alaska in the winter, you learn to accept the cold. If you are stuck in the traffic, you learn to accept there is nothing you can do but to wait. By the same token, if you failed an examination and want to pass it the next time, you learn to accept the result, without wasting time criticising yourself and/or emotional energy worrying about the future. Otherwise, you might fail again.

In using this technique, the therapist and the client can first discuss setbacks in life, and then shift the discussion to mental health problems. The therapist can say:

> Rather than demanding that you mustn't have a setback in your progress or the progress should be a smooth one, there are things you can learn to accept and make the best of. For example, perhaps you need some setbacks before you can learn to take control of your life and make a sustainable recovery from your mental health problems, and to appreciate/enjoy the progress you have made. Rather than criticising yourself for having a setback (e.g. I am a failure. I am mental) and magnifying its consequences (e.g. I will never be able to come off medication), you can say to yourself that 'I accept that a setback in my progress is normal and necessary, and now I will try to learn from it.'

Process

Therapist: Is it possible not to have setbacks in life, I wonder?

Anne: Yeah, I suppose not. Life is or could not be like that. There are ups and downs in life.

Therapist:	Absolutely. It is true that life has its ups and downs. As long as you are human, it is there and will be there in future, whether we like it or not. Did you have any setbacks previously?
Anne:	Yes, I did.
Therapist:	Can you think of any examples?
Anne:	The house we wanted to buy fell through a few years ago; my eldest son did not manage to get to his chosen university last year; there have been problems with the kitchen we are installing at the moment and it is hard work to harmonise these professionals.
Therapist:	How did your son cope with it?
Anne:	He was very good and philosophically accepted it. He is happy where he is now.
Therapist:	How do you cope with the problems with the kitchen?
Anne:	No choice but to accept it and do the best we can.
Therapist:	What conclusion can we draw about it?
Anne:	Well, it is life.
Therapist:	Why is a setback in life okay and acceptable, but not so for the setback in your progress? How logical is it?
Anne:	Yeah. Oh. I never thought of it in this way. I suppose it is the worry and fear.
Therapist:	About what?
Anne:	Going into depression again and never being able to come off medication.
Therapist:	What could be the benefit of worrying about it and of criticising yourself for being a failure?
Anne:	Nothing. It will make me worse.
Therapist:	Is that what you want?
Anne:	No.
Therapist:	Suppose you were to aim for accepting the setback and saw it as a valuable learning opportunity for making further progress, rather than judging yourself and worrying about the future, what could be the benefit?
Anne:	Oh, I could become less preoccupied with it and therefore have less worry and anxiety.

Homework

Anne was asked to:

- Write down the costs and benefits of not accepting setbacks as well as accepting them.

- Draw a conclusion on the usefulness of criticising herself (e.g. 'I am a failure and mental') for learning.
- Keep a diary of self-criticism.
- Devise a strategy to capitalise on setback.

Technique: Seeing the event from the other side

Rationale and focus

There are two sides to a coin. If you move over to the other side to see an event (e.g. losing a job, failing an examination, or being involved in a car accident), you can see there is something different and less negative about it. Being able to view the 'whole' picture, or put things into perspective, will have the effect of modifying unhelpful thoughts about setback. It also helps to reduce emotional reactions.

The therapist can use an analogy to illustrate what could be the costs of viewing just one side of a coin relative to the benefits of also seeing it from the other side. For example, 'An expensive car is written off in a car accident, but the driver escaped unharmed.'

Process

Therapist: What were your feelings about your car being written off in a car accident? You love this car and it was expensive too.

Anne: It would be very upsetting and terrible.

Therapist: Because of?

Anne: I would have no car to drive and it would be so inconvenient. I need a car to go to work and to socialise. It would cost me a lot of money to replace it. And I simply do not have the money to do it now.

Therapist: You are only seeing one side of it: the costs of losing your car. What could you see from the other side?

Anne: I don't understand.

Therapist: What would be the worst things that could happen in a car accident?

Anne: Oh, I see what you mean.

Therapist: Now, what could you see from the other side in a helpful way?

Anne: At least I did not end up in the hospital with my family around my hospital bed, or even worse I could have died. They would be so upset. It would be a lot more upsetting and terrible than losing a car. After all, it is just money and inconvenience. And it is not the end of the world.

Therapist:	It is true. Coming back to your setback, what could you see from the other side in a helpful and realistic way?
Anne:	Yeah. Oh. I suppose the other side is that it is a learning opportunity.
Therapist:	Suppose you can learn from it, then what?
Anne:	Less similar setback and more in control of myself.
Therapist:	If this is so, should you be fearful or not about a setback?
Anne:	No. I shouldn't.

Homework

Anne was asked to:

- List the benefits of being able to see things from the other side.
- Identify the helpful ways to deal with a setback and to give the rationale for the actions.
- Keep a diary of her feelings when she was able to see things from the other side.

Other techniques

Other relevant techniques include 'Rewriting assumptions', 'Cognitive continuum' and 'Read it out loud'.

Notes for therapists about setback and relapse

- Every setback is a step closer to a successful and sustainable recovery. The more setbacks you have, the more you learn and the faster progress you make.
- Setback is a prevention of relapse.
- It is an invaluable learning experience for acquiring psychological maturity and developing emotional toughness.
- No pain, no gain and no 'staying' better.
- Tolerate the short-term discomfort for the long-term interest or benefit.

Part IV

Client's perspective

Self-prejudice and interpersonal difficulties

Chapter 17

Others' criticism

Criticism is a fact of life and is an experience of every human being during the course of their lives. People criticise each other, irrespective of the nature of their relationships. It is hard to find a person who has never been criticised. Similarly, it is also hard to find a person who never criticises other people. Therefore, there is no logical reason for it not to happen. It would be more pleasant and preferable if we were not criticised, or if it was done in a kind and supportive manner, without feelings being hurt. But we do not live in an ideal world.

When we are praised and appreciated, we feel good about it. By the same token, it is not unusual for us to feel a bit upset, annoyed, irritated, hurt or angry for being criticised, rightly or wrongly. These feelings are both normal and appropriate. It is best to accept and tolerate them. We also learn to accept that we do not have *control* over what people say or do. As such, criticism is not usually regarded as a real issue or a problem, particularly for people with self-confidence and stable self-esteem. The crucial issue is to decide whether there are grounds for it and to exercise a *choice* of either accepting and viewing it as a learning opportunity or rejecting it for being unreasonable and unjustifiable. We do not see it as a personal attack, or link it to our self-worth, or allow it to affect our self-esteem. When a criticism becomes a personal attack (e.g. 'You are stupid and incompetent'), it will be rejected (e.g. 'Doing things well is satisfying, but it is human to make and learn from mistakes. Of course, I am not stupid and incompetent at all'). In this respect, there is no real harm in criticism. Quite the opposite: it can be helpful to personal and professional growth and business success.

'I hate criticism. It makes me feel bad as a person,' said Annette in an anxious and upset tone of voice. When criticism is linked to one's self-worth, self-image is distorted and this can affect one's confidence to deal with it appropriately and effectively. Often, it is being viewed through the beliefs of should/must, mind reading, fortune telling, magnification, mental filter, and black and white (Burns 1999), thus causing clients to be oversensitive to what is said, or even paranoid. Suggestions, comments and/or silence are often misinterpreted as criticisms, although these are not, nor are they intended to be, so. These beliefs are unhelpful and illogical, not only causing damage to clients' mental and emotional health, but also encouraging the use of unhelpful behaviours to avoid it, such as avoidance, safety-seeking behaviours, pleasing behaviours, aggression, or a tendency towards perfectionism.

In many cultures, criticism or pointing out what children have done wrong is usually seen as an appropriate way of learning and growth. They learn, as commonly believed, through correction (e.g. pointing out mistakes) and punishment (e.g. not allowing them to watch television, having no pocket money). However, when it is not balanced with praise and recognition for successes and efforts, criticism can become a contributing factor in the development and maintenance of mental health problems such as depression and anxiety disorders. Imagine a person you know who is quite self-confident. Imagine that he is being followed around, with every little mistake he makes being pointed out, being told that what he has done is all very well but he could have done it better, faster or more effectively, and being called names (e.g. stupid, useless or not good enough). At the same time, there are no rewards of love, affection, praise and recognition. As the days, weeks, months and years go by, what impact would correction and punishment have on his self-confidence, on his ability to cope and succeed in life? It is not surprising that a fear of criticism develops as a result.

Why is others' criticism a clinical issue?

Clients who are sensitive to criticism or even paranoid often have problems relating to people in general. Their sensitivity to criticism can negatively affect their response to and engagement with therapy; it can therefore become a barrier to achieving therapeutic goals.

Clients may mistakenly take what was said in therapy as criticism (e.g. 'We need to work harder together'), thus triggering unhelpful thoughts of 'He does not like me; I am stupid; I'll never be able to get better; nobody can help me'. These 'self-prescribed' labels in the form of unhelpful thoughts are harmful to clients' confidence and self-esteem and to their recovery from their mental health problems. Some clients may even believe that their problems are biological and are in the genes, which they cannot do much about.

The case of Michael

'I am open, decent, hard-working, and a fair person and I expect other people to behave the same to me,' Michael said in a frustrated tone of voice. He believed that people around him had not been treating him in a fair manner. He was resentful and hurt by the way people criticised him, and was particularly upset by the lack of support from his wife, his young son and people at work. He found it difficult to get on with people and did not understand why he was picked on. Either shouting or avoidance was his typical way of responding to criticism, although this was not an appropriate or adult behaviour, but he did not know any other way of coping with the criticism. There were occasions when he tried to stay calm to deal with people, but the sense of injustice or unfairness just took over and he lost control. He went back to his typical coping behaviour. A sense of shame and guilt hit him hard once his intense negative emotions subsided. He criticised his behaviour and himself as a person: 'I am a failure and a bad person.'

There was a cycle of being sensitive to people, responding to criticism with anger and shouting or avoidance, and a sense of guilt, shame and remorse afterwards. Michael recognised this pattern from his early years, but felt that there was not much he could do to break the cycle and he was angry with himself for being so useless. Apologising sometimes did not work in reducing the guilt and shame, as people were used to or even fed up with 'I am sorry'. When people refused to accept his apology, this could provoke another wave of anger because it was perceived as a criticism and a rejection. Although he said that he had no problem with people constructively criticising him, the reality was that, constructive or not, his pattern of response was the same. He knew that. Being sensitive to, anxious and worried about it caused problems at work and created tension in the family. Even his wife and son tried to minimise conversations with him because they were anxious that what they said would be mistakenly taken as a criticism. They were treading on eggshells and he knew it. The sense of increased isolation and of not being able to cope with life caused him to seek refuge in drink. He was hospitalised for alcoholism and depression on two occasions.

He did not have a good relationship with his parents, his father in particular. He was resentful of the way he was brought up. He described his father as a cold and emotionless person. He knew that his parents did love and care about him; however, his father's critical behaviour had quite a negative impact on him as a person. When he was a child, his father always pointed out what he had done wrong, instead of helping him to build on what he had done right. There was not much recognition and praise for doing well. He felt inferior and inadequate and that he was a reject, which resulted in his being sensitive or oversensitive to criticism, however constructive it might be.

Cognitive behaviour therapy approach to others' criticism

Criticism is a fact of life. Being criticised is *not* the cause of emotional upset, is *not* the reason for individuals not being able to get on with others, and is *not* the explanation for individuals not being able to perform at work. If criticism is the problem, one would expect that every human being criticised would be emotionally upset (or even have mental health problems), have relationship difficulties, and/or would not be able to perform at work.

When criticism is interpreted as an attack on an individual's self-worth and competence, it can provoke rage in response, and create a sense of guilt, shame and remorse afterwards. There is a need for these individuals to examine their interpretation of and assumptions made about criticism and for them to learn to deal with criticism in an appropriate and adult manner. In working with people who are sensitive to criticism, the CBT message is that:

- Criticism is a fact of life and is unavoidable.
- Criticism is not an indication of one's self-worth.
- The benefits of bring criticised far outweigh the costs in terms of personal and professional development and growth.
- Refusing to accept it as a fact of life is a case of wasting emotional energy and can damage emotional and mental health.

Technique: The law

Rationale and focus

We learn to respect the law in the society in which we live. The law says that we have to pay for eating in a restaurant, for travelling on public transport and for shopping in supermarkets. By the same token, the law also says that illegal or socially unacceptable activities such as drug selling and taking drugs, domestic violence and sexual abuse are forbidden. People do not question the validity of the law but accept it. Clients who are sensitive to criticism or resentful about being criticised often use expressions such as 'He mustn't criticise me; it is terrible to be criticised; it is unfair; it hurts; I don't like it'. When an expression of 'mustn't' or 'shouldn't' is used, strong negative emotions, such as anger, hurt and resentment, often evolve as if someone had just broken the 'law'. Does criticising somebody constitute breaking the law?

In using this technique, the therapist and the client can have a general discussion about what is allowed or not allowed in society, as far as the law is concerned, and then explore the issue of criticism within the framework of the law.

Process

Therapist: The beauty of living in a civilised society is that we are protected by the law. The law defines what is acceptable or not acceptable to do. Isn't it right?

Michael:	Yes.
Therapist:	Is it lawful or unlawful to eat in a restaurant without paying for it?
Michael:	Unlawful.
Therapist:	Is it lawful or unlawful to drive a car without insurance or MOT?
Michael:	Unlawful.
Therapist:	If a couple are having an argument in their house, is it lawful or unlawful?
Michael:	There is nothing wrong with this. We all do it from time to time; so long as it doesn't affect other people or happen in a public place.
Therapist:	Absolutely. This is the good thing about having the law telling us what we can or can't do. Agree?
Michael:	Yes.
Therapist:	Coming back to criticism. What is the problem with being criticised by other people?
Michael:	I don't like it.
Therapist:	And?
Michael:	It hurts.
Therapist:	You don't like it and it hurts and therefore people mustn't criticise you. Is that right?
Michael:	Yes.
Therapist:	Is there a law to say that just because you don't like it and it hurts, people mustn't criticise you?
Michael:	No. But it is not fair.
Therapist:	Suppose it is the case. Is there a law to say that just because it is not fair, criticism should not have happened?
Michael:	No.
Therapist:	Did you criticise people before? Do you criticise people? Will you criticise people in future?
Michael:	Yes.
Therapist:	Is there a law to say that you can criticise people and they can't do it to you? How logical is it?
Michael:	Oh. No. There is no such law and it is not logical.
Therapist:	Criticism is a fact of life. We criticise each other and this is the way life is. The reality is that even if it is not intended to be a criticism, you may take it as such because of your fear and because you are sensitive.
Michael:	Oh. Yes, it did happen in this way.
Therapist:	It is not the criticism that is the problem, but the way you link it to your self-worth and the way you react to it. Dealing with

criticism is not about demanding that people mustn't criticise you, but learning to deal with it in an appropriate and adult manner. If you are able to do that, this will give you a feeling of being in control and you will feel good about yourself. In this case, criticism is not a problem.

Homework

Michael was asked to:

- Talk to five people to find out whether or not criticism was a universal experience and to discuss with them a helpful way to deal with criticism. He was to write a summary of what people said and then draw a conclusion.
- List the costs and benefits of being criticised.
- Come up with an appropriate way to deal with criticism and to give a rationale for it.

In reviewing the costs and benefits of being criticised, the objective is to show that the benefits far outweigh the costs, and that most of the costs are often short-term discomfort, whereas the benefits are long term.

Technique: Cognitive continuum

Rationale and focus

Being criticised by others is often perceived as a terrible experience. This is particularly so when clients see it as a personal attack, or as an attack on their self-worth or integrity. Rather than reassuring the client that it is a universal experience, or asking the client not to take it personally, the therapist can compare the client's terrible feeling of being criticised with events that could be seen as even worse, such as redundancy, burglary, car accident or serious illness to see how terrible it actually is to be criticised. Is it really that terrible in comparison?

This comparative approach helps the client to put criticism into perspective. The therapist can say:

Rather than demanding that people *shouldn't* or *mustn't* criticise you, there are things you can learn from it. For example, perhaps you need some criticism before you can develop the skills and confidence to be assertive with people, and to work on your shortcomings. Rather than making it worse than it actually is, start with 'I don't like it, but this is life and I will learn to cope with it.'

Process

Therapist: You don't like criticism and see it as terrible, is that right?

Michael: Yes, I hate it. It is terrible to be criticised. For example, when my work is criticised, it makes me feel inadequate and inferior. It is unfair. People should know that I have worked hard.

Therapist: On a scale of 1 to 100, 100 being very terrible or bad, how terrible is it to be criticised?

Michael: 99.

Therapist: So it is really bad. Do you have a son?

Michael: Yes, he is 10 years old.

Therapist: Do you love him?

Michael: A lot. He is fun to be with.

Therapist: *Suppose* your son is in hospital because of a car accident. How terrible is it in relation to being criticised?

Michael: It is really terrible.

Therapist: What is your rating *relative* to being criticised?

Michael: 100 with my son in hospital and being criticised 70.

Therapist: It is quite a drop from 99. Why is that?

Michael: When you put it like that, being criticised does not seem to be that terrible.

Therapist: *Suppose* the doctor says that your son is critically ill and may not pull through and asks you to prepare psychologically. How terrible would it be in relation to being criticised?

Michael: There is no comparison. It is absolutely terrible to lose my son. Being criticised is nothing.

Therapist: What is your rating *relative* to being criticised?

Michael: 10 or even 5.

Therapist: From 99 to 70, now to 10 or even 5. It is a huge drop. What conclusion can we draw about it?

Michael: I need to stand back to look at the whole thing. Being criticised is not the end of the world and I need to accept it as a fact of life.

Therapist: Absolutely. The reality is that there is no need to link being criticised to your self-worth (e.g. 'I am inadequate and inferior'). There is no logic in that. If you can see it from the other side, you perhaps can see that you need some criticism in order to develop the skills and confidence to cope with adversity and to work on your shortcomings. The conclusion we can draw is that being criticised is unpleasant in the short term, but the long-term benefit can be substantial.

Homework

Michael was asked to:

- Keep a diary of events in which he was criticised: what were the criticisms, how did he deal with them, to what extent did he agree or disagree with each criticism? He was also asked to write down his (unhelpful) thoughts about each of the criticisms and rewrite them as helpful and realistic alternatives.
- Read and evaluate two chapters on communication to help him to be more able to deal with criticism: 'Good and bad communication' and 'The five secrets of communication' in *The feeling good handbook* (Burns 1999).

Other techniques

Other relevant techniques include 'Seeing the event from the other side', 'Acceptance' and 'Rewriting assumptions'.

Notes for therapists about others' criticism

- Demanding not to be criticised is a waste of emotional energy. It may damage our emotional and mental health.
- Criticism is a fact of life and could be useful for personal and professional development and growth.
- We do not have control over what people say to us, but we have a choice whether to accept or not accept what is said.
- Self-worth has got nothing to do with criticism.
- We criticise other people; there is no logical reason why they can't criticise us.

Chapter 18

Good and bad communication

'With no disrespect, I don't understand why you have asked me to read a chapter on communication. What is wrong with my communication? I honestly don't see there is any problem,' said Gary, who was clearly irritable and annoyed. It seemed that there was no connection between his low self-esteem, depression, substance misuse (alcohol), anger problem and communication. After all, Gary was quite an articulate person. He had a good honours degree in English and had worked in the financial industry for many years.

Communication seems easy and we all can do it. You just open your mouth and the words come out. Some believe that they're good at it or that they're experts. It was therefore understandable that Gary was upset and might even have felt insulted when asked to work on his communication skills as part of the treatment. It is true that we have been talking since we were young, and it comes naturally to all of us to be able to speak, to communicate what we want, and to express our feelings, views and opinions. When you feel happy and comfortable with someone, it's easy to communicate well. When others are supportive, kind, accommodating and encouraging, it's easy to express your feelings, views and opinions or even to disagree. You feel good, they feel good and everything seems perfectly in harmony. When you have a strong disagreement, a conflict with someone, or are being unfairly criticised, it is then you find out whether you can really communicate well. What do you say when the other person undermines you, is being unreasonable or refuses to listen to your point of view? How well do you communicate when you feel vulnerable and hurt, or if you are a person with low self-esteem who needs other people's recognition and acceptance in order to feel good?

Burns (1999) asserts that people who can communicate effectively in these situations are exceedingly rare. But these are the situations where good communication is vital. The key to intimacy, friendship and success in business is the ability to handle conflict successfully or to be open in the honest and appropriate expression of your feelings, views and opinions. Some people have a problem with this. For example, when husbands and wives don't communicate well, it may cause rows and arguments, attacks and counterattacks. This can cause mistrust and animosity in the relationship, possibly leading to divorce or even to the development of a mental health problem (e.g. depression). When friends don't communicate well, not only can friendship be affected, but it may also reduce social opportunities and lead to the problem of loneliness. Loneliness can be a social and psychological problem for people with mental health problems. When family members don't handle conflict and disagreements well, it may lead to the disintegration of the family unit, which is regarded as a contributing factor in the development and maintenance of mental health problems such as eating disorders, bipolar disorders and schizophrenia.

When people with anger problems believe that other people are unfair, inconsiderate, pick on them, or take advantage of them, it may affect their ability to deal with these situations and therefore their relationship with others. People with low self-esteem and anxiety problems may find it difficult to express their views and feelings, or have problems in dealing with requests or criticism. These examples illustrate that when working with people with mental health problems it is important to identify what their communication problems are in order to help them with their self-confidence and self-esteem.

Why is good and bad communication a clinical issue?

Imagine that a client suffering from a panic disorder actively avoids certain places or situations for fear of having a panic attack, that a client with a health anxiety problem constantly seeks reassurance in order to be less anxious about his or her health, and that a client suffering from obsessive-compulsive disorder keeps checking (physically and mentally) in order to keep anxiety-provoking intrusive thoughts at bay. Although these behaviours may have the short-term benefit of lowering anxiety levels, their mental health problems are unlikely to get better but to get worse.

'I asked her to learn to say "no" to people. Why can't she do it?' said a doctor, who was concerned about a client not being able to be assertive and to express her feelings and views. The concern was understandable as the communication problem partly contributed to the maintenance of her low self-esteem and her confidence levels, thereby affecting her prospect of recovery from depression and substance misuse (alcohol). Some clients may not know who they really are and what they want in life because of their inability or unwillingness to express their feelings, views or opinions. Graham, for example, said:

> I have had many 'masks' for use in different situations and with different people. I do not know who I am and what I want as I tend to say what people want to hear. I am good at it.

Communication problems are a clinical issue that underlies depression, eating disorders and anxiety disorders.

Cognitive behaviour therapy approach to good and bad communication

Cognitive behaviour therapy takes the view that poor communication skills partly contribute to the development and continuation of mental health problems. For example, Monica always had a problem in saying 'no' to people. 'No' was not in her vocabulary. 'I don't want to upset people. It is not nice to say "no". I can't do it,' said Monica, who had a fear of being disliked or rejected by people and tried to please others to avoid rejection or criticism. It did not come across to her that not only was it all right to say 'no', but also the benefits from it were important to her recovery from the problems of low self-esteem and depression. In CBT, the issue is not about saying 'no' but how to say it in a reasonable and appropriate manner. Clients can benefit from this in terms of helping with self-confidence and improving their self-esteem.

'How can I say "no" to people, especially to my boss, my best friends and my family?' said Lisa. 'I don't know how to do it. I simply do not have the skills and confidence.' What Lisa said highlighted a number of important points in the CBT approach to communication problems. First, although it is not difficult to understand the concepts, putting them into practice can be scary. Anxiety, worry and guilt can affect the person's confidence or motivation to carry it out. These emotions were due to Lisa's thoughts about the consequences of saying 'no' (or dealing with criticisms). Second, they do not know what to say or how to say it in an appropriate, assertive and reasonable manner. There is often a mistaken view that once clients understand that their thinking is unhelpful, they will have the confidence and be able to change their behaviour and say 'no'. This is far from true. Third, skills training (social and assertive) in the form of role-play and demonstrations are necessary in CBT sessions, as it helps clients develop self-confidence and acquire effective communication skills, thereby improving their ability to deal with interpersonal difficulties and alleviating the problem of self-prejudice (e.g. 'I am a reject').

To become a better communicator, it is important to understand what constitutes good and bad communication. Being able to distinguish between the two helps the client to be more aware of bad communication and therefore make an effort to reduce it. At the same time, good communication can be learnt and practised.

Good communication

Good communication is about being able to express your feelings, views, opinions and preferences openly and honestly and allow the other person to do the same. When the other person is talking, you try to listen and understand what is being said. This is the basic ingredient of good communication. It sounds easy, doesn't it? However, putting it into practice can be problematic. There is evidence that communication is a prevalent problem with people from all walks of life and bad communication may affect family, marital, work and social relationships. Note that poor communication can be the source of human stress.

Nobody will disagree that it is important to be open and honest in our communication. If we don't, other people will not know what we think, how we feel and what we want. It seems that good communication is not just *what* we say (open and honest); it is also about *how* we express it. 'Right and wrong', timing and our emotional state can influence the way we communicate with one another.

Technique: Turn the table round

'Turn the table round' is a useful technique to deal with the issue of expectation (or 'right and wrong'). Benedict said: 'I was cross with my wife for being critical of what I did. I told her about my feelings and my preference, but she wouldn't listen. What is the point of communication, if she doesn't change her behaviour?' Not surprisingly, Benedict was upset and angry, believing that if he was open and honest, his wife should accept his views and change. Such a belief, however reasonable to Benedict, undoubtedly made the situation worse, thereby affecting the way they talked to each other and their relationship.

Process

Therapist: You were angry and upset with your wife for not changing her behaviour, which, to you, was critical and unfair.

Benedict: Yes. I talked to and told her about how I felt and what I wanted. Why didn't she listen to me and change?

Therapist: If I turn the table round to look at an area of disagreement, will your perception and thinking be the same as that of your wife? [Note the use of 'Turn the table round' technique]

Benedict: What do you mean?

Therapist: Are your views about things always the same as those of your wife?

Benedict: No. We are different.

Therapist: Suppose your wife told you that she was not happy with what you did or said. She said that your behaviour was critical and unfair but you did not agree with what she said. In fact, you believed that you were right and she was wrong. Does it mean that just because she was open and honest in talking about it, you must accept her view and change your behaviour?

Benedict: Ah. Oh. I suppose not. We are all entitled to our views.

Therapist: How logical is it that she must listen and change, but you don't need to?

Benedict: I see what you mean. I can't impose my views and values on her.

This dialogue illustrates that good communication is not just about being open and honest; it is also about respecting that the other person has a right either to accept or to reject the point being made. This right applies to both parties. However, if you believe that you are right (fair or reasonable) and the other person is wrong, you may keep pushing the point. Inevitably, emotions on both sides are running high and the arguments that follow can result in a breakdown of communication. This may affect the relationship and make it more difficult for the other person to see things from your point of view. The other person is more likely to perceive your 'pushing' behaviour as aggressive and unreasonable and to view you as being immature.

If you stop pushing, the other person is more likely to be receptive to what you say with an open mind, which is helpful in the communication process and outcome. The most important point about good communication is that it is not just about expressing something openly and honestly, it is also about *not* imposing your view on the other person: 'I am right and you are wrong.' Good communication is not about getting rid of the disagreement. It is about sharing feelings, views and opinions.

Timing

Another important aspect of good communication is timing. 'Graham, I can see that you are busy, but I feel concerned about our son's school report and we need to talk. Shall we talk now or should I come back later?' said Nicola. Another way of putting it is: 'Graham, we need to talk now as I feel concerned about our son's school report.' Graham was busy preparing for a presentation scheduled for the next day.

The first request was thoughtful and gave Graham the option of whether to talk now or later. This communication was likely to be beneficial and productive, whereas the second one seemed to be imposing and demanding, which could lead to arguments.

Emotional state

'Don't communicate while you or the other person is emotional' is what I usually say to clients. Research shows that emotion can not only colour our judgement, but also affect the way we react. Frustration, anger, resentment, hurt and irritability at high levels are likely to make communication worse, affecting our ability to deal with interpersonal difficulties such as criticism or conflict and to get the message across clearly. For example, Andy was angry at being treated unfairly and disrespectfully by his boss, who was ten years younger than him and had less management experience than him. While he was so angry, not only was he unable to think rationally, but also he lost control over his behaviour. When he became less emotional, he started to feel ashamed of himself and wished that he had not behaved in the way he had. However, it was too late and the damage was done. He lost his job. An awareness of your emotional state (e.g. anger, irritability, frustration) is an art in communication (see the section on 'Emotional awareness' in Chapter 19 'Developing effective communication skills', pp. 173–175).

Bad communication

In order to be a better communicator, we need to know that bad communication involves a refusal to share your feelings openly or to listen to what the other person has to say. It may be difficult for an emotional person *not* to do it. For example, while Jeremy was so hurt and angry, he did not allow his wife to say anything nor would he listen to what she tried to say. Jeremy was shouting at the top of his voice, insisting that his wife listened to him. In the end, she became extremely upset and started crying. Jeremy felt guilty about the hurt he was causing her and ashamed of his behaviour. 'I behaved like a child having a tantrum,' said Jeremy. He condemned himself as a bad person. These people are slaves to their emotions rather than being the masters. Similarly, individuals who are anxious and worried about what others think about them have a problem being truthful about their feelings to others. A few years ago, a client said that she would not 'allow people to get close to her or find out anything about her' because she didn't want others to think less of her or reject her.

Burns (1999) provides a list of fifteen characteristics of bad communication and suggests that we need to be more aware of what *not* to do when we are trying to resolve a conflict with someone, to say 'no' to a request, or to deal with a criticism (whether it is constructive or not). Recognising those characteristics that get us into trouble and changing them can make a remarkable difference to the way we relate to people in different interpersonal settings. It also saves us endless emotional upset. Below is the description of twelve of these characteristics of bad communication. More information on them can be found in the excellent *Feeling good handbook* (Burns 1999).

- **Truth** – You insist that you're right and the other person is wrong.
- **Blame** – You say that it is the other person's fault or that he or she is the cause of the problem. You refuse to accept that you may also have

contributed to the problem. For example, 'We did not enjoy the party as much as we would have liked. It was his fault.'

- **Put-down** – You label the other person as 'a loser, a failure, stupid or useless' because he or she always or never does certain things. For example, 'You never learn from your mistakes, what a loser you are!'
- **Denial** – You insist that you don't feel anger, hurt, envy or jealousy when you really do. You don't want others to find out your true feelings. For example, 'My husband left me for a younger woman after fifteen years, but it doesn't upset me at all.'
- **Passive-aggression** – You sulk, withdraw or say nothing. You may storm out of the room or slam doors.
- **Self-blame** – You blame yourself for the problem or situation which may not have anything to do with you. For example, 'My 16-year-old son is not doing well at school. It is entirely my fault. I am not a good mother.'
- **Helping** – You try to solve the problem for the person, which may come across as controlling, domineering or patronising. For example, 'It is so simple and straightforward; you should do it like that.'
- **Sarcasm** – You say the exact opposite of what you think in order to mock another person. Sarcasm expresses scorn, disapproval or annoyance. For example, 'How unselfish you are,' said a girl as her brother took the biggest piece of cake.
- **Defensiveness** – You attempt to justify your actions when criticised or when expecting criticism. For example, 'I always do it this way. There is nothing wrong with it.'
- **Defensive counterattack** – Instead of acknowledging how the other person feels or a suggestion that the person has made, you respond to his criticism by criticising him. For example, 'Well, you've done the same thing to me plenty of times. What is the problem?'
- **Diversion** – Instead of dealing with the emotional issue or the problem here and now, you divert attention and talk about something else. For example, 'How about going out for a walk? The weather is nice.'
- **Scapegoating** – You suggest that a person, a group of people, or something else is responsible for the problem and it has nothing to do with you. You're not involved in the problem. For example, 'People from Eastern Europe are responsible for ruining the health care system of the UK.'

Homework

Benedict was asked to:

- Read a chapter on 'Good and bad communication' in Burns (1999).
- Read the fifteen characteristics of bad communication and identify his most frequently used types of bad communication.

- Rate those fifteen characteristics of bad communication on a scale of 1 to 10 (1 is least like me and 10 is most like me).
- Keep a diary to identify the frequency with which the most common types of bad communication were used (e.g. event, what did you say or do, forms of bad communication, others' response).

Notes for therapists about good and bad communication

- Good communication is about expressing feelings openly and honestly and allowing the other person to do the same.
- Bad communication is about refusing to share feelings openly or to listen to what the other person has to say.
- Effective communication is not just about what to say but also how to say it.
- Timing, emotional state, and 'right and wrong' can affect how things are expressed.
- Skills training (e.g. social, assertive) in the form of role-play and demonstrations in CBT sessions can make a great difference to the way clients relate to others in everyday situations, thereby giving them confidence and saving them endless emotional misery.

Chapter 19

Developing effective communication skills

Being a people pleaser, Susan always worried about upsetting people, especially her husband. When her husband came home from work, he didn't say much, looked grumpy, and sat in front of the television for the whole evening. She didn't know what had happened or what the trouble was. She was anxious and tense, wondering whether she had done anything to upset him. When she asked him if he was upset with her, he responded in an irritated tone of voice: 'I am not upset with you. Don't be so sensitive. Why don't you leave me alone?' Susan did not know what to say and left the room in tears. Rose had not answered the phone and opened her mail for three weeks. She was anxious and nervous about people contacting her about the work she had promised to do. She said:

> I am struggling. There is so much to do. I feel guilty for not being able to do the things I promised to do. I just find it difficult saying 'no'. I want to, but I don't know what to say or how to say it.

Rose had been the treasurer at a church for many years and was actively involved in church activities. She was a popular, friendly person and was good at what she did, which made her the first port of call for help for many of her friends. However, being a mother of three young children, she found it increasingly difficult to meet other people's requests or needs. As a result, she was anxious about going out, answering calls or opening the mail in case people asked her a favour. She felt guilty about saying 'no' and letting people down. Karl did not have a good relationship with his father, who was described as a cold, controlling and domineering person. Although they worked together in the same company, which his father owned, there was little communication between the two of them, even at a business level. They often 'talked' to each other either through their secretaries or by email. 'He was unsupportive in a meeting last Friday. He did not give me any credit for what I had done, but criticised me in front of other people for what I had done wrong. I felt stupid and incompetent,' said Karl, who was angry with his father for being critical and unsupportive and with himself for not defending himself. He said: 'I wish I knew how to deal with criticism. He puts me down and undermines my self-confidence.'

These examples illustrate how poor communication or an inability to communicate well in social, work and family situations can affect people's self-confidence and self-esteem. Some clients may even stigmatise themselves for being weak, useless, stupid or incompetent. Self-stigmatisation is likely to make their mental health problems worse, causing them to feel pessimistic about their chances of recovery.

Interpersonal difficulties are believed to be an important contributing factor in the development and continuation of mental health problems such as depression, anxiety disorders, eating disorders, bipolar disorders or schizophrenia. Clients' low self-esteem and poor self-image are likely to be maintained by their efforts not only to avoid dealing with difficult situations, but also to please other people, to avoid criticism and get recognition and acceptance. Note that some clients want to change the way they communicate with people, but do not know how. Therapists' support is vital to develop their confidence and skills in order to help them be better communicators.

Cognitive behaviour therapy approach to developing effective communication skills

Cognitive behaviour therapy takes the view that helping clients to learn to deal with difficult situations and be at ease in social situations is just as important as modifying their negative thoughts about self, others, events and the future. Being able to do so is beneficial to clients with low self-esteem and poor self-image. It also helps them realise that their unhelpful behaviour (e.g. avoiding saying 'no' to unreasonable requests or pleasing people to avoid criticism or rejection) is *not* a personality trait but is acquired through learning. As such, these behaviours can be changed through improving their ability to communicate.

The CBT treatment approach is to identify clients' deficits in communication and to explore ways to help them communicate with someone who refuses to talk to them or is stubborn and argumentative; and deal with someone who is hostile, critical, judgemental and manipulative, or puts them on the spot and makes unreasonable demands. Being confident and skilful in communication is closely related to the therapist and the client working together (see Chapter 6 on 'A shared responsibility approach in the change process'). Without the support of therapists helping clients develop skills and confidence, it is difficult for them to become better communicators. If clients do not put learning into use or practice, it is difficult to develop confidence and effective communication skills. This is similar to people learning to swim; they need to practise in the pool, after demonstrations by the instructor.

Emotional awareness

An awareness of your emotions at the time of dealing with a difficult situation (e.g. a disagreement) can make a considerable difference to how well you get the message across and to how receptive you are to listening and understanding a different point of view. Anger, frustration, anxiety or guilt at high levels can not only affect your judgement, but can also affect your ability to communicate effectively.

The case of Jason

Part of Jason's job was to handle customer complaints. 'You have to keep cool and be seen as helpful when dealing with a complaint. Being able to see things from their perspective is important,' said Jason. One evening, he and Wendy were happily discussing their forthcoming wedding, which they were very much looking forward to. However, the conversation soon turned into an argument over how much would be considered reasonable to spend on the wedding, who should be invited and where they could go on their honeymoon. Jason felt annoyed and frustrated about Wendy's insistence that the wedding should be a 'big' one. 'If we are going to make it "big", we will be in debt and may not be able to buy a house. Surely, we need to be sensible and get our priorities right,' said Jason, who was trying to be reasonable and get her to see things from his perspective. However, Wendy felt that as the wedding was a once-in-a-lifetime experience it was worthwhile making the occasion as memorable as possible. 'If you really love me and respect how I feel about the wedding, you wouldn't be so mean. If we can't buy a house now, it is not a big deal. We can buy it later. We both have good jobs,' said Wendy, who was upset and not happy at all that buying a house should take priority over their wedding.

'She is just so stubborn and unreasonable,' said Jason, who was becoming emotional and was about to explode. His muscles tightened, his face went red and he was uncomfortable. He clenched his fists and his voice got louder. At this point, not only did he refuse to listen, but he also started to shout and criticise her for being difficult to reason with. Wendy was extremely upset and started crying. Jason didn't comfort her, but instead walked out and slammed the door behind him. 'I lost my cool. I should have stopped talking to her when things did not go well,' said Jason, who felt guilty about the hurt he was causing her and he was ashamed of his behaviour.

'I should have stopped talking to her when things did not go well' really means that it is best *not* to talk or communicate any more when emotions are running high. Note that an awareness of the expressive features of each emotion is important in the communication process. For example, the features of anger can include a red or flushed face, feeling nervous or uncomfortable, tightening of muscles, clenching of fists, or using a loud voice. These features serve as a warning signal that 'it is time to stop talking or arguing before things go from bad to worse'. The example of Jason illustrated how important it is to be aware of this warning signal when the 'talk' is not going well. 'When things are getting too hot, get out of the kitchen' is my advice. The benefit of 'get out of the kitchen' is to allow you to cool down, to prevent an escalation of the emotional upset, and to work out a better way to handle the situation. For example, Jason could have suggested, 'We are both getting too emotional, let's cool down before we talk again. Is that okay?' before removing himself: going out for a walk or going into another room. Note the use of 'we are both getting too emotional' rather than 'you are getting too emotional'. The latter sounds critical and judgemental.

An emotional awareness of the expressive features of other emotions (e.g. guilt, shame, sadness) can make a considerable difference to the way we communicate (Linehan 1993). Table 19.1 shows the expressive features of different emotions.

Communication skills

In a survey of recruiters from companies with more than 50,000 employees, communication skills were cited as the single most important decisive factor in choosing managers. The survey, conducted by the University of Pittsburgh's Katz Business School, points out that communication skills and an ability to work with others are the main factors contributing to job success. In spite of the increasing importance placed on communication skills, many individuals continue to struggle and are unable to communicate their thoughts and feelings effectively.

For people with mental health problems, being able to communicate thoughts and feelings effectively in social, work and family situations is one of the main contributing factors to their recovery. This is important not only for clients' self-confidence and self-esteem, but also for how they respond to therapy. Although negative thinking is seen as the primary cause of mental health problems, an ability to communicate is a key factor for self-confidence and self-esteem, which, in turn, can affect the way clients think (realistically or negatively) and react. Cognitive behaviour therapy believes that in order to help clients reintegrate into society, cope with stress in daily life and prevent relapse, helping them develop their ability to communicate effectively and confidently in interpersonal settings should be part of the treatment focus. Active listening, disarming technique, empathy, enquiry

Table 19.1 Emotional awareness

Emotion	Expressive (observable) features
Anger, frustration or irritability	• Tightness or rigidity in the body • Flushed face or getting hot • Nervous tension, anxiety or discomfort • Feeling as if going to explode • Muscles tightening • Wanting to hit, bang the wall, throw something or blow up • Loud voice, yelling, screaming or shouting • Clenching hands or fists • Withdrawing from contact with others
Sadness	• Tired, run-down or low in energy • Lethargic • Crying, tears, moaning • Feeling empty • Low, quiet, slow or monotonous voice
Fear or anxiety	• Sweating • Feeling nervous or jumpy • Shaking or trembling • Choking sensation, lump in the throat • Muscles tightening • Feeling sick • Breathlessness or breathing fast • A shaky or trembling voice
Shame	• Sense of dread • Blushing, hot, red face • Wanting to hide or cover your face • Eyes down • Apologising
Guilt	• Apologising • Eyes down • Try to compensate by being nice and generous • Self-critical

and 'I feel' statements are some useful communication skills that the client can practise in CBT sessions (with the therapist) and in everyday situations.

Technique: Active listening

'I don't think that you're interested in what I am saying. Do you want me to come back some other time?' said a student, who came for academic supervision. I was taken aback by what she said, then responded in a reassuring tone of voice, 'Of course, I am interested in what you have been saying. I can repeat everything that you have said to me so far.' The student was right to point out that while she was talking, I was busy doing other things such as checking my diary, opening the drawers, going through some papers on the desk and looking at my watch. I hardly looked at or engaged with her. If I were in her position, would I have had the same impression that 'my teacher is not interested in me or in what I am saying'? I am afraid the impression would have been the same. She then said, 'I am sure you are able to repeat what I have said, but you're not listening.' 'What is the difference?' I said to myself.

There is a real difference between merely hearing the words and listening for the message. Research shows people speak at 100 to 175 words per minute, but they can listen intelligently at 600 to 800 words per minute. This means that only a part of our mind is involved in communication and it is easy to go into mind drift: thinking about and doing other things while listening to someone. Not only will we be unable to fully understand what the person is saying, but it is also disrespectful to that person. My student was right to assert that I wasn't listening, even though I had heard and could repeat the words. When we actively listen for the message, we understand not only the meaning of the words, but also the feelings or intent beyond the words. In other words, we listen with a purpose. It may be to gain information, obtain direction, understand others, solve problems, share an interest, see how another person feels, show support, etc. Active listening allows us to stand in that person's position (or in the other person's shoes), see through his or her eyes and listen through his or her ears. Active listening involves:

- Giving the speaker your full attention.
- Watching the person's non-verbal communication or body language. Are they looking away or fidgeting?
- Showing that you are listening through attentive body language such as smiling appropriately, gestures, eye contact and posture.
- Not interrupting.
- Checking your understanding by 'paraphrasing' – repeating what the person said in your *own* words. For example, 'Am I correct that you have said . . . ?'
- Checking how the person is feeling behind the words. For example, 'You look really upset when you say that' or 'It sounds like that made you really angry.'
- Not staying totally silent – add in simple and brief words (e.g. 'I see') or a sound to show you are listening like 'Oh. Ah'.

An effective way of dealing with conflict or difficult situations is by not being defensive, counterattacking, sarcastic, or jumping to conclusions, but by listening first. Active listening is a very effective *first* response when the other person is angry, hurt or expressing hard feelings towards you, especially in relationships that are important to you. Active listening helps you to identify areas of agreement for the disarming technique (discussed below) to be used and gives you time to think about ways of resolving areas of disagreement. When the disagreement is put into perspective and dealt with rather than being magnified through bad communication, it helps to keep costly, time-consuming misunderstandings to a minimum (see Chapter 18 on 'Good and bad communication').

Without interruption, the person being listened to is likely to think more rationally, be less emotionally upset and more willing to consider an alternative view. This helps soften his or her position. Active listening may also have the effect of helping the person realise the fault in his or her reasoning or argument and recognise the different levels of expectation that are going on below the surface. This helps to bring things into the open where they can be more readily resolved.

Technique: Disarming

Active listening (discussed above) illustrates that if you want to be listened to, then listen to the other person first. Similarly, if you want respect, you have to give respect first. These examples illustrate the basic concept of the disarming technique, which is regarded as one of the most important techniques in good and effective communication. When you have a strong disagreement, a conflict with someone, or are being unfairly criticised, you may have an urge to defend yourself or argue with the other person. When you're angry or feeling hurt, a voice inside your head will be screaming, 'Don't let him get away with this.' When emotions (e.g. anger, hurt) are running high, you're likely to give in to the voice and start a pointless and frustrating battle. Not only will you be unable to deal with the disagreement, conflict and criticism effectively, but you may also end up wasting a lot of emotional energy and damaging your emotional health. You may then either criticise yourself for being so useless or feel sorry for yourself. Burns (1999: p. 378) asserts that 'arguing with a critic almost never works. Agreeing with a critic almost always builds rapport. The effects can be quite magical!'

Disarming technique is about *not* arguing with the other person, but is about finding out what you can agree with in what the person said. Your own viewpoint may be different and you may not necessarily agree with everything, but as you listen, you understand the other person's perspective and may therefore be able to find a convincing way to agree, no matter how unreasonable the person's criticism might seem to you. Epictetus, a Greek Stoic philosopher, started the idea of disarming technique nearly 2,000 years ago when he wrote: 'If you hear somebody has criticised you, do not bother with excuses or defences but agree with them at once. Tell the person that if only s/he knew you well, s/he would not bother to criticise only that!' In other words, it is all right to agree with some of the criticism or the entire criticism, if there is some truth in it. Epictetus cautioned us not to be afraid of the criticism of others. Only the morally weak feel the need to defend or explain themselves to others. Furthermore, we can't control the impressions of others, and the effort of defending ourselves only demeans us. Note that agreeing with a valid criticism is not a sign of weakness. It is a sign of courage for which you will gain respect.

If you agree with some of the criticism or the entire criticism in a sincere way, it can have a profound and sudden calming effect on the other person, who is likely to be more willing to listen, less likely to argue and put you down. Areas of agreement and disagreement can be brought to the surface where they can be readily resolved. For example, your husband criticised you for being too emotional and overreacting all the time: 'Why don't you use a little logic and be a bit more rational?' If there was some truth in what he said, you could say, 'I agree with you. I sometimes overreact and get illogical and irrational. I am working on it.' You could then go on to say, 'But I am afraid that I can't agree with you that I am too emotional and overreacting all the time.' This important technique needs to be practised over and over again before you can become good at it.

Technique: Empathy (the foundation of emotional coaching)

'You don't understand how I feel,' a client said in a resentful and irritated tone of voice. 'Don't try to be clever with me.' 'What does he mean by "Don't try to be clever with me"?' I said to myself. I did not know what I had said or done to provoke such a response from him. What was wrong with being empathic ('I understand how you feel') to his complaint?

This client complained that it had taken too long before he received cognitive behaviour therapy for his anger problem. His general practitioner was very concerned about the impact of his anger and aggressive behaviour on his heart condition, thus referring him for anger management and low self-esteem. He had recently had a stroke and had had a heart bypass operation a year earlier. He was told that unless he did something about his anger he might have a heart attack and die. His anger problem had not only taken a toll on his heart, but also affected his relationships with others such as neighbours, friends and relatives. His wife and children were scared of him and they tried to keep conversation to a minimum so as not to provoke him. He said that he was lonely and didn't have anybody to talk to. He didn't like people saying that they understood how he felt in response to his anger and believed that they were trying to be 'clever with him'. It was therefore not surprising that he responded to my empathic response in the way he did. It seems that expressing empathy is not just saying, 'I understand how you feel'. The dialogue below illustrates the use of empathic skills:

Therapist:	What's wrong with people saying 'I understand how you feel'?
Client:	They don't. How can they understand my feelings? They are not me.
Therapist:	True, they are not you. How does it make you feel when they say that?
Client:	Angry.
Therapist:	Because of?
Client:	They are trying to be clever with me.
Therapist:	Meaning?
Client:	You know what I mean. Don't try to be clever with me.
Therapist:	When I use this phrase, I know exactly what I mean. I don't know what *you* mean when you say it. But I am willing to listen.
Client:	Oh. They look down on me, thinking I am stupid and useless. They are trying to make fun of me.
Therapist:	How does it make you feel?
Client:	Angry.
Therapist:	When people say they understand how you feel, you become angry because you believe that they look down on you, in the sense you are stupid and useless. It is not fair and right for them to think of you in this way. When you believe this is how people make fun of you, it can make you mad. [Note the use of thought empathy]
Client:	Yes.
Therapist:	That's why you said: 'Don't try to be clever with me'.
Client:	Yes.
Therapist:	You were angry with me because you thought that I looked down on you or tried to make fun of you.
Client:	Yes.
Therapist:	When you believe this, you become angry. When you are angry, you shout and may even be aggressive in a physical way. People are scared of you and are anxious about upsetting you. They therefore say as little to you as possible and try to keep their distance. In a way, your anger and aggressive behaviour drives them away. We can now understand why you feel lonely and do not have many people to talk to. [Note the use of action empathy]
Client:	Oh. Ah. You're right about what you said. You really understand how I feel.

There were signs of relief in his eyes that he was really being understood and that I wasn't looking down on him or trying to make fun of him. I genuinely understood what was going through his mind that made him angry, which in turn affected his reactions. He was calmer and more responsive as I was using the empathic skills to show my understanding of his anger, not just simply saying, 'I understand how you feel.'

Empathy is often characterised as the ability to 'put oneself into another's shoes', or experiencing the emotions of another being within oneself. This is quite difficult to understand, let alone to be able to do. How can we 'put ourselves into another's shoes'? Does saying 'I understand how you feel' mean that you're putting yourself into another's shoes? When you say that you understand how they feel, some clients may cast doubt over how much you really understand, whereas others may perceive it as similar to when people say, 'Have a good day.' In other words, you (the therapist) don't really understand how they feel. Some clients may even take it as offensive, as illustrated by the client above.

Empathy is commonly defined as one's ability to recognise, perceive and feel the emotion of another. We can recognise, perceive and feel another's emotions through observing their *behaviour and actions*. For example, when someone uses a loud voice (yells, screams or shouts), throws or breaks things or slams doors, you know they are angry. When someone is in tears, feels tired, is lethargic, is not interested in doing things or in socialising, you know they may be feeling sad. When someone asks for forgiveness and tries to make up for some wrongdoing, they may feel ashamed or guilty. Alternatively, we can recognise, perceive and feel another's emotions through their *thinking and thought*. For example, if someone believes that they are being treated unfairly or being taken for granted, they are likely to feel angry. If someone has done something ethically or morally wrong, they may feel ashamed or guilty. If someone believes that something bad or terrible is about to happen, they may be fearful or anxious. These examples show that empathy cannot be adequately reflected in a simple statement: 'I understand how you feel.'

In order to understand the client's emotions, it is important to demonstrate that understanding either through *thought empathy*, *action empathy*, or both (illustrated in the dialogue above). Thought empathy is about paraphrasing the other person's thoughts or beliefs that are causing the emotion. For example, you are angry because you believe that the person does not respect you or takes advantage of you. Action empathy is about specifying what behaviour is caused by a particular emotion. For example, you shouted, threw things and then walked out of the room because you were so angry about what the person said. Putting them together, we can say, 'You were so upset emotionally (angry, hurt, anxious or guilty) because you believed that . . . [thought empathy], that's why you reacted in the way you did [action empathy], is that right?' A good understanding of the connection between thinking, emotion and behaviour helps with developing effective empathic skills. (This is illustrated in the next chapter in Table 20.2.)

Technique: Enquiry

Enquiry is a useful skill for learning more about what the other person is thinking and feeling in order to bring things out in the open where problems or misunderstandings can be more readily resolved. Some clients find it very hard to express their (painful) feelings and choose not to think or talk about them, in the hope that these feelings will diminish with time, whereas some don't want to admit that they feel hurt. Others may not feel comfortable finding out what the other person is feeling because they do not know what to say to help the person who is angry or in distress (e.g. bereavement).

'It hurts to talk about these feelings. I am so confused,' said Sarah, who was one of identical twins brought up in a wealthy and competitive family. Her father was a successful novelist. Out of the twelve books he had written, five were best-sellers. Her mother was a prominent politician whose job required her to travel extensively. Sarah described her parents as loving and caring, but they didn't have much time for her and her sister, Emily, when they were young. Because her parents were so successful, there was pressure on the twins to do well. She and Emily went to the same private school but were in different classes. Emily was a sporty, active and friendly person with many friends, whereas Sarah was introverted and had only a few friends. Her parents tried to treat them both the same, but it didn't come across as such to Sarah. Rivalry, jealousy, envy, resentment, hurt and anger were some of the emotions she felt, but she was confused about having these feelings and was reluctant to talk about them. The dialogue below shows the use of enquiry skills (Table 19.2) and the words in parentheses indicate the type of enquiry skill being used.

Therapist:	You said that you are confused about having these feelings. Can you tell me more . . . ? (Encouraging)
Sarah:	I don't want to talk about it. It is just too painful.
Therapist:	It is difficult, isn't it? (Validating)
Sarah:	It is.
Therapist:	Will the pain and the problem go away just because you don't want to talk about it? (Clarifying)
Sarah:	Oh, I suppose not.
Therapist:	Have you considered that there may be benefits in talking about it, however painful it may be? (Building)
Sarah:	Ah. No.
Therapist:	One thing we can be sure of is that the problem and the pain are unlikely to go away, just because you don't want to talk about it. The longer you try to hide them, the bigger the problem will be and the more pain you will experience. Is this what you want? (Summarising)

Table 19.2 Enquiry skills

Enquiry skill	Purpose	Example
Encouraging	To encourage the other person to keep talking	Can you tell me more . . . ?
Clarifying	To help you clarify what is said	Are you saying . . . ? What do you mean by . . . ?
Reflecting	To show that you understand how the other person feels	You seem quite keen about this idea. You look sad about . . .
Summarising	To review progress	Let me make sure I understand you . . . These problems seem to be . . .
Validating	To acknowledge the worthiness of the other person	I appreciate your willingness to share this difficult issue with me.
Building	To offer other opinions/options	Have you considered . . . ?

Sarah:	No.
Therapist:	Would you like to feel better and have less of this emotional pain?
Sarah:	Yes. I really would, but I am scared.
Therapist:	While you are feeling scared, I also notice that you want to do something about it. (Reflecting)
Sarah:	I do. I really do.
Therapist:	Can you tell me more about your confusion? (Encouraging)

Some clients don't want to talk about their painful feelings or to open 'the box' and let all the nasty monsters out because of the pain. However, these painful feelings can get stronger and become more destructive if they are allowed to stay unchallenged inside the person's system. A few years ago, an American lawyer said that she would only open the lid if I could guarantee that I would be able to put all the 'worms' back into the box. Paradoxically, keeping the 'worms' in the box had actually inflicted more pain on her.

Not only is enquiry used to learn more about how the other person is thinking and feeling, but it can also help you to be more proactive in dealing with a problem or an issue in a more productive manner. Suppose you are trying to get a promotion and your boss is not sure whether you have sufficient experience for the job. Using the enquiry skill, you can ask, 'What kind of experience do you feel I lack?' This helps clarify the requirements for the promotion, prepare you for the challenge and improve your market-ability. It will also demonstrate your ability to listen and learn.

Technique: 'I . . .' statements

When dealing with a disagreement or a conflict, it is more effective to express your feelings using 'I . . .' statements. For example, 'I feel angry', 'I feel put down', I prefer' or 'I wish that you'. These statements are in sharp contrast to 'You . . .' statements which can make the disagreement or the conflict worse. Ask yourself how you would respond, when you find yourself getting defensive or argumentative. Do you find yourself using some or all of the following expressions?

- You're wrong about that.
- You don't care about anything.
- You've no right to say that.
- You're stupid and incompetent for making such a simple mistake.
- You make me angry. You're so inconsiderate.
- You obviously don't care about anyone but yourself.
- You're wrong about this. You're such a stupid jerk.

If you are a frequent user of the 'You . . .' statements, you may have a problem communicating your thoughts and feelings to others in an appropriate manner. This is particularly so when you have a strong disagreement, a conflict with someone, or are being unfairly criticised. Perhaps by putting yourself on the receiving end of the 'You . . .' statements, you would be able to see how you would feel and how it would affect how you would react. You may feel angry, irritable and hurt because these 'You . . .' statements can come across as critical, blaming and judgemental. You feel that you have to defend yourself even if the other person has a point, is fair or reasonable. 'You have no right to talk to me like that', 'You hurt me', 'You're so unfair', or 'You put me down' may well be what you would say in return. In the end, the communication doesn't get anywhere, as each person is attacking or blaming the other: 'I am right and you are wrong.'

People have immense trouble expressing anger, hurt, resentment, frustration or jealousy in an appropriate and assertive manner. These emotions can colour their judgement and affect their behaviour. We learn to attack when we're angry, hurt, or frustrated or we act out our feelings instead of expressing them openly. It's far easier to attack or blame rather than saying, 'I feel annoyed about this, let's talk it out.' 'I . . .' statements are an effective way of telling the other person that you are not happy and that you want to sort things out in a civilised way. These statements do not give the impression that you are critical, blaming or judgemental. Note that good communication is not about right or wrong, or winning or losing an argument. It is about expressing your feelings and preferences and not pushing the point to try to win an argument (see Chapter 18 on 'Good and bad communication').

Homework

The following homework is helpful in developing effective communication skills:

- Read the chapter on 'The five secrets of intimate communication' in Burns (1999).
- Read the chapter on 'How to deal with difficult people' in Burns (1999).
- Keep a diary of events in which each of these good communication skills was used and, to indicate how effectively it was used, on a scale of 1 to 100.

Notes for therapists about developing effective communication skills

- Being able to communicate thoughts and feelings effectively is a contributing factor to clients' recovery from mental health problems.
- An ability to communicate is a key factor in building self-confidence and self-esteem.
- Therapists' support and encouragement is vital to clients' developing effective communication skills.

Part V

Therapeutic approach

Skills and techniques

Chapter 20

Assessment skills

Assessment and cognitive case formulation

Some mental health professionals tend to make diagnoses by classifying symptoms within different categories, based on a selection of symptoms or behaviours. Making a diagnosis helps a doctor to assess what treatment is needed and to predict what is likely to happen. It can also be a relief to the client with a mental health problem to be able to put a name to what is wrong. However, each client's experience of mental distress is unique and it can be misread, especially if there are cultural, social or religious differences between doctor (or therapist) and client. Different doctors may give the same client completely different diagnoses. Simply focusing on the symptoms or on identifying the symptoms to make a psychiatric diagnosis can mean that not enough attention is paid to the client as a whole. It fails to take into account the way in which personal, social, family and work experiences contribute to the development and continuation of mental health problems. Medical diagnosis may therefore be too simplistic or mechanical in the description and understanding of the person's symptoms or problems (Lam 2004). If a diagnosis becomes a stigmatising label (e.g. bipolar disorder), it can be damaging, demoralising and confusing for the client with mental distress, which in turn may affect his or her engagement with and response to treatment.

It has been suggested that a useful approach to assessing the client's mental health problem (e.g. depression) is to understand how symptoms (e.g. tearfulness, withdrawal, lack of concentration, problems in sleeping) of the problem developed and what factors (e.g. psychological, social and environmental) are involved in the continuation of these symptoms. In the assessment therapists can pay attention to the client as a whole by assessing the client's background, presenting problems and current functioning, psychiatric diagnoses, previous treatment success and/or failure, educational development, family dynamics and relationships, developmental profile and crises, cognitive profile, and the client's self-perception and belief about the cause and nature of their mental health problem (Lam 2005). Assessment data from these areas enables the development of a cognitive case formulation, which helps not only to understand the client's mental health problem better, but also to develop appropriate treatment strategies for the problem.

The ABC model for assessment

The ABC model described in Chapter 1 is useful for the assessment of various areas as outlined above. 'A' is known as an activating event (e.g. divorce), 'C' is the emotional response (e.g. anger, depression) and reactions of the individual (e.g. self-blame, blaming others). According to cognitive behaviour therapy theory, a divorce (A) does not cause the person to be depressed or to blame self and others (C). It is the person's beliefs about the divorce (B) that are largely responsible for the emotional and behavioural reactions (C). For example, if a person experiences depression after a divorce, it may not be the divorce itself that causes the depressive reactions but the person's beliefs about the divorce: being a failure, being responsible for the cause of the divorce and being unable to find another partner. Otherwise, everybody going through a divorce would end up with depression.

We know that the way we think (positively or negatively) about an event can affect our mood and our behaviour. Similarly, our emotional state (anger or happiness) can affect the way we think and the way in which the event is dealt with. The way we deal with the event (in an aggressive or friendly manner) can in turn affect our state of mind and our emotional state in a circular fashion. Researchers in the United States showed that emotion plays a part in making judgements between right and wrong, fairness and unfairness. Judgements are coloured by emotion, rather than by the application of thinking alone. This helps to explain why people are not wholly rational. For example, if Patrick felt that he was being treated unfairly, he tended to respond to the situation or other person angrily. The emotion of anger tended to have a negative impact on the way he perceived the situation or other person and on the way he reacted. While he was so angry, not only was he unable to think rationally, but his anger also perpetuated a negative view of the situation or other person unjustifiably, thereby affecting his judgement. This circular relationship between thinking, emotion and behaviour thus provides a useful assessment framework to understand the way in which the symptoms of a mental health problem (e.g. depression) have developed and what factors are involved in the continuation of these symptoms (e.g. problems in sleeping, difficulty in getting out of bed, withdrawal, poor concentration or memory, tearfulness).

Technique: Socratic questioning

An accurate assessment is important to the way in which the therapist works with the client and to the treatment success. Effective questioning skills help to understand and clarify what the client thinks about and how he or she reacts to an emotional situation. Take thinking as an example: there are two possible ways in which the client's *thinking* about an upsetting or anxious event (e.g. doing a presentation) can be determined. We can use one of the following:

- The client's emotional experience ('What were you thinking about the presentation that made you anxious [E → **T**]?')
- The client's behaviour ('When you were having a problem concentrating on your work, what thoughts did you have about the presentation [B → **T**]?')

A similar approach can be used to assess clients' **emotional** state using either their thinking (T → **E**) or their behaviour (B → **E**). By the same token, clients' **behaviour** or reactions to an emotional event can also be recognised using their thinking (T → **B**) or their emotion (E → **B**). Note that the letter in bold indicates a target area for assessment. For example, **T** means thinking is being assessed. Note also that the formula (T → **B**) means that behaviour (**B**) is being assessed using the client's thinking (T). Table 20.1 shows questioning skills for the assessment of thoughts, emotions and behaviour, using the ABC model framework. The case of Jack, described below, shows how an assessment is conducted using a range of questioning skills.

The case of Jack

Jack was asked to do a presentation on a project which he had been working on with a team of people for the past two years. The president of the company, who was visiting from the United States, was going to attend the presentation, along with some senior managers and some important customers. It was estimated that around 100 people would listen to the presentation. Jack said that 'he was stressed and couldn't cope'.

Therapist: When you were stressed, what was going through your mind about doing the presentation? [E → **T**]
Jack: I just thought what if I couldn't cope.
Therapist: Meaning what? [**T**]
Jack: People would see me as incompetent and not up to my job.
Therapist: And? [**T**]
Jack: If this was the case, I am not as good as I thought I was.
Therapist: Suppose this was so, how would it make you feel? [T → **E**]
Jack: Upset and disappointed.
Therapist: Because of? [E → **T**]

Table 20.1 Questioning skills

Target	Questioning skills
T	• What is going through your mind about the event (A)? • What thoughts do you have about the A? • What does it mean to you in relation to the A? • What are you thinking about the A?
T → E	• What is going through your mind about the A that makes you so . . . (upset, angry, or anxious)? • Suppose your thinking is correct, how does it make you feel? • What did you say to yourself that made you so . . . (upset, angry, or frustrated)?
T → B	• What did you do, when you believed that . . . ? • How would your thinking affect your behaviour at the time? • What was the impact on your relationship with . . . when you believed that . . . ?
E → A	• What did he say that you felt guilty about? • What was the situation like that you felt anxious about? • What did she say or do that you felt angry about?
E → B	• When you were so upset, what did you do at the time? • How did it affect your coping, when you were so angry? • How did your anxiety affect the way you coped at the time?
B → T	• By avoiding the situation, what was your thinking at the time? • What were your thoughts when you stayed in your 'shell'? • What were your thoughts about yourself when you made a fool of yourself?
B → E	• Would the way you behave make you feel better or worse? • How would you feel about not facing the anxiety-provoking situation? • How did you feel when you beat yourself up?

Jack: I must do it perfectly. I mustn't let people down, especially my manager who, like me, is a perfectionist and expects a lot of me.

Therapist: What if you couldn't do it perfectly, how did you feel about it? [T → **E**]

Jack: Angry, frustrated and irritable.

Therapist: And then what did you do, when you were feeling like that? [E → **B**]

Jack: I beat myself up and did not do much work for the presentation. I found it difficult to concentrate when I was emotionally tired. I upset my family with my irritable behaviour and shouted at them over little or trivial things.

Therapist: How did it make you feel? [B → **E**]

Jack: Terrible. I felt guilty and ashamed of my behaviour towards my family. They hadn't done anything to upset me. It was my fault.

Therapist:	What did you do, when you felt guilty and ashamed? [E → **B**]
Jack:	I apologised to them and tried to be nice. But I lost the plot again and again. In the end, my wife and my children were fed up with me saying 'sorry'. On a number of occasions, she was so upset she cried.
Therapist:	How did it make you feel? [B → **E**]
Jack:	Worse. I couldn't do the work for the presentation. I wasn't in the mood.
Therapist:	What went through your mind, when you weren't in the mood and didn't do much work for the presentation? [B → **T**]
Jack:	I just thought that if I didn't do it well, my future would suffer. Promotion would be out to start with. I might even lose my job, lose my home and . . .
Therapist:	How did these thoughts make you feel? [T → **E**]
Jack:	Scared, anxious and panicky. The more I thought about it, the worse it became.
Therapist:	How can we make sense of the whole thing? Is it the presentation or the way you think about it and your reaction that is the problem?
Jack:	Oh. Ah. Yes, it is not the presentation, isn't it?

This example of Socratic questioning illustrated that the problem with Jack being 'stressed and not being able to cope' might have little or nothing to do with the presentation itself (see Figure 20.1 on page 193). After all, he had been doing this project for two years and was good at what he did. His thoughts (e.g. incompetent, not up to the job, let people down, my future will suffer) about the presentation were the most likely cause of his stress and the way he reacted (e.g. beat himself up, found it difficult to concentrate, shouted at his family) could also have made the stress levels worse.

An effective use of questioning skills allows the therapist (and the client) not only to explore the thoughts, emotions and behaviour in relation to an emotional event, but also to understand how they interact with one another in the development and continuation of a mental health problem. Note that Socratic dialogue is a style of questioning that attempts to have clients discover the answers for themselves. The therapist asks questions that bring out information the client already knows but has not assimilated. Once the client is able to think objectively and rationally, the strength of his or her irrational thoughts weaken, leading to doubts about the authenticity of the thoughts. Jack realised and accepted that the problem had little or nothing to do with the presentation. His thoughts and reactions were largely the cause of his stress levels.

Table 20.2 illustrates the connection between thinking (thoughts), emotions (moods) and behaviour (reactions). An understanding of this

Table 20.2 Connection between thinking, emotion and behaviour

Emotion	Thoughts that lead to this emotion	Emotions that lead to this behaviour
Sadness or depression	You believe that the loss is so bad, so terrible, and such a catastrophe that life will never be the same again. There is nothing much you can do to change the situation. Thoughts of loss include: the death of a loved one, the loss of a job, or the failure to achieve an important goal.	• Tearfulness and withdrawal • Procrastination • Self-criticism • Self-harm
Anxiety, fear, nervousness or panic	You believe that you are in danger because you think something bad or terrible is about to happen and that you cannot cope with the threat. The threat can be related to social, work, health or bodily sensations.	• Withdrawing physically or mentally from the threat • Constantly seeking reassurance • Constantly checking to make sure that everything is all right • Experiencing uncomfortable bodily sensations such as heart pounding
Guilt	You believe that you have hurt someone or that you have failed to live up to your own moral and ethical standards. Guilt results in self-condemnation because you assume that.	• Begging forgiveness • Trying to compensate for what you did by being nice to people • Self-criticism/self-punishment
Shame	You believe that you have done something ethically and morally wrong and are anxious about people's reactions or about losing face when they find out.	• Removing self from the gaze of others • Isolating self from others • Saving face by attacking others • Hiding problems away from others
Anger, annoyance, irritation or frustration	You believe that life falls short of your expectations and insist that things should be different. It might be your own performance ('I shouldn't have made that mistake'), what someone else does ('He should have been on time'), or an event ('Why is the traffic always slow when I'm in a hurry?').	• Tantrums and aggressive behaviour • Quietness and withdrawal • Criticising others • Self-criticism
Worry	You feel uneasy or concerned about something that may happen in the future such as job, finance, and health of yourself and your family. You can also worry over more minor matters such as deadlines for appointments, keeping the house clean, and whether or not the workspace is properly organised.	• Restlessness • Muscle tension • Sleep disturbance • Difficulty in concentrating or the mind going blank • Difficulty in controlling worry

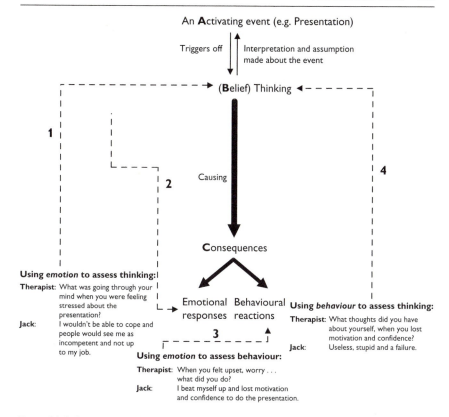

Figure 20.1 Socratic circular process of assessment

connection will make it easy for the therapist to know what to look for or expect when the client's thinking, emotion and behaviour is assessed. Following assessment, the next step in the therapeutic process is to dispute the client's irrational or negative thinking.

Notes for therapists about assessment skills

- Knowing the connection between thinking, emotion and behaviour (Table 20.2) is essential to the assessment, to cognitive case formulation and to the understanding of the client as a whole person.
- Socratic questioning skills help the therapist (and the client) understand the way in which thinking, emotion and behaviour interact with one another in the development and continuation of mental health problems.
- This circular relationship between thinking, emotion and behaviour thus provides a useful assessment framework for understanding the way in which the symptoms of a mental health problem developed and what factors are involved in the continuation of these symptoms.

Chapter 21

Disputing approach and techniques

Technique: Territory model (an effective disputing approach)

It is hardly surprising that disputing or trying to change the way clients think about their unhelpful thinking could be one of the most difficult parts of the therapeutic process. When challenged, clients are often able to support their thinking or beliefs with evidence, due to the selective and habitual nature of their thinking process. It has been suggested that if the client is resistant to change, the therapist can 'psychologically remove' the client from his or her subjective 'territory' to a 'different' psychological territory (Figure 21.1). When a disputing technique being used in the 'different territory' can highlight an experience or an example that the client can relate to, the client is likely to become more objective and less emotionally charged. This objective thinking would then act as a catalyst or a mirror for the client to reflect on his or her unhelpful way of thinking when the disputing is shifted back to the client's territory. This approach has the positive effect of reducing the client's resistance to change (Lam 1997; Lam and Gale 2004). Therapists often find it difficult to help those clients who are highly emotionally upset or those who seem to have evidence to support their way of thinking.

Some of my students often say that it is so difficult to change clients' negative thinking. Clients' negative thinking is obviously unhelpful, does not make sense and is detrimental to their mental health and their recovery. However, they can be resistant to change and may even argue with you, particularly when they are emotionally upset. Therapists often have trouble helping clients to make sense of an emotive event and are sometimes frustrated by not being able to change the way they perceive such an event. An ineffective therapeutic approach may cause frustration and despair to both the therapist and the client. An example of such a problem is shown as follows:

'It is not fair and right to say that my thoughts are irrational,' said a client who was not happy with her thoughts being described as irrational in

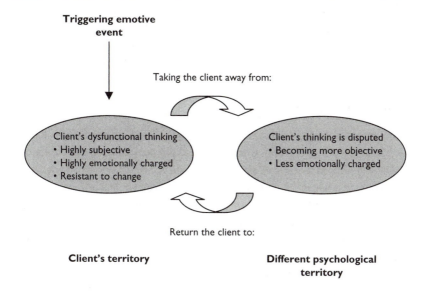

Figure 21.1 Territory model: effective dispute approach

nature. 'I do have evidence to support my beliefs.' In the eyes of the client, the emotional and upsetting thoughts or beliefs are both logical and rational and can, of course, be supported by some selective evidence that the client chooses to use. Aaron T. Beck (1976) describes these thoughts as plausible and automatic, specific and discrete, idiosyncratic and unhelpful. However, the client tends to believe in the authenticity of these thoughts and feels that her emotional upset is justifiable. For example, Sally was angry with her husband for coming home late from work and that he did not have the courtesy to let her know. Her husband was regarded as a good father and husband and a hard-working person, although he was a bit forgetful at times. When she was emotional, Sally believed that her husband was inconsiderate, unsupportive and did not appreciate how difficult it was to be a wife and mother. Such beliefs inevitably stirred up quite a bit of emotional upset which in turn caused her to be even more sensitive and selective to what her husband said and did. Not only did she look for supporting evidence for her beliefs, but she also chose to ignore any conflicting evidence about the circumstances in which the lateness occurred. There was a tendency for evidence from past events to be used to support her irrational way of thinking. For example, 'You were even late getting to our wedding. You don't care.' Their wedding took place ten years earlier. The tendency to use negative past events to support negative or irrational thinking about the present event is what I call the contamination of the present thinking by past events.

The idea of disputing the client's irrational thought in a different territory and then coming back to the client's territory or irrational thought to further the process of disputing it is an effective approach, which is illustrated using the case of Judith.

The case of Judith

Judith reported feeling guilty and depressed because of her inability to help her daughter (15 years old) with her geography schoolwork. She blamed herself and insisted that she was a failure, despite the fact that she had tried to help, contacted her daughter's teacher to air the problem and advised her to contact other friends. In a 'traditional' way of disputing (client's territory), I pointed out to her that she had done more than some parents would have done under the circumstances and therefore she should not view herself as a failure. Furthermore, how could she be a failure when she had a degree, a good job and a family? Not only had she discounted this evidence but she had also repeatedly come up with evidence that supported her unhelpful thinking. For example, 'I am a mother. I should be able to help her. She was shouting and stressed for not getting the help.'

Realising that it was pointless to try to convince her that she was not a failure, I decided to take her away from her territory and asked the question: if she talked to 100 mothers about not being able to help their daughters (same age) with their schoolwork (same subject), how many mothers would feel guilty and regard themselves as failures? The following dialogue shows the usefulness of pursuing the disputing at a different territory, before returning to the client's problem (client's territory).

Therapist:	Suppose, let us suppose, that you have talked to 100 mothers, how many would feel guilty and regard themselves as failures? [Note the use of 100 people technique]
Judith:	I don't know.
Therapist:	Would 100 per cent of them feel guilty and regard themselves as failures?
Judith:	I suppose not. It can't be 100 per cent, can it?
Therapist:	60 per cent, 70 per cent, or 80 per cent?
Judith:	I don't know, but I don't think it would be that high.
Therapist:	Good. I wonder why?
Judith:	Ah. Oh. I suppose not every mother would know or be good at all subjects at school. It is impossible. So long as they have tried to do whatever they can to help their children, it is good enough.

Therapist:	And?
Judith:	Well, their children are not young. You can't be protective of them all the time and do everything for them.
Therapist:	Absolutely. If these mothers have tried their best, would you regard them as failures?
Judith:	No. I would not.
Therapist:	Suppose your best friend was also in similar circumstances and you knew that she had tried hard to help her daughter, would you see her as a failure? [Note the use of best friend technique]
Judith:	Of course, she was not. How could she be a failure?
Therapist:	Because of?
Judith:	She loves her children and is good to them.
Therapist:	Do you love your daughter?
Judith:	Yes.
Therapist:	Are you good to her?
Judith:	Yes.
Therapist:	Have you tried to help her?
Judith:	Yes.
Therapist:	If this is so, how is it logical to say that your best friend and the other 100 mothers are not failures but you are? [Note that the dispute is shifting back to Judith's territory]
Judith:	Oh. I am too harsh on myself. You are right. How can I be a failure just because of that?
Therapist:	How helpful is it to be harsh on yourself and to call yourself a failure?
Judith:	It makes me anxious, feel guilty and depressed.

The Socratic dialogue, conducted within the framework of the 'Territory model', not only has the positive effect of lowering the levels of her emotional upset and reducing her resistance to change, but also helps her to develop a more reality-based thinking. An effective disputing approach is therefore closely related to the therapist being able to understand the rationale, the focus and the process of the technique being used.

Disputing techniques: rationale, focus and process

We can train somebody to be good and effective in the treatment of a mental health problem such as obsessive-compulsive disorder. However, to be good and effective in the treatment of a range of mental health problems, 'talent' is needed.

(Paul Salkovskis, Professor of Clinical Psychology and Applied Science at the Institute of Psychiatry at King's College and Clinical Director at the Centre for Anxiety Disorders and Trauma, Maudsley Hospital, said this when he was giving a speech at a conference: Salkovskis 2003.)

What Professor Salkovskis said did make sense. It is not that difficult to treat a mental health problem such as depression, obsessive-compulsive disorder, panic disorder, health anxiety or post-traumatic stress disorder. However, it is a challenge to be good and effective in the treatment of a range of mental health problems. 'What is it? How can it be obtained? Can we learn to be talented?' were some of my thoughts when I left the conference.

'Talent' is about being skilful in what we do, as in the case of a good bricklayer, an efficient accountant, an effective lawyer or a competent teacher. If a person has the knowledge and understanding to do a job but does not have the skills (or techniques), it means that the person is unlikely to be able to do the job or do the job well. Skills or techniques are something that can surely be learnt or developed. However, to be good and effective in the treatment of a range of mental health problems requires therapists not only to be creative and flexible in the use of a particular technique for a particular unhelpful thought, but also to be able to adapt the same technique for other thoughts. For example, the daughter's technique (Table 21.1) is effective in modifying the thoughts of a depressed client (e.g. 'I am a failure') but it can also be adapted to use with a client with low self-esteem (e.g. 'People do not like me') or with an anxious client (e.g. 'I can't cope').

Although an understanding of a specific CBT model for each mental health problem is important for the assessment and planning of treatment strategies, being able to be flexible and adaptable in the use of a technique is just as important in the change process. In CBT, knowing the rationale, the focus and the process of the particular technique to use is almost like having a 'map', which enables the therapist not only to effectively dispute an unhelpful thought, but also to adapt that technique for disputing other types of unhelpful thoughts. Note that a particular technique should not be exclusive to just one particular unhelpful thought. I am often asked by students what technique could be used for a particular unhelpful thought. 'You can use "almost" any one of the techniques that you have learnt about if you understand the rationale, the focus and the process of that technique,' is my usual response. A wide range of cognitive and behavioural techniques described in various sources (A. T. Beck and Emery 1995; J. S. Beck 1995; McMullin 2000; Leahy 2003) and the techniques and skills (Table 21.1) illustrated throughout this book may be adapted for use on different types of unhelpful thoughts.

The rationale for the 100 people or the best friend technique (illustrated above) is that given the same circumstances it was not logical that the other

Table 21.1 Disputing techniques

Chapter	Content	Technique
1	Mental illness stigma	The ABC model
2	Biological and genetic explanations of 'mental illness'	Developing an alternative explanation Costs and benefits analysis
3	Prejudice, discrimination and 'mental illness'	Balloon Confirmation
4	Cognitive behaviour therapy of emotional upset	100 people: developing an objective point of view 100 people: challenging negative labels
6	A shared responsibility approach in the change process	Education An athlete and a sports coach
7	Dealing with negative thoughts	Judge Law in the universe
8	Dealing with unhelpful behaviour	Swimming analogue Prediction
9	Homework assignments	Bricklaying Prediction
10	Drug treatments	The brain
11	Approval and approval-seeking behaviour	Assumption Rewriting assumptions
12	Perfectionism and competitiveness	Define the term Benefits of being fallible and infallible
13	Healthy and unhealthy negative emotions	Survey Sun and rain
14	Fear of failure and procrastination	Define the term Cognitive continuum
15	Self-criticism	Read it out loud Follow your son around
16	Setback and relapse	Acceptance Seeing the event from the other side
17	Others' criticism	The law Cognitive continuum
18	Good and bad communication	Turn the table round
19	Developing effective communication skills	Active listening Disarming Empathy Enquiry 'I . . .' statements
20	Assessment skills	Socratic questioning
21	Disputing approach and techniques	Territory model Daughter 100 people Best friend

100 mothers and Judith's best friend were not failures but she was. In other words, there were two sets of rules being used: the helpful and unhelpful ones. It was inevitable that Judith was emotionally upset because she applied the unhelpful set of rules to herself. The focus was to point out such a discrepancy in the therapeutic process. Knowing what the focus is will

help the therapist keep the therapeutic process within the boundary of the rationale in order to achieve the therapeutic goal.

In short, knowing the rationale, the focus and the process of a particular technique can help the therapist adapt it to use on other types of unhelpful thoughts. For example, the 100 people or the best friend technique can also be used for a client with social anxiety; this is illustrated using the case of Leo.

The case of Leo

Leo avoided going to parties where there were a lot of people as he did not like talking to people he either did not know or did not know well. Holding a conversation with people had always been a problem, as he felt that he needed to be interesting and to be able to come up with topics that would interest people. He was invited to a wedding which he knew that he needed to attend. He said: 'If people do not find what I say interesting or appear to be bored in my company, I will feel like a reject.'

Therapist: How strongly will you feel that you are a reject, if people do not find what you say interesting, on a scale of 1 to 100?

Leo: 95.

Therapist: How strongly do you believe that you're a reject, if people look bored in your company, on a scale of 1 to 100?

Leo: 95 again.

Therapist: The rating is rather high. What you are really saying is that unless people at the wedding are interested in what you say and do not find you boring, you are a reject.

Leo: Yes.

Therapist: Will it be everybody you talk to or only some people?

Leo: Pretty much everybody.

Therapist: Suppose you talk to 100 people at the same wedding, would they all see themselves as rejects if what they say is not found to be interesting by some people? [Note that Leo was taken away from his 'territory', using the 100 people technique]

Leo: Oh, I suppose not.

Therapist: Would they all see themselves as rejects if some people do not enjoy their company?

Leo: Oh, I suppose not.

Therapist: Because of?

Leo: I suppose it is impossible to make everybody interested in what you say and/or enjoy your company all the time.

Therapist:	I agree. If these 100 people or most of them do not see themselves as rejects, what would they say?
Leo:	It is a waste of time and emotional energy needing people's recognition and acceptance in order to feel good. Just be yourself and enjoy the drink and the food.
Therapist:	How helpful is it to think in this way?
Leo:	It is very helpful.
Therapist:	Suppose your daughter sees herself as a reject if some people at the party do not enjoy her company or what she said, is she a reject? [Note the use of daughter technique]
Leo:	Oh, no. She is not.
Therapist:	As a father, what will you say to her in a helpful and realistic manner?
Leo:	I will tell her that she does not need everybody to enjoy her company or what she says. Otherwise, she won't enjoy the party.
Therapist:	Help me to understand why your daughter and the 100 people are not rejects in similar circumstances but you are? [Note that the disputing is shifting back to Leo's territory]
Leo:	Oh. Ah. It is my expectation, isn't it?
Therapist:	How helpful it is to have such an expectation?
Leo:	I can see that it is not helpful. I have been avoiding people I don't know or don't know well. In fact, I hate going to parties.
Therapist:	How helpful is it to your self-confidence and self-esteem to label yourself as a reject just because of . . . ?
Leo:	You're right. I am not a reject.

Techniques: Best friend and Daughter

Note that the focuses of the 'best friend' technique (in the case of Judith) and the 'daughter' technique (in the case of Leo) are very similar in principle, which is to 'psychologically remove' the client from his or her emotive and subjective territory to a rational and objective one. The idea of successful disputing requires the therapist and the client to work together to search and evaluate a range of evidence (best friend, daughter, neighbour, colleague and relative) that can be used to establish the helpfulness of a negative thought. Using just one piece of evidence (for example, best friend) may not be or is often not sufficient to change some negative thoughts, particularly the underlying assumptions and core beliefs (see Chapter 7 on 'Dealing with negative thoughts'). These thoughts are learnt early in life and can have a powerful and enduring impact on thinking, feeling and behaviour, and affect self-beliefs (e.g. 'I am successful and likeable', or 'I am a reject and a failure').

Changing them can be a challenge, but is also highly rewarding to both the client and the therapist if the client is able to develop a helpful thinking perspective in relation to an emotive situation.

From clinical experience, 'best friend' and 'daughter' (compared with neighbour, colleague or relative) approaches are more likely to get the client to respond in a rational and helpful manner. The daughter technique is a better one in terms of reducing the client's resistance to change and clinical effectiveness as it draws on the notion of 'love' (see the dialogue below), whereas the best friend technique relies on 'friendship'. Although best friend and daughter techniques are pretty much similar in their use, combining them in clinical work, one technique used after another, can have a powerful effect in challenging or disputing the client's unhelpful thought, thus enabling the client to question not only its reliability but also the benefits of holding on to it.

One student commented that one of her clients didn't have a family and therefore the daughter technique would not be appropriate to use. The alternative is to use the best friend technique. However, knowing the rationale, the focus and the process would provide the therapist with the confidence to adapt a particular technique to situations often thought to be inappropriate. For example, we can adapt the daughter technique to use on a client who does not have a family (see the dialogue below).

Therapist: Do you have a daughter? [Note that the therapist might choose to ask about a son instead – sometimes it may be more beneficial to use 'son' instead of 'daughter' because of the different cultural values placed on the gender differences]

Judith: No. I am single.

Therapist: Suppose you have a daughter. Do you think you will love her?

Judith: Oh, well, I think so.

Therapist: Because of?

Judith: Because I am the mother.

Therapist: Absolutely, because you're the biological mother and therefore it is right for you to love her. How much do you think you'll love her – your own daughter, on a scale of 1 to 100?

Judith: Very much so. I will say 100.

Therapist: Great. Suppose your daughter (she is now a mother with her own daughter) was also in similar circumstances and you know that she had tried very hard to help her daughter (your granddaughter), would you see her as a failure?

Judith: Of course, she was not. How could she be a failure?

Therapist: If this is so, how logical is it to say that your daughter is not a failure but you are? [Note that the disputing is shifting back to

Judith's territory to further the process of challenging and to highlight the use of two sets of rules: the helpful and unhelpful ones]

(See the dialogue in the case of Judith on pp. 196–197.)

The benefits of knowing the rationale, the focus and the process of the technique are to provide an effective and flexible approach in disputing an unhelpful thought and to give the therapist the confidence to adapt that technique to enable it to be used on other types of unhelpful thoughts. Therapists can also learn to create their own disputing techniques, with the help of such knowledge.

Notes for therapists about the disputing approach and techniques

- Effective disputing is closely related to the therapist knowing the rationale, the focus and the process of the technique being used.
- Knowing the rationale, the focus and the process of the technique gives therapists the confidence to adapt that technique for use on other types of unhelpful thoughts and to develop their own techniques.
- If a disputing technique being used in the 'different territory' can highlight an experience or an example that the client can relate to, the client is likely to become more objective, less emotionally charged and less resistant to change.

Part VI

Taking control
New models for helping change

Chapter 22

Control and choice in mental health

Cognitive behaviour therapy takes the view that mental health problems are related to a number of interacting causes, including psychological, emotional, social, environmental, behavioural, biological and genetic ones. Throughout this book it is clearly shown that an emphasis on a 'diseased' brain or 'chemical imbalance' explanation as the primary cause of mental health problems is unhelpful, may be counterproductive in treatment terms, negatively affects clients' self-perception and self-esteem, and has the unwanted effect of maintaining the problems of stigma, prejudice and discrimination. Case examples also illustrate that such an explanation does not empower and motivate clients to change nor give them a feeling of being in control over their moods and behaviour (e.g. 'I can't control my anger, frustration and irritability'; 'Depression just happens'; 'I am just anxious for no reason'). It also makes them feel different from the rest of society (e.g. 'I am mental'), creates fear of a possible relapse (e.g. 'How long can I be well?'), and affects their confidence or willingness to reintegrate into society (e.g. 'I can't cope').

Research and clinical observations show that some clients may even use the 'diseased brain' or genetic explanation to justify their antisocial, aggressive or avoidance behaviour or tantrums or to try to get away from behaving responsibly ('I can't help the way I behave'). This attitude may make their mental health problems worse. One alcoholic client said that he had no control over his drinking because 'the doctor said that I have an addictive personality'. An anxious client said that 'because of the anxious genes in my body' it would be difficult for her to leave her 'shell' to go on a holiday, to a party, or to return to work. Her mother and a sister were also described as anxious people. An angry client with a low frustration tolerance said that he had no control over his shouting, swearing and aggressive or moody behaviour because he was born with such a condition as his father was also a hot-tempered person. Some clients may use the 'sick' role to gain attention, sympathy, understanding and support, and, at the same time, to avoid responsibility for moving on with their lives. Blaming the brain or their personality traits may additionally affect their motivation or willingness to work on their unhelpful behaviour such as perfectionism, competitiveness, self-criticism, approval-seeking and self-harm, which in part can contribute to the development of mental health problems.

There is growing evidence to indicate that the 'blaming the brain' approach has not been effective in de-stigmatising mental health problems. Although an emphasis on biological information in mental health issues is often assumed to have the effect of reducing guilt and shame for clients and relatives, evidence does not support such a claim. In view of the de-stigmatisation campaigns not being as effective as was hoped to date and of the potential impact on clients' self-confidence and self-esteem, it may be necessary to review the 'blaming the brain' approach not just in the de-stigmatisation campaigns, but also in helping people with mental health problems.

It is suggested that society (and therapists as part of society) needs to rethink the way it seeks to help people with mental health problems. The therapist is more like a personal trainer or a sports coach (helping people to do better) than a doctor who cures diseases. New models of helping people to change should therefore concentrate on helping people to do better rather than curing disease. *Control* and *choice* are at the heart of these new models of change. When symptoms of 'mental illness' are blamed on a 'diseased' brain, clients often believe that they do not have control over their moods (e.g. depression, anxiety, anger, guilt, fear and irritability) or their bodily sensations (e.g. shaking, sweating, racing heart, choking and feelings of unreality), nor is there a choice in the way they behave (e.g. aggression, tearfulness, procrastination, self-harm and self-criticism). Clients with a physical illness such as cancer, diabetes and heart disease know that they have little or no control over their symptoms and drug treatment is seen as the main mechanism for recovery. By the same token, clients with obsessive-compulsive disorder and post-traumatic stress disorder often believe that their symptoms of intrusive thoughts or images, anxiety, fear, trembling, sweating and lack of concentration are beyond their control and are related to a problem in their brain. Drug treatment is therefore seen as the main mechanism for curing the 'brain disease'.

Control and choice

New models of helping clients to change aim to give them (back) control and choice to help them do better in personal (see Part III) as well as inter-personal situations (see Part IV). Some research (McCombs 1991) suggests that what underlies control (or internal locus of control) and choice is the concept of 'self as agent'. This means that our thoughts control our moods and actions. When we realise this important function of thinking, we can positively affect our moods, beliefs, motivation and performance. 'The self as agent can consciously or unconsciously direct and regulate the use of all knowledge structures and intellectual processes in support of personal goals, intentions, and choices' (McCombs 1991: 6). McCombs (1991: 7) asserts that 'the degree to which one chooses to be self-determining is a function of one's realisation of the source of agency and personal control'. We can say to ourselves:

> I choose not to be frightened by my anxiety or feelings of inadequacy. I choose what I want to say and do and not what others expect me to. I choose to view making mistakes as part of life, as inevitable, and as learning experiences and not to view making mistakes as being stupid, incompetent and a failure. I choose to view and accept myself as a whole person with positive qualities and shortcomings and not to undermine myself because of these shortcomings.

Knowledge, understanding and action

The 'self as agent' or a sense of control and choice can be achieved through knowledge, understanding and action which are a cornerstone of the cognitive behaviour therapy approach.

Ralph Waldo Emerson, a leader of the transcendentalists in the early nineteenth century, said: '*knowledge* is the antidote to fear.' Similarly, knowledge is the antidote to people's ignorance about the nature and cause of mental health problems. Socrates (470–399 BC), an ancient Greek philosopher who is widely credited for laying the foundation for Western philosophy, believed that 'the only good is knowledge and the only evil is ignorance'. Ignorance is in part the cause of stigmatisation, prejudice and discrimination and contributes to clients' fear of their symptoms or illness. Francis Bacon, best known as a philosophical advocate and defender of the scientific revolution, said that 'knowledge is power'. One way to motivate clients to start the process of change is to empower them with helpful knowledge about the nature and cause of mental health problems and about the way in which they can learn to change.

Thomas Alva Edison, one of the most prolific inventors in history, holding 1097 US patents in his name, said the concept of *understanding* comes from two simple words *under* and *stand*. He said that 'when one acknowledges that s/he stands below someone or something else, s/he makes him/herself receptive to obtain and retain information from it, thereby allowing for understanding to occur'. If clients are encouraged to 'stand below their symptoms', they can be receptive to information about why these symptoms have developed and what made these symptoms continue (or get worse). In other words, 'standing below their symptoms' is to stand back and observe these symptoms instead of reacting (overreacting) to them. For example, instead of reacting to headache as a symptom of a brain tumour, the client can stand back and observe, thereby allowing him/herself to understand that the headache may also be due to working too hard and/or not having enough rest or relaxation. It is thought that an understanding of the cause-and-effect relationship can motivate and empower clients to take action to change. Some people believe knowledge is the simple awareness of bits of information. Understanding is the awareness of the connectedness of this information. It is understanding which allows knowledge to be put to use or into action.

Confucius said that 'the superior man is modest in his speech, but exceeds in his action' and Florence Nightingale asserted that 'actions bring results'. Ralph Waldo Emerson advised: 'Don't be too timid and easily upset about your actions. All life is an experiment. The more experiments you make the better.' This wisdom simply illustrates that actions speak louder than words. In the context of therapeutic change, knowledge and understanding without action represents little or no change. If clients with depression, panic disorder, obsessive-compulsive disorder or low self-esteem do not change their unhelpful behaviour (e.g. avoidance, checking, scanning, self-criticism, procrastination) or therapists do not equip them with skills (e.g. communication, social and assertive skills) and confidence for the change, there is little or no prospect for them to achieve a sustainable change: to stay better. *Action* provides evidence that can be used to question the incorrect and misguided knowledge or belief about the nature and cause of mental health problems. Action deepens understanding about the way in which mental health problems or symptoms (e.g. depression, panic disorder) are developed and maintained within the psychosocial framework (e.g. stress). Action also helps to develop self-confidence, to improve self-image, and to acquire a stable self-esteem. Albert Ellis (1994), who is regarded as one of the founding fathers of CBT, makes an important distinction between intellectual insight and emotional insight as it relates to the therapeutic change process. Intellectual insight refers to knowledge and understanding, whereas emotional insight refers to conviction. Clients who have attained intellectual insight understand the relationship between dysfunctional thoughts and the self-defeating emotional and behavioural consequences they experience. Clients with emotional insight, however, not only have achieved a degree of conviction about the relationship between thoughts and consequences, but are also able to act on changing the consequences. This distinction is of immense clinical importance. A successful therapeutic change is about engaging with clients and encouraging them to work at the emotional insight level, not just the intellectual level. Note that treatment failures are often due to CBT therapy being conducted at the intellectual level (e.g. identifying negative thinking and changing it to positive thinking). Clients simply do not have the self-confidence and skills (social, assertive and communicative) to change their unhelpful behaviours at personal (see Part III of this book) and interpersonal levels (see Part IV of this book). Action therefore helps clients to reintegrate into society, thereby enabling them to live a productive and fulfilling life. Burns (1999: 7) believes that learning 'how to cope with a realistically negative situation is just as important as learning how to rid yourself of distorted thoughts and feelings'.

Put simply: to know it (knowledge) is good, to understand it (understanding) is better, and to apply it (action) is best. Remember the Chinese saying, 'A journey of a thousand miles begins with a single step.' If you take a single step (action) and see how that works out, you are on your way, and who knows how many miles you will travel?

Notes for therapists about control and choice

- Knowledge, understanding and action are cornerstones in the cognitive behaviour therapy approach.
- To know it (knowledge) is good, to understand it (understanding) is better, and to apply it (action) is best.
- A successful therapeutic change is about engaging with clients and encouraging them to work at the emotional insight level, not just the intellectual level.
- Control and choice are at the heart of the new models of change.

Chapter 23

An illustration of the cognitive behaviour therapy approach to panic disorder

A case example

Introduction

'Will I ever be cured?' said Celia in a desperate tone of voice. She was pessimistic about her chance of recovery after three years suffering from a panic disorder. Her pessimism clearly showed in her facial expression of fear, anxiety, sadness and worry. Her eyes showed her helplessness and hopelessness and she was tearful at times. Her mother, who accompanied her to the first session for assessment, was clearly worried and, at a loss to know what she could do to help, asked: 'Will my daughter ever be able to be normal again? Is there anything wrong with her brain? What is wrong with her brain?' Celia was feeling low and down and started to feel depressed, saying that there was no point in carrying on like that. It was sad to see a young and intelligent woman of only 27 in such emotional turmoil.

Background

Celia had graduated with a first-class honours degree from a prestigious university and had been working in a management consultancy firm since she left university. She was an attractive, confident, able and ambitious person with an active social life and was in a relationship with a man who worked in a different department in the firm. They were talking about getting married after having been together for almost two years and a date had been set for the wedding. However, she was soon in doubt about the marriage and, as the days went by, it was getting worse. She wasn't sure about her choice of partner, about whether they were compatible with each other, or about the timing of the marriage as her career was progressing well. There was a likelihood of her being promoted to a senior management position although it was unusual for the firm to consider promoting a person as young as her. This excellent prospect and the challenge that came with the promotion excited her, but it also increased her doubts about her imminent marriage.

Celia's sister was a successful lawyer, but she stopped practising soon after the birth of a second child due to postnatal depression. Her younger brother was an engineer working for an international company and the job required him to travel a lot. Their parents were described as supportive and they always encouraged their children to develop their careers. They were both disappointed that their elder daughter could not continue with her law practice because of the 'illness'. Her father was the managing director of an international IT company and her mother did not work. Celia said that her mother was caring and supportive, but she was also an anxious person.

Celia was deeply troubled by the thoughts of the marriage and was confused, worried and anxious. She was feeling guilty about her decision to cancel the wedding. This caused her to feel tense, nervous and sick, and she was unable to concentrate or sleep. She did not know what to say or how to break the news to her partner, as he did not know about her concerns and was enthusiastic and excited about the forthcoming marriage. One Saturday, Celia decided that she had to get it over and done with by telling him that the wedding was off. However, her anxiety was at such a level that, without being able to say anything to him, her heart started to beat faster and faster and her stomach was churning. She felt sick, faint, dizzy and was sweating and her legs were shaking. Her breathing was very fast and she started to feel breathless, as if she couldn't get enough air. Not knowing what had happened to her, the thoughts of 'I will not be able to breathe, I will suffocate, I will die, and I will lose all control, go "crazy" and be taken to a mental hospital' scared her so much that she went into a massive panic attack.

An ambulance was called and she was taken to an accident and emergency department in a local hospital for examination. However, the doctor did not find anything wrong with her physically and sent her home. When she woke up the next day, she noticed her legs were shaking and the thought of 'here it comes again' frightened her and triggered off a series of panic attacks. More attacks subsequently occurred, thus affecting her confidence to stay at home by herself or to go to crowded places. Her general practitioner diagnosed her problem as being anxiety related and medication was prescribed. Although the medication initially helped, the panic attacks did not stop. She said that she had at least one anxiety or panic attack a day or every other day. As a result, she was nervous, fearful and feeling physically and emotionally drained, causing her moods to get even worse. The psychiatrist had referred her to psychotherapy on a number of occasions over the past three years but it had little or no long-term benefit.

It was then suggested that her panic problem could be related to particular parts of the brain being involved in the triggering of panic attacks. Panic disorder is probably a biological condition and may be the result of genetic factors, involving biochemical imbalances. Part of the brain is overactive which causes anxiety to increase and trigger off bodily sensations and feelings of panic. Although she was relieved to know that the problem was not due to a psychological weakness, she was nevertheless ashamed of having an anxiety disorder and was worried how others would see her.

Cognitive case formulation

She said that an attack could happen any time, anywhere, and that she did not have any control over it. According to cognitive behaviour therapy, her recurrent panic attacks may be the result of her negative beliefs about bodily sensations of anxiety such as shortness of breath, breathing very fast, feeling faint, and shaking legs. These beliefs (e.g. 'Something is wrong with my brain, I am mental, I will not be able to breathe, and I will collapse and die') were more dangerous than the reality and caused Celia more anxiety. This further increased her bodily sensations and so on in a vicious circle. Other beliefs (e.g. 'I am going to make a complete fool of myself in front of everyone, people will think less of me and see me as weak') caused her to feel ashamed, worried and anxious, thus affecting her self-confidence and self-esteem. She tried to hide her anxiety from other people and constantly scanned for signs of bodily sensations. Scanning was seen as a 'protective' mechanism against panic as she did not want to have a panic attack in front of people. Scanning had a paradoxically harmful effect of increasing her preoccupation with her body and therefore maintaining high levels of anxiety in a vicious circle. She avoided taking business trips or holidays whenever she felt anxious or her legs were shaking. She cancelled a holiday to Australia at the last minute and came home early from a two-week holiday in Thailand because of her bodily symptoms of anxiety. Shaking legs were particularly troublesome to her. Her parents' home was her shelter: she needed somebody to be there if she had a panic attack, in case she passed out or suffocated. These avoidance, escape, safety-seeking and scanning behaviours not only did not help to confront her unhelpful fears and beliefs, but made them even worse. She said: 'Had I not cancelled the trip to Australia and come back early from Thailand, something terrible would have happened.' How did she know that? Figure 23.1 shows a cognitive case formulation of a panic attack.

The idea of a panic attack being biological in nature did not empower her and give her the confidence to work on the panic and to reduce the use of avoidance, escape, safety-seeking and scanning behaviours. She said that she

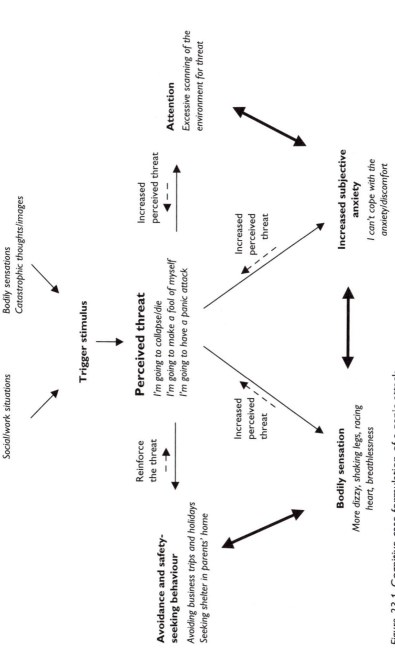

External
Social/work situations

Internal
Bodily sensations
Catastrophic thoughts/images

Trigger stimulus

Perceived threat
I'm going to collapse/die
I'm going to make a fool of myself
I'm going to have a panic attack

Increased
perceived threat

Attention
*Excessive scanning of the
environment for threat*

Increased
perceived
threat

**Increased subjective
anxiety**
*I can't cope with the
anxiety/discomfort*

Increased
perceived
threat

Bodily sensation
*More dizzy, shaking legs, racing
heart, breathlessness*

Reinforce
the threat

**Avoidance and safety-
seeking behaviour**
Avoiding business trips and holidays
Seeking shelter in parents' home

Figure 23.1 Cognitive case formulation of a panic attack

needed to 'protect' herself with these behaviours as she couldn't 'trust' her brain. She was pessimistic about her chance of recovery and was worried about the impact it might have on her career and future.

Treatment strategy

The treatment objectives were:

- To weaken the biological and genetic explanations for a panic attack.
- To understand anxiety and its relationship to beliefs, bodily sensations and behaviours.
- To reduce (and stop) the use of avoidance, escape and a range of safety-seeking behaviours.
- To weaken unhelpful beliefs about panic attacks and develop helpful alternatives.
- To reduce and stop medication.

First three sessions after intake

Celia was conditioned to believe that her panic attack was most probably due to something wrong with particular parts of her brain. It is not unusual for clients with such a condition to subscribe to a biological belief, especially those with a recurrent panic problem or those who had been given a biological explanation. However, following the explanation of the specific cognitive behaviour therapy model of anxiety and panic disorder (Clark 1999), Celia could relate it to her panic and anxiety experience. She now realised that panic often begins as a result of stress (e.g. the wedding was cancelled), other painful feelings (e.g. anxiety, worry and fear) and/or bodily sensations such as breathlessness and shaking legs. Teaching her the ABC model (Lam 1997) helped to consolidate her knowledge/understanding of anxiety and its relationship to beliefs, bodily sensations and behaviour. 'My thinking is the problem,' said Celia with a sigh of relief, giving her a glimmer of hope that her panic could be 'cured'.

Celia was asked to read an excellent booklet on panic disorder and a chapter ('You can change the way you feel': Burns 1999), keep a stress diary based on the ABC format (see Lam 2005 on the format of the stress diary), and to write down the costs and benefits of accepting the biological explanation. Useful therapeutic techniques for the first three sessions include 'the ABC model', 'Developing an alternative explanation', 'Balloon', 'Costs and benefits analysis' and 'The brain' (see Table 21.1, page 199 on disputing techniques).

Celia:	It makes sense. I did not realise that 'thoughts' can have such strong effects, but I can relate to everything you have said and the things I have read about anxiety, sensations and . . .
Therapist:	How strongly do you now believe that your problem is biologically based, on a scale of 1 to 10?
Celia:	7.
Therapist:	What was it before?
Celia:	10.
Therapist:	Because of?
Celia:	What you have said does make sense. Knowing and understanding it is one thing, but whether it will make a difference to my anxiety level is another.

Celia achieved an intellectual insight into her problem. Her biological belief was still quite strong, although it was not as strong as before (10 out of 10). She was feeling 'good' in the first three weeks. Her anxiety and panic feeling was still there, but it was not as bad as it used to be and she had not had a massive panic attack since the treatment started. She was tearful with fear and her body was shaking when she came to the fourth session, saying that she had had a relapse.

Next two sessions

'I let you and everybody down. I have had a relapse. It is terrible. I will never be cured,' said Celia, who beat herself up for having a relapse, which, in CBT terms, was in fact a setback. Note that there is a crucial difference between a setback and a relapse. Celia was asked to read Chapter 16 on 'Setbacks and relapse'. Setbacks prevent relapse and are an invaluable experience for acquiring psychological maturity and developing emotional toughness.

Celia:	I was feeling quite good in the past three weeks. I know my thinking is the problem, but why is it I am still having panic attacks?
Therapist:	Knowing thinking is the problem is just the first step in the change process. What is also important is to identify the sort of thinking that causes anxiety and so on, challenge it, and then change it into something helpful and believable. Otherwise, the panic problem will not go away.
Celia:	Oh.
Therapist:	For example, if a person keeps telling himself that he is a failure and stupid for making mistakes, he comes to believe that he is

such a person in the event of a mistake being made. Knowing that the thinking is negative is not enough to reduce the anxiety and worry, he needs to question the soundness of such thinking and change it into something that is realistic and believable. What can it be?

Celia: Ah. Yeah. I suppose he can say that he is not a failure and stupid for making mistakes.

Therapist: And?

Celia: I don't know.

Therapist: How about saying that making mistakes is not about being a failure and stupid and that doing things well is satisfying, but it is human to make and learn from mistakes?

Celia: Oh, yes. It is good.

Therapist: Because of?

Celia: It makes sense and will help to lower worry and anxiety in the event of a mistake being made.

Celia's stress diary from previous sessions was beneficial. She now accepted that her thoughts were largely the cause of her panic and that she could learn to take control over her anxiety and panic through making a choice in her thoughts and behaviour. She also realised that her thoughts about stressful events (e.g. meetings, business trips, holidays), painful feelings (e.g. 'My god, I am anxious. I mustn't be anxious'), and/or bodily sensations (e.g. 'My legs are shaking. My heart is racing') were more dangerous than they really were and these caused her more anxiety. This further increased her bodily sensations and so on in a vicious circle. These thoughts included black and white thinking, should/must statements, magnification, jumping to conclusions, emotional reasoning, over-generalisation and mental filter (Burns 1999).

From the stress diary, five unhelpful thoughts were randomly picked out and Celia was asked to change them into more realistic alternatives, using the criteria of:

- Does the new thought challenge the old one?
- Is it believable?
- Does it make you feel better?

For example, 'Making mistakes is not about being a failure and stupid. Doing things well is satisfying, but it is human to make and learn from mistakes' is an alternative to the 'I must not make mistakes, otherwise I am a failure and stupid'. This alternative challenges the old one, is believable and does make the feeling better. Celia was then asked to work on other unhelpful thoughts from the diary and was encouraged to continue with the diary for another two months. Useful therapeutic techniques (Table 21.1) for her problems include 'Rewriting an assumption', 'Define the term', 'Survey', '100 people' and 'Best friend' (see Table 21.1, page 199 on disputing techniques).

Next four sessions

Celia was less anxious and the frequency of her panic attacks was less than it used to be. There were some occasions on which she did not have a panic attack for the whole week. This gave her a glimmer of hope and confidence about the prospect of being 'cured'. Her mother started to believe that the therapy could make a difference to her panic attacks. Intellectually, Celia was more able to accept that her panic attacks were triggered off not just by her thoughts, but also by her reactions (or over-reactions).

Despite the progress, she still avoided crowded places and carried tranquillisers, other tablets, 'just in case' something happened. Travelling abroad was particularly worrying, whether it was on business or holiday. It became clear that a fear of anxiety (sometimes called anxiety about anxiety), the use of safety behaviours, a low tolerance of bodily sensations, and worrying about people knowing her anxiety problem were preventing more progress being made. Another way that panic attacks may be kept going is through scanning (sometimes called 'hypervigilance'). Celia became oversensitive to picking up possible threats, particularly to normal bodily signals (see Figure 23.1 on cognitive case formulation of a panic attack). These signals are always there, but ordinarily we do not notice them. Because they are so common, if we start to look for them, we will probably find something. The frightening thoughts then start up ('What does this mean? Am I having an attack? Here it goes again') and the spiral into a panic attack may begin. As a result, reducing the medication was viewed as a risk. These problems illustrated the importance of engaging clients to work at the emotional insight level in order to achieve the objective of 'staying' better (see the section on 'Knowledge, understanding and action' in Chapter 22, pp. 209–211). Useful techniques (see Table 21.1, page 199) for dealing with the above problems include 'Bricklaying', 'Prediction', 'Survey' and 'Daughter' techniques.

It is also important to note that the objective of CBT was to help Celia do better in the management of her panic or anxiety attacks rather than curing the 'disease', in a way similar to the way people learn to manage their anxiety prior to a presentation, an interview or an examination. The notion of panic being a disease is counterproductive in terms of helping clients to do better.

When clients perceive or regard it as such, the fear of anxiety can cause them to avoid or escape any situations that may trigger anxiety. It also affects their ability to tolerate bodily sensations, however little.

The following two incidents made Celia realise that actions in the form of *exposure* were necessary to achieve more progress.

First incident: 'I won't be able to cope for four days in Paris. What if I can't cope and have a panic attack? What will other people think?' Celia was anxious, panicky and worried about a business trip to Paris in a week's time. Medication did not calm her down and she had another panic attack as a result. The locum doctor (her consultant psychiatrist and therapist were both away) gave her more medication, said that she should not go, that she wouldn't be able to cope, and that she would have more panic attacks if she did go. Celia did not find the meeting helpful and was angry with the way he undermined her confidence. The thought of cancelling the trip was there, but she went in the end and the experience was not as bad as she had imagined.

Second incident: Celia was contemplating cancelling her two-week holiday in Cuba with a friend. She was anxious about ruining her friend's holiday because of her panic attacks and was ashamed to admit her problem to her friend. Knowing that such a decision would not help her to overcome her anxiety and panic attacks, she told her friend about it and went ahead with the holiday. She was a bit anxious in the first few days (no panic attacks) and for the rest of the holiday she had a fantastic time.

Celia was asked to keep an anxiety diary in which she would record her anxiety levels before, during and after each exposure to a range of anxiety-provoking situations such as supermarkets, lifts, restaurants, trains, planes and foreign trips. A range of techniques were used during the exposure, including relaxation, controlling breathing, and distraction (Clark 1999). Celia also learnt to challenge her anxious and worrying thoughts by asking, 'What is the worst that could happen? Is this a realistic worry? What is going through my mind? Am I exaggerating the bodily sensations? What is a constructive way of dealing with the anxiety?' Through repeated exposure, it was found that the anxiety was not as bad as it used to be and the frequency of panic attacks was much lower. For example, Celia found that after about ten exposures to crowded places her anxiety levels became progressively lower following each exposure and this gave her confidence about her future prospects. Note that an efficient way is to start the exposure from the least to the most anxiety-provoking situations. Note also that it is important to teach clients a range of techniques that can be used during the exposure. A useful homework to motivate the client is to ask him/her to make a list of the benefits of exposure and the costs of avoidance/escape.

Celia was also asked to read Chapter 13 on 'Healthy and unhealthy negative emotions', Chapter 15 on 'Self-criticism' and Chapter 7 on 'Dealing with negative thoughts' in this book.

Next session

Therapist: How have you been doing since our last meeting two months ago?

Celia: Okay.

Therapist: Meaning?

Celia: I am feeling better and happier. Since our last session, I haven't had a massive panic attack. I did feel anxious and panicky at times, but, as you said, it was normal and appropriate to have anxiety at a low level. The panic attack was less intense and was shorter.

Therapist: Good news. What could be the reasons for the progress?

Celia: I know more about panic and understand that it is often due to stress and to the way I think about anxiety and bodily sensations. The exposure work really helped and my medication is being reduced.

Therapist: In view of the progress you have made, how strongly do you now believe that your panic is biologically based, on a scale of 1 to 10?

Celia: 4.

Next session (final session)

Therapist: Let us review your progress over the past four months.

Celia: I am feeling much better and I have not had a massive panic attack. My medication is now down to 25 per cent of what I used to take and I am okay with it.

Therapist: It sounds as if more progress has been made.

Celia: Yes.

Therapist: What could be the reasons for the progress?

Celia: I now feel that I have control and choice in the way I think about anxiety, panic and bodily sensations. The way I deal with them has also changed and this has given me a lot of confidence.

Therapist: Given the confidence you have, how strongly do you now believe your panic problem is biologically based, on a scale of 1 to 10?

Celia: 2.

Therapist: What was the rating before?

Celia: It used to be 10.

Therapist: It went from 10, to 7, to 4, then to 2. It is a big change. How likely is it that you will relapse, on a scale of 1 to 10?

Celia:	I think it is very low, if I continue putting learning into practice.
Therapist:	And the rating is?
Celia:	2.

Summary

These few sessions illustrate the diversity, adaptability and flexibility of the cognitive behaviour therapist in the use of a range of techniques and homework assignments to target problems, difficulties and setbacks and promote change. Through Socratic dialogue, the therapist helps the client to know more and understand better the nature and causes of mental health problems, thereby reducing the problems of stigma, prejudice and discrimination. It is understanding which allows knowledge to be put to use or into action. It is action that enables the client to see ways of doing things better both in the management of his or her negative emotions and in coping with adversity, thereby giving him or her control and choice.

Celia was a 'different' person and she felt different too. Her medication was reduced and then stopped. She was gaining control over anxious and fearful thoughts about panic and was able to exercise choice in the way she behaved in anxiety-provoking situations. More importantly, she no longer viewed panic as being caused by a 'diseased' brain or related to genetic factors, as reflected in her ratings, from 10 (totally believing that it was biological) to 2. She said that she was now half way through her Master in Business Administration (MBA) studies, which was an achievement and was a credit to her and her determination.

Cognitive behaviour therapy approach to the treatment of mental health problems

'The therapist is more like a personal trainer or a sports coach (helping people to do better) than a doctor who cures diseases' represents a radical departure from the current medical view of mentally ill clients and its treatment approach of 'mental illness'. This part of the book and the case of Celia, as described in this chapter, illustrates and summarises the concepts, principles and process of the contemporary CBT approach to the treatment of mental health problems. Celia was empowered with knowledge and understanding about panic and was motivated and encouraged (what a personal trainer does) to put these to use or into action in order to do better. Florence Nightingale rightly stated that 'actions bring results'.

When an athlete is doing better, it is a rewarding experience for both the athlete and the personal trainer or the sports coach. The reward for the client, as in the case of Celia, is control and choice and for the therapist a sense of satisfaction.

Notes for therapists about cognitive behaviour therapy

- Therapeutic success is closely related to the therapist and the client taking their respective responsibilities in the change process, as an athlete and a personal trainer do.
- Negative emotions (e.g. anxiety, worry, frustration) at a *low* level are normal, appropriate and healthy.
- An understanding of the mechanisms involved in the development and continuation of mental health problems is the *first* step in the process of change.
- Adherence to a particular explanation (biological versus psychological) of the cause of mental health problems by professionals tends to influence the way in which these problems are explained to clients, relatives and the public. It also influences the way in which they work with clients: 'either as a doctor or as a personal trainer'.

References

Ashton, H. (2001). 'A view from the shoulders of giants: A review of David Healy's "The Psychopharmacologists III".' *British Journal of Psychiatry* **179**: 277–278.

Barsa, J. A. and Kline, N. S. (1956). 'Use of reserpine in disturbed psychotic clients.' *American Journal of Psychiatrists* **112**: 684–691.

Beck, A. T. (1976). *Cognitive therapy and the emotional disorders*. New York: International Universities Press.

Beck, A. T. and G. Emery (1985). *Anxiety disorders and phobias: A cognitive perspective*. New York: Basic Books.

Beck, J. S. (1995). *Cognitive therapy: Basics and beyond*. New York: Guilford Press.

Burns, D. D. (1999). *The feeling good handbook*. New York: Plume.

Clark, D. A. (1999). 'Case conceptualisation and treatment failure: A commentary.' *Journal of Cognitive Psychotherapy* **13**: 331–339.

Crisp, A. H. (1999). 'The stigmatisation of sufferers with mental disorders.' *British Journal of General Practice* **49**: 3–4.

Day, D. M. and Page, S. (1986). 'Portrayals of mental illness in Canadian newspapers.' *Canadian Journal of Psychiatry* **31**: 813–817.

Denber, H. C. B. and Bird, E. G. (1957). 'Chlorpromazine in the treatment of mental illness. IV: Final results with analysis of data on 1,523 clients.' *American Journal of Psychiatrists* **113**: 972–978.

Double, D. (2002). 'The limits of psychiatry.' *British Medical Journal* **324**: 900–904.

Dyer, W. (1996). *Your erroneous zones*. London: Warner.

Ellis, A. (1962). *Reason and emotion in psychotherapy*. New York: Lyle Stuart.

Ellis, A. (1994). *Reason and emotion in psychotherapy: A comprehensive method of treating human disturbances*. Toronto: Birch Lane Press.

Fennell, M. J. (1999). *Overcoming low self-esteem*. London: Robinson.

Franzoi, S. L. (1996). *Social psychology*. London: Brown & Benchmark.

Goffman, E. (1990). *Stigma: Notes on the management of spoiled identity*. Harmondsworth: Penguin.

Green, D. E., McCormick, I. A., Walkey F. H. and Taylor, A. J. W. (1987). 'Community attitudes to mental illness in New Zealand twenty-two years on.' *Social Science Medicine* **24**: 417–422.

Greenberger, D. and Padesky, C. A. (1995). *Mind over mood: Change how you feel by changing the way you think*. New York: Guilford Press.

Gussow, J. and Tracy, G. S. (1968). 'Status, ideology and adaptation to stigmatised illness: A study of leprosy.' *Human Organisation* **27**: 316–325.

Hennessy, S., Bilker, W. B., Knauss, J. S., Margolis, D. J., Kimmel, S. E. et al. (2002). 'Cardiac arrest and ventricular arrhythmia in clients taking antipsychotic drugs: Cohort study using administrative data.' *British Medical Journal* **325**: 1070–1072.

Hill, D. J. and Bale, R. M. (1981). *Measuring beliefs about where psychological distress originates and who is responsible for its alleviation.* New York: Academic Press.

Hinshaw, S. P. and Cicchetti, D. (2000). 'Stigma and mental disorder: Conceptions of illness, public attitudes, personal disclosure, and social policy.' *Development and Psychopathology* **12**: 555–598.

Jacobson, N. S. (1994). 'Behavioural therapy and psychotherapy integration.' *Journal of Psychotherapy Integration* **4**: 105–119.

Kazantzis, N., Deane, F. P. and Ronan, K. R. (2000). 'Homework assignments in cognitive and behavioural therapy: A meta-analysis.' *Clinical Psychology: Science and Practice* **7**: 189–202.

Kent, H. and Read, J. (1998). 'Measuring consumer participation in mental health services: Are attitudes related to professional orientation?' *International Journal of Social Psychiatry* **44**(4): 295–310.

Kessler, R. C., Nelson, C. B., McGonagle, K. A., Edlund, M. J., Frank, R. G. and Leaf, P. J. (1996). 'The epidemiology of co-occurring addictive and mental disorders: Implications for prevention and service utilisation.' *American Journal of Orthospsychiatry* **66**: 17–31.

Kinross-Wright, V. (1955). 'Chlorpromazine treatment of mental disorders.' *American Journal of Psychiatrists* **111**: 907–912.

Koro, C. E., Fedder, D. O., L'Italien, G. J., Weiss, S. S., Magder, L. S. et al. (2002). 'Assessment of independent effect of olanzapine and risperidone on risk of diabetes among clients with schizophrenia: Population based nest-control study.' *British Medical Journal* **325**: 243–247.

Lam, D. C. K. (1997). 'Cognitive behaviour therapy territory model: Effective disputing approach.' *Journal of Advanced Nursing* **25**: 1205–1209.

Lam, D. C. K. (2004). 'The effects of labelling on perceptions of therapists, therapy and clients.' St George's Hospital Medical School, London. University of London. PhD thesis.

Lam, D. C. K. (2005). A brief overview of CBT techniques. In S. M. Freeman and A. Freeman (eds) *Cognitive behaviour therapy in nursing practice.* New York: Springer.

Lam, D. C. K. and Cheng, L. (2001). 'Cognitive behaviour therapy approach to assessing dysfunctional thoughts.' *Counselling Psychology Quarterly* **14**(3): 255–265.

Lam, D. C. K. and Gale, J. (2000). 'Cognitive behaviour therapy: Teaching a client the ABC model – the first step towards the process of change.' *Journal of Advanced Nursing* **31**(2): 444–451.

Lam, D. C. K. and Gale, J. (2004). 'An evidence-based clinical framework for working with dysfunctional thoughts.' *Counselling Psychology Quarterly* **17**(1): 53–67.

Lam, D. C. K. and Salkovskis, P. M. (2007). 'An experimental investigation of the impact of biological and psychological causal explanations on anxious and depressed clients' perception of a person with panic disorder.' *Behaviour Research and Therapy* **45**: 405–411.

Lam, D. C. K. and Salkovskis, P. M. (in press). '"Judging a book by its cover": An experimental study on the impact of personality disorder diagnosis on clinicians' judgements.' *Behaviour Research and Therapy*.

Lam, D. C. K., Salkovskis, P. M. and Warwick, H. (2005). 'An experimental investigation of the impact of biological versus psychological explanations of the cause of "mental illness".' *Journal of Mental Health* **14**(5): 453–464.

Leahy, R. L. (2002). *A model of emotional schema*. Warwick, UK: British Association of Behavioural & Cognitive Psychotherapy.

Leahy, R. L. (2003). *Cognitive therapy techniques: A practitioners' guide*. New York: Guilford Press.

Linehan, M. M. (1993). *Cognitive-behavioural treatment of borderline personality disorder*. New York: Guilford Press.

McCombs, B. (1991). *Metacognition and motivation in higher level thinking*. Chicago, IL: American Educational Research Association.

McMullin, R. E. (2000). *The new handbook of cognitive therapy techniques*. New York: Norton.

Moncrieff, J. (2003). *An examination of the influence of the pharmaceutical industry on academic and practical psychiatry*. London: Institute of Psychiatry.

Moncrieff, J. and Pommerleau, J. (2000). 'Trends in sickness benefits in Great Britain and the contribution of mental disorders.' *Journal of Nervous and Mental Disease* **189**: 288–295.

Mother Jones (2002). 'Disorders made to order.' *Mother Jones* (magazine) July–August.

Moynihan, R., Heath, I. and Henry, D. (2002). 'Selling sickness: The pharmaceutical industry and disease mongering.' *British Medical Journal* **324**: 886–891.

Nunnally, J. C. (1950). *Popular conceptions of mental health: Their development and change*. New York: Holt, Rinehart, Winston.

Person, J. B. (1989). *Cognitive therapy in practice: A case formulation approach*. New York: Norton.

Phelan, J. C. (2002). 'Genetic bases of mental illness – a cure for stigma?' *Trends in Neurosciences* **25**(8): 430–431.

Read, J. and Harre, N. (2001). 'The role of biological and genetic causal beliefs in the stigmatisation of "mental clients".' *Journal of Mental Health* **10**(2): 223–235.

Read, J. and Law, A. (1999). 'The relationship of causal beliefs and contact with users of mental health services to attitudes to the "mentally ill".' *Journal of Social Psychiatry* **45**(3): 216–229.

Rimes, K. A. and Salkovskis, P. M. (1998). 'Psychological effects of genetic testing for psychological disorders.' *Behavioural & Cognitive Psychotherapy* **26**(1): 29–42.

Riskind, J. H. and Wahl, O. F. (1992). 'Moving makes it worse: The role of rapid movement in fear of psychiatric clients.' *Journal of Social and Clinical Psychology* **11**: 349–364.

Roth, A. and Fonagy, P. (2005). *What works for whom? A critical review of psychotherapy research*. New York: Guilford Press.

Salkovskis, P. M. (2003). 'Third generation cognitive-behavioural therapy: A clinical update on empirically grounded psychological treatments in anxiety problems.'

Paper presented at St George's Hospital Medical School, London, February 2003.

Sayce, L. (1998). 'Stigma, discrimination and social exclusion: What's in a word?' *Journal of Mental Health* **7**(4): 331–343.

Sayce, L. (2000). *From psychiatric client to citizen: Overcoming discrimination and social exclusion.* New York: St Martin's Press.

Scambler, G. (1989). *Epilepsy.* London: Tavistock.

Tringo, J. L. (1970). 'The hierarchy of preference toward disability groups.' *Journal of Special Education* **4**: 295–306.

Van Praag, H. M. (2002). 'Why had the antidepressant era not shown a significant drop in suicide rates?' *Crisis* **23**: 77–82.

Wahl, O. F. (1995). *Media madness: Public images of mental illness.* New Brunswick, NJ: Rutgers University Press.

Wahl, O. F. (1999). *Telling is risky business: Mental health consumers confront stigma.* New Brunswick, NJ: Rutgers University Press.

Walker, I. and Read, J. (2002). 'The differential effectiveness of psychosocial and biogenetic causal explanations in reducing negative attitudes toward "mental illness".' *Psychiatry* **65**(4): 313–325.

Whittington, C. J., Kendall, T., Fonagy, P., Cottrell, D., Cotgrove, A. and Boddington, E. (2004). 'Selective serotonin re-uptake inhibitors in childhood depression: Systematic review of published versus published data.' *Lancet* **363**: 1341–1345.

Whittle, P. (1996). 'Psychiatric disorder and the development of a causal belief questionnaire.' *Journal of Mental Health* **5**(3): 257–266.

Index